The Healing Tradition

Reviving the soul of Western medicine

David Gι

Senior Lecturer in Me   ιanities
Centre for Philosophy, Humanities and Law in Health Care
School of Health Science
University of Wales, Swansea

Forewords by

Kenneth M Boyd

and

Howard Brody

Radcliffe Publishing
Oxford • San Francisco

Radcliffe Publishing Ltd
18 Marcham Road
Abingdon
Oxon OX14 1AA
United Kingdom

www.radcliffe-oxford.com
Electronic catalogue and worldwide online ordering.

British Library Cataloguing in Publication Data

A catalogue record for this book is available from the British Library.

ISBN 1 85775 963 X

Typeset by Aarontype Ltd, Easton, Bristol
Printed and bound by TJ International Ltd, Padstow, Cornwall

Contents

Foreword

The best physician, according to Hippocrates, is also a philosopher, a lover of wisdom. But while long experience has made many physicians philosophical in the colloquial sense, few have developed their insights into a coherent philosophy of medicine. Nor have many professional philosophers articulated their technical analyses in ways readily accessible to the everyday concerns of physicians and patients. David Greaves, however, is a notable exception, and this collection of his papers is greatly to be welcomed for bringing his work to a wider readership.

Many people sense that something vital has been lost amidst the undoubted scientific and technological achievements of medicine in recent centuries. But the remedies offered by physicians or philosophers are often piecemeal or polemical. Greaves, by contrast, has no quick fixes or knock-down arguments. Addressing the morally problematic aspects of contemporary biomedicine with exemplary patience and perceptiveness, he illuminates their human hinterland, making sometimes unexpected connections (between ancient humoral and modern alternative systems of medicine for example) which deepen understanding of what has gone wrong and how it might in time be remedied. His carefully crafted studies, in the earlier chapters of this book, of the conceptual and contextual aspects of familiar topics, such as sudden infant deaths, heart attacks and dementia, prepare the reader to appreciate the pertinence of the larger questions he raises, in his final chapters, about medical humanities and a new medical cosmology.

Greaves emphasises an integrated approach to contemporary problems and demonstrates the distinctive contributions that philosophy and medicine can make to their resolution. His essays embody the highest aspirations of both disciplines – to provoke thought and to be open to new insights. This collection of papers, reflecting the growth of a physician-philosopher's mind, is a much-needed prelude to the discussion we now need to have, if modern medicine is to fulfil its healing potential.

Kenneth M Boyd
Professor of Medical Ethics
College of Medicine and Veterinary Medicine
University of Edinburgh
May 2004

Foreword

When interest in medical humanities began to develop in US medical schools in the 1970s, philosophy was among the first of the traditional humanities disciplines to come aboard. The *Journal of Medicine and Philosophy* began publication in 1976; and many early issues of that journal were devoted to analyzing concepts of health, disease, and medicine itself. Many of the early philosophical papers on these topics were collected in a volume in 1981.[1] The interest in this set of issues then seemed to die out. Some philosophers who had become interested in medicine turned to other topics; others became immersed completely within the burgeoning field of bioethics.

It was my own impression that considerably more work could profitably be done on further clarifications of the nature of health, disease, and medicine. I am therefore pleased to see that our British colleagues are picking up where we left off. Dr Greaves begins from the assumption that medicine is unlikely to solve the problems that beset it today unless it better understands what sort of activity it is and what it aims to accomplish. He rejects an 'additive' model of the role of humanities in medical education – what some of my own mentors referred to as the 'finishing school' idea, that a little bit of humanities added on the surface as a veneer would polish some of the rough edges off scientist-physicians and make them more educated and civilized. Humanities in medicine is not worth paper and ink, much less curriculum time, unless it engages medicine at its core and wrestles with basic questions, transforming the nature of medicine in our day.

Dr Greaves employs a helpful method. He works back and forth between concrete medical issues and abstract concepts. He begins with matters such as the nature of cot deaths and heart attacks, how to take care of dementia patients, and why so many long-stay hospital beds have been closed. He eventually travels to the level of medical cosmology – a 'paradigm shift,' which is as high as most of my American colleagues choose to aim, is too limited for him – and sketches out the way we need to rethink the role of medicine in the world over the next several decades. Nothing abstract is here for its own sake. It all has a purpose – problems we trip over in the everyday world of medicine are ultimately rooted in these matters, as Dr Greaves argues persuasively. The cost of continuing to butt our heads against these problems solely at the concrete level is to render the problems insoluble.

One of the most puzzling aspects of contemporary life in Britain and the US is the resurgence of interest in complementary and alternative medicine (CAM), at precisely the time in history when conventional Western medicine seems to be at the height of its scientific powers to influence the course and outcome of disease. Many physicians view the CAM phenomenon indulgently as evidence of public quirkiness. Sadly, more than a few medical leaders view CAM in a purely entrepreneurial way – if the public wishes to throw away its money on such nonsense, let's at least be sure that we get our share, by opening up 'integrative medicine' centers at conventional hospitals and clinics. Dr Greaves approaches CAM in the spirit of diagnosis. He asks what ingredients CAM might possess that are part of the long cultural and historical heritage of Western medicine, but that have been pushed aside by the dominance of scientific biomedicine in the last century. He boldly asks what conventional medicine might learn from CAM in this regard, even going so far as to suggest that the humoral system of medicine that was supplanted by biomedicine contained important truths that the medicine of the future must not neglect.

We can only hope that Dr Greaves's thoughtful work will stimulate others on both sides of the Atlantic to undertake further development of these important inquiries.

Howard Brody MD, PhD
University Distinguished Professor
Family Practice, Philosophy, and Center for Ethics and Humanities in the
Life Sciences
Michigan State University
East Lansing, MI
USA
May 2004

Reference

1   Caplan AL, Engelhardt HT and McCartney JJ (eds) (1981) *Concepts of Health and Disease: Interdisciplinary Perspectives.* Addison-Wesley, Reading, MA.

Preface

In the early 1970s I had been puzzling about the problems posed for Western medicine by the dichotomy between the group and the individual, cause and meaning, and quantitative and qualitative method. Then in 1976 it dawned on me that perhaps these divisions could be abolished. Maybe there was the possibility of a different configuration where they could be brought into a new relationship. This held out the prospect not only of providing a novel way of re-examining the basis of medicine and healthcare, but also of opening a window on the problems of Western society more generally.

I was so excited by these ideas that I wanted to tell everyone about them, but in whatever direction I turned I was met either by cautious scepticism or more commonly by blank incomprehension or outright hostility. This taught me a painful lesson, that having a new insight is of little use on its own; it has to be developed, articulated and aligned with the parallel insights of others if it is to have any impact. This then has been the central task that has engaged me, on and off, ever since. It has become the subtext of my professional life, as well as a personal pilgrimage, with this book representing a synthesis of my thoughts and a staging post of my progress so far.

In 1976 I had just started work on a thesis in medical sociology, and my first attempts to communicate something of these ideas were incorporated into an empirical study of the role of blood pressure measurement in general practice. One of the most important conclusions I reached was the need to challenge the status of medical research methods, and especially the part played by the randomised controlled trial (RCT) as the 'gold standard'. I also ended the thesis with a more general reflection on the nature of Western medicine, which was published in 1979 as a paper entitled 'What is medicine? Towards a philosophical approach', in which I asked:

> Why, though, should contemporary twentieth century medicine have failed to develop a coherent philosophy of medicine (meaning, as Carr does, a self-questioning attitude) when history along with the majority of other subjects, and notably for medicine the biological sciences, have developed a philosophy of their subjects.[1]

In the ensuing years, my work as a public health doctor afforded me little opportunity to pursue this question further, until in 1984–85 I studied for a Diploma in Medical Ethics and Law for which I had to prepare a dissertation. The subject I chose to focus on was cot deaths, as a particularly elegant example through which to examine how medical knowledge is constructed within the framework of biomedicine. This work was published in 1988 with the title 'Sudden infant deaths: models of health and illness',[2] but the main conclusions still hold good. It also represents an early attempt on my behalf to explore some of biomedicine's presuppositions, and because this is an important theme running throughout this book, I have included it as the first chapter.

Shortly after this I moved to the Centre for Philosophy and Health Care in Swansea, where I had the opportunity to undertake a more major study for a PhD thesis. Between 1990 and 1995 this gave me room to reflect on Western medicine more generally and develop an overall critique. Entitled *Mystery in Western Medicine*, this thesis was published as a book in 1996,[3] the central argument being that for the past two centuries medicine has been embarked on an 'Enlightenment Project' which, in seeking absolute 'scientific' objectivity, has largely denied or rejected the role of uncertainty.

It was only while I was writing this thesis that the term 'medical humanities' began to be used in Britain, although it had been coined in the United States at least 20 years earlier. Gradually, I began to see that when interpreted in a particular way, this newly emerging field could provide the conceptual foundation for my work, and I have come to view it as a way of approaching the philosophy of medicine which embodies several distinctive elements. First, it is not a new subject, but more an interdisciplinary perspective that aims to break out of the constraints imposed by particular academic disciplines. Second, this interdisciplinarity does not only involve the arts or humanities, but also the sciences in their relationship with the arts. Hence it explicitly challenges the division between arts and sciences in medicine. Third, it avoids the use of the word 'philosophy' and so the 'clever shallowness' of the detached Oxford tradition that has characterised mainstream philosophy in Britain.[4] Rather, it focuses attention on human values, which implies commitment rather than detachment, and goes with an engagement with practice as well as theory, seen as two sides of a coin which are inextricably linked.

This awareness led me to become involved with developing medical humanities at Swansea University and more generally in Britain, and so to writing a series of papers which relate to medical humanities, either directly or indirectly. Because of the eclectic nature of medical humanities, these papers might appear at first sight to be so diverse in subject matter and approach as to have little in common. Relatedly, there have until recently been no journals devoted to medical humanities, so these papers have appeared in what may seem a surprising variety of journals and books, whilst others have remained unpublished. So even those who have been closely involved with medical humanities will not have had the chance to read all of them. I have therefore brought them together in this book, in order to show that they constitute a body of work which has a collective bearing on medical humanities, even though they were not originally written with this in mind. Obviously this means that there is no predetermined order in which they were designed to appear, but I have placed the topic-related papers before those providing a more general analysis, as they raise a number of specific issues which are dealt with in a more comprehensive way in the later chapters.

The commentary provided in the introduction which precedes the chapters is not intended as a means of summarising what is to follow, but rather of showing that there is one particular theme, that of healing, which is capable of providing a unifying analysis. A criticism that some colleagues made of *Mystery in Western Medicine* was that although it offered a coherent critique, it failed to provide details of a more positive and tangible alternative. In this book I have addressed this issue by arguing that Western medicine is fundamentally flawed because it fails to provide a healing environment for both individuals and society, but that this deficiency is potentially correctable, so leaving room for optimism about the future. It serves then as a warning of what is in store if we fail to change course, but also shows that constructive alternatives are available if we are prepared to grasp them. Further, these are most likely to be realised not through any dramatic revolution, but rather by the evolution of old ideas and practices, reconfigured so as to suit the circumstances of the twenty-first century.

Jonas claims that Western society has replaced the older assumption of vitalistic monism (the doctrine that emphasises the oneness or unity of reality, and that living organisms cannot be explained ultimately in physical or chemical terms) with its opposite mechanistic monism: '... as formerly panvitalism so now panmechanism is the comprehensive hypothesis'.[5]   However, the most notable feature of Western medicine is that although it has gone a long way down this route, it has shown more resistance to it than most other institutions. Thus what we have in practice is not mechanistic medical monism, but lopsided medical dualism, with the technical and the sciences dominant, and the personal and the arts recessive, but without any complete supremacy. So despite the fact that there are those who continually press for mechanistic monism (by means of technical rationalism) from various theoretical perspectives, e.g. sociobiology, most recently formulated in terms of 'genetic fundamentalism', they are never completely successful. This is inevitable because medicine is not only a theoretical project, but also a practice, which ultimately can never escape dealing with man as a unity of body and soul. Toulmin paints the wider historical and philosophical context:

> From classical Greece on, indeed, medicine has presented philosophers with a peculiarly rich and close alliance of mind and hand, theory and practice, universal and existential. The art of medicine demonstrates that human reason is practical as well as theoretical, existential as well as universal; that is, reason is concerned not just with abstract, but also with *flesh and blood* issues.[6]

So the continuing existence of medicine's duality, and its paired characteristics, although they have become distorted by biomedicine, nevertheless provides a starting point from which to restore a better balance between them, and then to go a step further in devising an integrated relationship. Dualism, which has continued throughout its history '... to drain the spiritual elements off the physical realm'.[7] would then be ended, so reviving the soul of Western medicine and facilitating its ability to heal the sick and contribute to the healing of society.

David Greaves
May 2004

References

1   Greaves D (1979) What is medicine? Towards a philosophical approach. *Journal of Medical Ethics*. **5**: 29–32.
2   Greaves D (1988) Sudden infant deaths: models of health and illness. *Journal of Applied Philosophy*. **5**: 61–74.

3 Greaves D (1996) *Mystery in Western Medicine*. Avebury, Aldershot.
4 Magee B (1998) *Confessions of a Philosopher*, p. 134. (First published in 1997.) Phoenix, London.
5 Jonas H (1982) Life, death and the body in the theory of being. In: *The Phenomenon of Life: toward a philosophical biology*, p. 10. (First published in 1966.) University of Chicago Press, Chicago, IL.
6 Toulmin S (1993) Knowledge and art in the practice of medicine: clinical judgment and historical reconstruction. In: C Delkeskamp-Hayes and MAG Cutter (eds) *Science, Technology and the Art of Medicine*, p. 231. Kluwer, Dordrecht.
7 Jonas B, op. cit., p. 13.

Acknowledgements

Much of the context of this book consists of a reworking of lectures that I gave on the MA in Medical Humanities at the University of Wales, Swansea, and I owe a great debt to Martyn Evans who developed and taught the course with me. I also wish to thank the students for their contributions, and our external examiner, Tony Hope, for his support and encouragement. Further, I am extremely grateful to my colleagues – Gillie Bolton, Anne Borsay, Wayne Lewis, Mike Sullivan, Kieran Sweeney, Paul Wainwright and James Willis – who read and commented on the book in draft. Other colleagues – Richard Bryden, Steve Edwards, Elizabeth James, Neil Pickering, Stephen Pattison and John Turner – also kindly gave their time to comment on particular chapters at different stages. I am also grateful to Chris Butler for the seminars he arranged with Martyn Evans and myself in the primary care department in Cardiff, which provided a forum for the discussion of a range of relevant philosophical issues. In addition, the medical humanities programme in Wales has led to a fruitful collaboration with a group of colleagues in Finland, and I would especially like to thank Raimo Puustinen and Anna Maria Viljanen for their enthusiasm and commitment.

I also want to remember and pay my deepest respects to Sue Sullivan, a friend and colleague, who died from cancer, and whose life and personal support were a source of comfort and inspiration.

Eight of the chapters in the book have been published before and I wish to thank the following for permission to reprint copyright material.

Blackwell Publications for:
• Sudden infant deaths: models of health and illness (1988) *Journal of Applied Philosophy*. **5**: 61–74.

Kluwer Academic Publishers for:
• What are heart attacks? Rethinking some aspects of medical knowledge (1998) *Medicine, Health Care and Philosophy*. **1**: 133–41.

The Institute for the Medical Humanities, Galveston, Texas for:
• The enduring appeal of the Victorian family doctor (1999) *Medical Humanities Review*. **13**: 44–56.

British Medical Journal Publishing Group for:
• Changing priorities in residential medical and social services (1997) *Journal of Medical Ethics*. **23**: 77–81.
• Reflections on a new medical cosmology (2002) *Journal of Medical Ethics*. **28**: 81–5.
• The nature and role of the medical humanities (2001) In: M Evans and IG Finlay (eds) *Medical Humanities*, pp. 13–22. BMJ Books, London.

University of Wales Press for:

- Contrasting perspectives of inequalities in health and medical care (2003) In: A Borsay (ed.) *Medicine in Wales c.1800–2000: public service or private commodity?*, pp. 226–44. University of Wales Press, Cardiff.

Cambridge University Press for:

- The creation of partial patients (2000) *Cambridge Quarterly of Healthcare Ethics.* **9**: 23–33.

Finally, I am indebted to Gillian Nineham of Radcliffe Publishing for her cheerful help from the inception of the book to its completion, and to Gwyneth Abbott for all her hard work in typing it.

Introduction

I was a student at a London medical school during the 1960s and have a vivid memory of the first hospital ward rounds I attended. They were led by a consultant surgeon of the old school. He was always smartly dressed in a dark suit, and was both punctilious and unfailingly courteous to the patients, hospital staff and medical students. He would appear on the ward at five to nine and greet the ward sister in her office, who would unfurl a newly laundered stiff white coat that was awaiting his arrival. Then after a few pleasantries, he would begin his slow procession around the 30 beds with sister, the junior doctors and six medical students in train.

Meanwhile the patients were all tucked up and quietly prepared for the big occasion, especially those who were to be operated on the next day. The medical posse would congregate at the foot of each bed, and the sister would pull out the appropriate set of patient's notes at just the right moment. The consultant, having acknowledged the patient with a formal 'Good morning', would then indulge in his favourite ward-round routine, drawing a sketch of the operation that was going to be performed. He always carried a notepad for this particular purpose, and as he was a good draughtsman his artistic performance was a reassuring demonstration to the patients, staff and students alike that his accomplished hands would be equally dextrous in the operating theatre.

The artist's models posed passively in their beds, and although already part of a dress rehearsal, had been allocated non-speaking parts. However, one day an unruly patient had the temerity to break the spell of this performance, and enquired of the surgeon what he was doing. The reply was short, firm and direct: 'Oh, you don't need to worry about this, it has nothing to do with you'.

When I relate this episode to my current students, it always elicits laughter, but I don't think any of us who were involved found it funny at the time. So what, I wonder, has changed in the past 40 years, and what lessons can we learn from this change of perception?

First, it is a dramatic cameo of the last throes of what was standard medical practice under traditional biomedicine which harks back to the Victorian era, and only strikes us as strange and so amusing now because our medical norms have moved on. Medical knowledge was derived from, and the property of, hospital medicine and research, and was held in trust by a hierarchy of doctors, with consultants as the leading exponents, and junior doctors and medical students as apprentices. The patients were conceived as having a dual identity which, although hidden from view when they were well, was made manifest when they entered hospital. On crossing the threshold they retained their personal identity, but implicitly relinquished their bodily identity. The latter was then placed in the care of the doctors for the duration of their stay, to do with as they judged best.

The patient's body thus became the temporary property of the hospital, to be publicly displayed, discussed and acted upon by the doctors. It had been entrusted to the hospital doctors, on the understanding that they both knew and would follow what was best, on the basis that the patient was neither fully capable of comprehending nor should be burdened with the details of medical knowledge and practice. Also, relieving him of such responsibility was thought to be the best way of restoring him to health.[1]

It might then be thought that although the patient's body was being taken care of, his personal identity was being neglected, but this was not so. It was frequently the case that patients would ask the consultant personal questions during the course of the ward round, but these would invariably be referred to the sister, to be dealt with later on a one-to-one basis. The sister was therefore taking responsibility for the person and acting as an intermediary between the consultant and the patient, a bridge between the disembodied person and their medicalised body, and in doing so attempting a reconciliation of the two disaggregated parts and so a reintegration of the person as a whole.

Seen in this light, the response '... it has nothing to do with you' would have been thought appropriate in relation to the patient's body, and '... you don't need to worry about this' reassuring and so in the patient's best interests. Thus our shared amusement when listening to this story now does not show that the consultant was a bad doctor, but rather that he was acting appropriately by the standards of an earlier and fading day. What it further shows is how far the norms of society and medical practice have changed since that time, and it is these that will now be examined.

In retrospect, the 1960s may be seen as a time of social and political uncertainty and unrest that was to be a watershed for Western society in general and medicine in particular. The student riots of 1968 and the anti-psychiatry movement, respectively, were perhaps the most visible signs of this. Hence the 'classic' ward round outlined above represented the end of a passing era, which had stretched back largely unchanged for 100 years or so. It had been forged in Victorian times, and the structural relationships had much in common with the dynamics of the Victorian family. The consultant (father) is the paternalistic figure who is master of the hospital (household). He knows what is best for the patient (child) who is expected to be seen and not heard when the consultant is present. The nursing sister (mother) communicates with the patient when the consultant is not present, dealing with the more mundane everyday questions, and in doing so spans the social distance, disparate knowledge and perceptual gap between them.

Now, by present-day standards, this degree of paternalism and lack of direct personal communication between the father and child, or consultant and patient, is no longer considered acceptable. I was made aware of this in 1994 when I attended another hospital ward round (an unusual event for me as I have not worked in clinical practice since 1970). This time there was just the consultant physician, the ward sister and myself as visitor. The doctor was less formally dressed but still wore a white coat. The ward was divided into six-bedded units and the atmosphere was far more relaxed. The patients wandered about or lounged in chairs, only returning to their beds at the time of their own consultation, when voices were lowered so as to procure a semblance of privacy.

Nonetheless, much had not changed. The consultant still greeted the patient from the foot of the bed (albeit in a more familiar manner) before turning to consult the patient's notes, which were handed to him by the sister. He then discussed the details of the case with me, including special investigations, before turning again to the patient. Then came the most significant change. He walked around the bed, sat down on it next to the patient and, holding her hand, addressed her directly with the words: 'Everything seems to be fine, and how are you in yourself?'.

When I relay this encounter to my students, it doesn't usually strike them as either odd or amusing, precisely because it chimes so well with our present-day medical norms. Yet, on reflection, the incongruity of the dislocation, which led us to laugh before, is still apparent. However, it seems to be dealt with in a different way now. There is an old message and a new one being presented simultaneously. The first, 'Everything seems to be fine', would seem to convey a very similar meaning to the whole of the earlier retort '... you don't need to worry about this, it has nothing to do with you'. Both statements refer to the bodily or technical component of the patient, and are the consultant's statement to the patient. The message is — you as a patient neither need to worry nor have any need to know about the bodily element of your identity, and it is our duty to take responsibility for it, and yours to be reassured and so be helped to get well. The second part of the communication did not have a counterpart before, though, and is therefore both new and quite different, being phrased as a question to the patient: '... and how are you in yourself?'. It is a personal enquiry about the patient's subjective feelings and experience, and the change mirrors changes from the Victorian to the modern family model. The consultant (father) is taking on some of the nursing sister's (mother's) more personal role, and she at the same time takes on more of his traditional responsibilities. The patient (child) meanwhile is positively invited to communicate directly with the consultant (father), but in matters of his choosing.

Now, these two ward rounds, although not necessarily typical of their times, nevertheless capture something of their spirit, and we can see that there is both a continuity and a discontinuity between them. They both involve the assumption of a patient duality, relating to a separate bodily and personal identity. The difference, though, is how the patient's personal matters are dealt with; in the earlier encounter there is a complete division of labour between the consultant and the nursing sister, with the latter dealing with all personal matters. In the later encounter the consultant assumes partial responsibility for dealing with them in a more informal manner than his general approach to the bodily or technical concerns. So while the consultant surgeon of the 1960s presented a single persona in dealing with his patients, the consultant physician of the 1990s presented a dual personality, principally unchanged in its technical component, but quite different in its personal component. So the relationships between the doctor, nurse and patient have in one way remained rooted in the past, and in another altered dramatically.

This more modern and complex relationship exposes inherent difficulties though. The doctor has personally to manage the two halves of his new persona, the technical and the personal, and he may have serious difficulties in keeping them separate. In the personal encounter, he (or now perhaps she) is directly engaged with the patient and, having acceded to dealing with personal questions, may no longer be able to resist dealing with queries about technical questions. There are those who believe that the resolution of this difficulty is already at hand because patients now have such ready access to technical medical knowledge, especially via the Internet, that they can negotiate with their doctors about their treatment and care on equal terms. This is the extreme version of the informed consent doctrine, but it is only applicable to acute self-contained medical episodes, and if applied elsewhere misrepresents the nature of most treatment and care, and the corresponding doctor–patient relationship. It is certainly true that in general patients now expect and demand to know more than in the past, but not in order to cast the doctor as merely a sophisticated technical adviser and so dispense with the need to trust him. Jacob describes the situation as follows:

> What does seem clear is that the amount of information now required to enable people generally to take courage is greater and that submission is no longer unreasoned: there is now an insistence on making reply and on reasoning why. I would agree that the medical profession has responded to this change. This is not to say that true self-determination has become common: rather it is to say those in authority, in particular, doctors, have recognised that greater degrees of explanation are required in order to secure the patient's compliance. The philosophical divide between compliance and liberty remains.[2]

However, the location of the boundary between compliance and liberty is no longer clearly marked but has to be constantly negotiated, and thus is a source of uncertainty for both doctor and patient. So this produces a problem for the consultant physician in his attempt to separate personal and technical matters and maintain the strict line between them, which he set out to establish through his opening remark 'Everything seems to be fine' (technically).

In the earlier relationship this was much easier to manage, because by never engaging with the patient directly (apart from a formal introduction), the consultant surgeon was effortlessly in charge when maintaining the boundary between technical and personal matters. He therefore controlled the extent of his own responsibility, and thus also that of the nursing sister and patients. By aggregation the hospital system as a whole was then clearly definable and so readily manageable. It had absolute and therefore definite limits which all the participants as well as the politicians could rely upon.

Dualism and healing

These two snapshots of medical encounters on ward rounds in the 1960s and 1990s demonstrate that although the traditional biomedical model had typically become modified over this period (as biopsychosocial model B describes in Chapter 11, and consonant with the additive model of medical humanities described in Chapter 9), dualism remained as a fundamental feature which had not changed.

The influence of dualism in Western thinking has a long lineage. Plato was a dualist and, as part of the Ancient Greek heritage, was an important inspiration for the Renaissance which lasted from the fourteenth to the sixteenth centuries. Then, in the first half of the seventeenth century, Descartes constructed his famous formulation of mind–body dualism. The focus here, though, is not directly on Cartesian dualism so much as the general trend in the historical development of ideas which his work has come to symbolise and sustain. Since Descartes' time, dualism has become firmly embedded in all Western thought and has had a profound effect on all knowledge, social structure and practice. Medicine then has been shaped by it, both in a general way as well as more obviously in relation to the separation of mind and body. Thus dualism has had an important impact on the following inter-related aspects of medicine – knowledge and research, conceptions of health, illness and disease, the nature of the human person, and the values and goals of medicine and healthcare – and these will be considered in more detail later.

Dualism then represents a fault-line which runs through the whole of modern Western medicine, and this contrasts with all the other mainstream systems of medicine, both historical and contemporary, which are rooted in humoralism (and particular attention is paid to these in Chapter 10). Now 'healing', as well as 'health', is rooted in the idea of wholeness, and so is in tension with the divisions produced by dualism. So the ability to engender healing is severely compromised by Western medicine in a way that does not apply to these other medical systems. It is commonly thought that this is the price that has to be paid as an inevitable corollary of Western medicine's scientific and technical achievements, but it will be shown that this is not so. Rather, there are serious flaws in biomedicine's scientific programme, which arise because of the dualistic assumptions of the system as a whole. However, these usually go unnoticed because the analytic framework is itself constrained by these assumptions. Western medicine has therefore, in large measure, sacrificed its healing tradition, which existed before biomedicine became predominant, and in order to restore it we will first need to examine the detailed workings of dualism in Western medicine. This will then provide a basis from which to explore some of the ways in which dualism might be overcome, not at the expense of science and technology, but with the prospect of their refinement and improvement.

The following diagram illustrates the way in which dualism affects knowledge in general and medical knowledge in particular, the focus here being on the latter.

Natural sciences	Social sciences	Arts
Quantitative		Qualitative
General or universal		Individual
Cause		Meaning

The assumption which underlies this general scheme is that by dividing medical knowledge into quantitative ('scientific') and qualitative ('non-scientific') aspects, the former will be concerned with generalisation and cause, and the latter with the individual and meaning. Problems arise, though, with maintaining this boundary once the social sciences and the arts are accepted as subjects which are not only relevant to medicine but are open to academic enquiry, as they have become increasingly since the 1960s. The additive model of medical humanities, through which a simple addition of qualitative to quantitative knowledge is envisaged, avoids this difficulty but, as I suggest in 'The nature and role of medical humanities' (Chapter 9), is untenable. The alternative integrated model, by breaching the dualistic division, changes the status of medical knowledge in all three epistemological categories, so that to a degree they merge into one another, and this also has implications for medical research. A more detailed examination of current orthodoxy concerning medical knowledge and research will help as a starting point for this analysis.

Medical scientists, who derive their classification from biomedical theory, picture a hierarchy of research methods, which relate to the three modalities of knowledge and which are ranked as follows:

- *highest value* – derived from the **natural sciences**, involving quantitative methods, with the randomised controlled trial (RCT) as the 'gold standard'
- *intermediate value* – derived from the **social sciences**, involving both quantitative and qualitative (or ethnographic) methods
- *lowest value* – derived from the **arts** (especially literature and poetry), involving narratives or stories.

What this ranking reveals is a circular argument. It assumes that the natural sciences take precedence over the social sciences, and the social sciences over the arts, because what is being sought is an absolute account of knowledge and so also of truth, which in its pure form is represented by the natural sciences and can only be revealed by the methods appropriate to them. In this positivist conception natural science is the final guarantor of all forms of knowledge, against which other forms of knowledge always fall short and so are of uncertain as well as lower status. The word most commonly used to describe this type of scientific knowledge is 'valid', indicating that it alone has ultimate reliability.

The additive model of medical humanities, and biopsychosocial model B which parallels it, demonstrate this priority. They are split into two components, one being 'scientific' and the other a 'non-scientific' supplement which, although it is recognised, necessarily produces knowledge of doubtful 'validity' and so of lower status and uncertain application.

A further question then is where to draw the line between these two realms, and because the social sciences are seen as being intermediate between the natural sciences and the arts, it is here that disputes have raged most fiercely. This itself is a demonstration of the weight that society and professionals place on the 'scientific' label. The most contentious issue has concerned how far it is appropriate to extend the use of quantitative methodology and so of 'science' to behavioural issues. From the traditional and purest biomedical perspective the word 'science' should be reserved for the natural sciences, so that it is improper to use the term 'social science' at all. Others, though, may permit an extension of 'science' to cover some or all psychological and social issues, or even further to cover the arts. So the dispute ranges over the whole of this continuum, and the different positions described in Chapter 9 represent particular stopping points on this spectrum.

There is currently no consensus about which of these positions to adopt, and a different way forward is to acknowledge the sovereignty of the three epistemological realms without ceding priority to the natural sciences. Each then provides its own account of what knowledge it produces and the methods appropriate to that knowledge. The three realms are then seen as developing knowledge and truths which stand alongside each other. The status of qualitative knowledge is thus raised, and this may be to the extent of regarding it as of equal, or even greater, worth than quantitative knowledge. This is the furthest limit to which the additive model can be stretched, but contradictions and problems still remain.

This is because earlier concerns about dualistic medical knowledge have not been resolved in favour of greater unity, but rather the reverse — a range of different and incommensurable types of knowledge have been produced with no common source of reference. The tension produced by dualism between universal medical knowledge based on scientific positivism and individually derived medical knowledge has then been converted into one of multiple categories of knowledge and so of multiple tensions between them. Such relativism, if extrapolated to its furthest extent, leads to subjectivism in which each individual's view is accounted as good as any other. Nietzsche anticipated the implications of this philosophical position for health over a century ago:

> For there is no health as such, and all attempts to define anything in that way have been miserable failures. Even the determination of what health means for your *body* depends on your goal, your horizon, your energies, your drives, your errors, and above all on the ideals and phantasms of your soul. Thus there are innumerable healths of the body; and ... the more we put aside the dogma of the 'equality of men', the more must the concept of a normal health, along with a normal diet and the normal course of an illness be abandoned by our physicians. Only then would the time have come to reflect on the health and sicknesses of the *soul*, and to find the peculiar virtue of each man in the health of his soul: in one person's case this health could, of course, look like the opposite of health in another person.[3]

So in trying to avoid the pitfalls of absolutism in the form of medical positivism, the danger is of resorting to its polar opposite, subjectivism as applied to health, which is equally untenable because it suggests an unbridgeable dialogue of the deaf, which is inimitable to healing. Social constructionism is commonly posed as a way out of this impasse by its claim that medicine is ultimately a social practice. However, although it does not view science as having a role in explaining medicine, it continues to acknowledge that medicine utilises science. Thus the two elements, 'scientific' and 'social', remain and the original dualistic structure is left intact.

The integrated model represents an attempt to deal with these problems by steering a course between the two extremes of medical positivism and either subjectivism or social constructionism, in order to provide a sustainable alternative which endorses man's healing potential. What it involves are the following positive features. First, that the three categories of medical knowledge, rather than being divided up in the traditional way, are on a continuum which provides a whole spectrum of viewpoints. This is not to propose a form of medical relativism but rather is an acknowledgement that because values are always involved, and are contestable, judgements have to be made about the appropriateness of these different viewpoints and the varieties of knowledge derived from them. So there is no absolute fixed knowledge, but equally some viewpoints and their associated conceptions are better than others, and this determination has to be continually revised. When the knowledge involved has enduring physical or material 'penetration' (e.g. in the biological aspects of certain conditions, such as tuberculosis which has been recognised since antiquity), radical revision may seem inappropriate, and for use in everyday practice it may well make sense to continue operating with traditional models. However, even in these 'hardest' of cases, the material as well as the non-material (or social) aspects can never be immune from revision, once they are properly understood as lying on a single continuum, and so are inseparable. An example of this new unified conception is dealt with in 'What are heart attacks? Rethinking some aspects of medical knowledge' (Chapter 2), and when applied more generally has several novel consequences.

First, it changes the status of all research methods, overturning the hierarchy derived from biomedicine (see above). It places the whole range of methods on a more equitable basis, each only being of value insofar as it is judged appropriate to the particular situation, which has to be continuously revisited and re-evaluated. Thus, the RCT, rather than representing a pinnacle of research methodology, becomes just one method amongst many, no longer providing automatically privileged knowledge.

Second, reductionism does not carry the same meaning as before because the knowledge which is sought is not being judged against an absolute standard. The knowledge derived from each viewpoint has its own strengths and weaknesses, and so has to be judged against other viewpoints. Hence the production of knowledge is by its nature a collective activity which has to be constantly revised. For practical purposes medical knowledge will need to be held constant at times, but only as a frozen frame may be in a continuously running film so it can be examined and analysed. Whilst the film is open to myriad possible interpretations, the still frame becomes for a moment the concrete focus of attention. This conception of knowledge is an attempt then to give weight to a more general or universal perspective, whilst at the same time allowing for the endless variety of individual views.

In more practical terms this allows the doctor's account and the patient's narrative to be brought together. At any one time they can be seen as being like two separate frames from the same film, neither of which, at any one moment, has to take priority, but both of which are important to the ongoing film. Thus the doctor in the second consultation would no longer be able to clearly distinguish his technical assessment from the patient's personal story, and dualistic medical knowledge would have given way to an ongoing exchange between doctor and patient in a unitary production.

One of my colleagues, John Saunders, points to Polanyi's analysis of personal and tacit knowledge as a route to understanding this type of relationship – 'There seemed to me to be a need to connect the personal, the experience of people and about people, with the world of our admittedly incomplete trials'[4] – and Polanyi argues that:

> ... we can reconnect science and the humanities; that personal participation and imagination are *essentially* involved in both science and the humanities and that meanings created in the sciences are no closer to reality than meanings created in the arts, moral judgements or religion.[5]

This fits well with my earlier theoretical analysis, but the way in which policy and practice are being developed at present, with biomedicine still predominant and the recent drive to implement evidence-based medicine (EBM), suggests that the possibility of its being generally accepted is severely compromised. This situation applied to hospital medicine for many years before the formal introduction of

EBM, but is getting progressively worse as hospital consultants become increasingly specialised. Those few general physicians still remaining in Britain may be able to maintain a practice style which combines personal and technical elements to a limited extent but, like Bernard Lown in America,[6] they are part of a dying breed.

The incursion that this approach is making into general practice is equally worrying, because as argued in 'The tradition of the healer' (Chapter 4) and 'The enduring appeal of the Victorian family doctor' (Chapter 5), general practice has acted as a counterweight to hospital medicine. Within orthodox medicine the traditional model of general practice has been the main locus of healing, and the general practitioner the continuation of the 'archetypal' healer. This has been possible because the traditional general practitioner has resisted dualism in practice, through not implementing biomedical theory as prescribed in the textbooks. However, such resistance has become increasingly untenable in recent years, as it is eroded by the imposition of quantitatively derived guidelines[7] and the fragmentation of the general practitioner's role.

The traditional disposition and role of nurses may also provide them with the potential to act as archetypal healers in the community, which would seem of vital importance now that they are beginning to be employed as first-line practitioners in primary care. The fact that their education and training are becoming increasingly driven by technical procedures could, however, be fatally damaging to this possibility. The paradox here is that just at the time when doctors are being encouraged to recognise the importance of more personal involvement, there is a real danger of nurses giving it less attention.

Turning more explicitly now to the arts and the epistemological spectrum of which they are part, it is sometimes suggested that studying literature can only be of relevance to individual medical cases – see, for example, Downie.[8] However, if the involvement of the arts in medicine is viewed as part of a single continuum of knowledge, which includes the natural and social sciences, the expectation would be that all aspects of medical knowledge would have some general as well as individual relevance, and so also break down the barriers between cause and meaning. Thus the greatest works of art, literature and poetry which touch on universal meanings must also have relevance to generalisation and its implications for causation.

Virginia Woolf, in her essay 'On Being Ill' (1926), bemoans the general lack of insightful literature about medicine – '... it becomes strange indeed that illness has not taken its place with love, battle and jealousy among the prime themes of literature'[9] – and it is probably because biomedicine has so clearly separated these two aspects, cause and meaning, that she came to this view. Her own work points to the underlying reason why this is so, and prefigures much of the subsequent philosophical debate which has only become topical very recently. The following passage brings out the central issue:

> ... literature does its best to maintain that its concern is with the mind; that the body is a sheet of plain glass through which the soul looks straight and clear ... People write always about the doings of the mind; the thoughts that come of it; its noble plans; how it has civilised the universe. They show it ignoring the body in the philosopher's turret; or kicking the body, like an old leather football, across leagues of snow

and desert in the pursuit of conquest or discovery. Those great wars which it wages by itself, with the mind a slave to it, in the solitude of the bedroom against the assault of fever or the oncome of melancholia, are neglected. Nor is the reason far to seek. To look these things squarely in the face would need the courage of a lion; a robust philosophy; a reason rooted in the bowels of the earth.[10]

What this shows is the deadening effect that mind–body dualism has and the way that it reduces the possibilities for the expression of illness. The reduction of the body to a mechanised thing limits the ability of even the most creative writers in what they are able to say about illness. Hence the cultural understanding of health and illness is diminished as the price that has been paid for 'scientific' ideas about causation. Yet at the same time these latter ideas have been distorted and so are crude notions precisely because they have excluded the creative impulses that those in arts and literature can provide. Thus these are two sides of the same coin, the primitive reductionism of medical scientism and the loss of creativity because of its restriction to the arts.

Merleau-Ponty, who was a phenomenologist, first raised these issues in his most celebrated book *Phenomenologie de la Perception* published in 1945, in which he described the need for a 'philosophy of the body'.[11] He dispensed with mind–body dualism by viewing mind and body as inextricably intertwined. Much of his focus, as well as that of subsequent work, has been on the implications for the nature of the person (see below), but those relating to epistemology are of equal importance, and these two aspects are inescapably linked.

Leder, who has done much in recent years to explain and extend Merleau-Ponty's work as it applies to medicine, brought out this linkage in the following quotation (*see also* Chapter 2):

> Just as the lived body is an intertwining of intentionality and materiality, subject and object, so we would arrive at a medicine of the *intertwining*. That is, our notions of disease and treatment would always involve a chiasmatic blending of biological and existential terms, wherein these terms are not seen as ultimately opposed, but mutually implicatory and involved in intricate 'logics' of exchange.[12]

Medical knowledge is then no longer seen as objective, but must be reinterpreted in the light of this reconceptualisation of the person as involving an intertwining of both subject and object.

In a later paper, Leder adds a further dimension, that of the relationship of reciprocity between the individual sick person and other people:

> World and self still lack their full depth, however, until reference is made to another schismatic relation: that which connects me to other perceivers. My perspective and that of the other intertwine in mutual validation, while never quite coinciding. The reality of the world is secured via its presence to other eyes, other hands, than my own. Even my own body is brought to fruition only through this gaze of another.[13]

This further insight is vitally important, not least because it demonstrates that medical knowledge is not produced by individuals in isolation, but is necessarily a collective and hence a social matter, and so avoids the extreme subjectivism which was referred to earlier in relation to Nietzsche. 'Conceptions of persons and dementia' (Chapter 3), which deals with the nature of the person in both individual and social terms and the complementary conceptualisation of dementia, attempts to show how all these ideas fit together.

From this new vantage, with its two strands of continuous interaction at individual and social levels, 'subject' and 'object' become somewhat redundant notions as they are no longer separable. This also applies to 'illness' (as subjective) and 'disease' (as objective), which then has further implications for concepts of health, and these issues will be explored further below.

The crucial steps in this reconfiguration of medical knowledge can now be seen in their relationship with the two models of medical humanities. The additive model involves the switch of attention from objective to subjective knowledge and from cause to meaning, whilst the integrated model involves a further move concerning the reciprocal interaction of object and subject at two levels, within the sick person and within the wider social world which that person inhabits. The very ideas 'subject' and 'object', 'cause' and 'meaning' can then only be understood in combination with each other, and so the traditional sense in which they are used tends to be lost. They emerge as part of a single unity, but in our present culture we find difficulty in expressing this unreservedly:

> 'Flesh and blood' expresses well the chiasmatic identity-in-difference of perceptual and visceral life. The expression itself appears in the dictionary as if one word. To be 'flesh and blood' is clearly to be one thing. A life entire unto itself. Yet the 'and' is never expunged. There is always an écart, a divergence of two existential levels.[14]

Nevertheless, 'flesh and blood' opens the way to overcoming dualism, and so to the possibility of a new meld of arts and science in medicine. The separation of technical and personal medical knowledge then disappears as well, and the doctor–patient consultation from the 1990s becomes problematic, as much as that from the 1960s.

Whilst this has direct significance for all medical practice and research, it also has relevance in relation to understanding knowledge more generally. It is only then by placing medical knowledge within this wider context that it is possible to fully comprehend the notion of healing which is being sought, and this will be explored in the next section.

From rationalism to reason and healing

In *Return to Reason*, Toulmin argues that:

> Seventeenth-century natural scientists … dreamed of uniting the ideas of rationality, necessity and certainty into a single mathematical package, and the effect of that dream was to inflict on Human Reason a wound that remained unhealed for three hundred years – a wound from which we are only recently beginning to recover.[15]

The programmes of philosophy set in train by Descartes, and of science by Galileo, in the 1630s, provided the foundation for this dream, and the dualisms of mind and body, as well as arts and sciences, were central to it. Now the argument made so far is that the long-standing developments of this histor-ical dualism had and continue to have a profound influence on medicine and healthcare, making healing in its fullest sense impossible to achieve even by the best healthcare providers. This is because of the epistemological, institutional and cultural constraints within which they work, which derive from this histor-ical framework.

In order to deal with this as a general issue, Toulmin sees the need to return to the source of the problem '... and re-establish the proper balance between Theory and Practice, Logic and Rhetoric, Rationality and Reasonableness',[16] the divisions between which were a consequence of the new seventeenth-century order. His proposal as to how to achieve this then involves recalling '... the prac-tical wisdom of sixteenth-century humanists, who hoped to recapture the modesty that had made it possible for them to live happily with uncertainty, ambiguity and pluralism'.[17]

Consideration will first be given to how this historical analysis applies specif-ically to medicine, and second to what implications may be drawn for the future of medicine and healthcare. In relation to the former, the particular issue that will be addressed is why this modernist programme based on rationalism, which began in the seventeenth century, did not have any substantial effect on the practice of mainstream medicine until the second half of the eighteenth century, or become dominant until the second half of the nineteenth century, and still continues to have such a hold on orthodox medicine today, when its influence has been de-clining in other spheres of life for the past century or so.

Let us consider two seventeenth-century English doctors, Harvey and Syden-ham, who today are widely celebrated as pioneers of modern medicine: Harvey for his work on the circulation of the blood (published as *De Motu Cordis* in 1628), and Sydenham for his systematic clinical observations on epidemics of infectious diseases (published in the 1660s and 1670s), which in the nineteenth century gained him the title of the 'English Hippocrates'.

The issue here, though, is that the retrospective construction of Harvey's and Sydenham's contribution to medicine became framed so as to fit with the assump-tions of a later orthodoxy. This involved the selection of particular aspects of their work, whilst other aspects were ignored or even denounced. Thus those features which have come to be regarded as radical and forward looking are highlighted, whilst others which have come to be regarded as conservative and backward looking disappeared from view. The focus here will be on the latter because they provide a more rounded picture of medicine in the seventeenth century, and so a firmer basis from which to gauge how medicine has developed in subsequent centuries, as well as a different view of future prospects.

What is missing currently from popular descriptions of Harvey's work is his technological account of the circulation of the blood, described in terms of vitalism, with the heart as the essential life-giving organ which enlivened the blood. Such ideas are now seen as 'unscientific' and are so outmoded as to have disappeared. Sydenham's work also contained notions now seen as outdated, notably his appeal to that part of the Hippocratic tradition that emphasises natural healing abilities, which also relied on the notion of a 'life-giving' or 'vital' principle.

Now this vitalist notion – which posits that the nature of living things cannot be explained only in physical or material terms – has been almost universally rejected by scientists since the nineteenth century, but is integral to the understanding of Harvey's and Sydenham's world views (although there were also differences between them). So focusing as we now do on the mechanical features of the circulatory system in Harvey's case, and the reductionist aspects of Sydenham's clinical observations, is a serious misrepresentation of their work. In fact, the abstraction of Harvey's and Sydenham's physical or material innovations is doubly distorting because it is not just one-sided, but also obscures the broader conception provided by the indivisibility of the physical and spiritual nature of the body as inseparable from the person. Neither of them were therefore relying on mind–body dualism, and so, far from being straightforwardly pioneers of modern medicine, had not dispensed with those vitalist or spiritual ideas, which continued to connect them with the earlier ideas of healing which derived from the Renaissance.

In the succeeding two centuries, vitalism and the spiritual dimension of man which it represented in medicine gradually lost ground as more and more emphasis came to be placed on the mechanical, physical and biochemical dimension, until the link between them was formally broken in the second half of the nineteenth century through the rise of biomedical orthodoxy. The medical establishment's interest in this is chiefly in celebrating how this process developed in what is seen as an unbroken chain but, as already indicated in relation to Harvey and Sydenham, the story is much less clear-cut than this. In fact, it involves turning the usual presumption on its head, and instead of marvelling at the progress made, raises questions instead as to why there was so much resistance to it that it took two centuries to become firmly established in medical theory and practice. This will require a brief re-examination of one centrally important aspect of the story, the emergence of the disease concept, as a way of presenting a contrary interpretation, which may be of assistance in reflecting differently on the current situation.

The Dutch physician Boerhaave had a seminal influence on the development of medical thought in the eighteenth century and '... created a history whose peaks were Hippocrates, Bacon, Sydenham and Newton'.[18] Galen is absent from this list, an omission that would have been unthinkable in previous centuries, and Sydenham was chosen to fill his place. The main reason for his selection was because by proposing that in infectious diseases all patients suffer from the *same* condition, he was seen as the first doctor to have initiated the transformation of medicine from being patient centred to being disease centred, or to be moving from a physiological to an ontological concept of disease. This is now seen as the first stage of a process, which we largely take for granted, and as having three elements which were discovered in three stages by great men between about 1650 and 1875: 'These are the clinical (Sydenham), the pathological (Bichat) and the causal (Pasteur and Koch).'[19] Sydenham, though, would undoubtedly have been resistant to his work being taken up in this way, and why this is so will now be explored in more detail.

Seventeenth-century physicians were private practitioners who relied on their wealthy clients in maintaining their high income and status, but because of his attachment to the 'good old cause' of the Commonwealth, Sydenham was politically tainted and so forced into the most unusual position for a physician of working mainly with the poor.[20] It was this aspect of Sydenham's work, though, which gave him licence to exploit his relative position of power, so distancing himself from his patient's individual concerns and seeing them in a way which allowed him to record clinical observations on them in a detached manner. The reductive elements of his newly minted knowledge had then been expropriated from the patients so as to pool them and subject them to mathematical calculation.

In 'The enduring appeal of the Victorian family doctor' (Chapter 5), it is shown how it was not until the second half of the nineteenth century that the general practitioner was able to routinely attend on patients from all levels of society. So this new era of political equality in medical practice did not arrive till some two centuries after Sydenham's original work. This delay relates most obviously to a general political resistance to the Enlightenment ideas of the social equality of man so that 'Democratic rhetoric on health citizenship failed to translate into reality in any late Enlightenment state',[21] but partly also to resistance to the idea of bodily equality. In 'Contrasting perspectives of inequalities in health and in medical care' (Chapter 7), it is shown that as late as 1800 there was a general assumption that officers in the army were physically as well as socially superior to their men, and this was seen as a natural state. It was only then in the nineteenth century that these attitudes slowly faded, and even so they persisted in a modified form in the eugenics movement.

Also there was considerable resistance to dissection of the human body till well into the nineteenth century,[22] and the practice of cremation only became accepted in England and Wales in the 1880s, having been contested for many years. In both these cases it was the violation of the integrity of the body which was at issue, with the objectors to change being cast as unscientific and irrational.

So these two deeply held assumptions about the body, concerning inequality and integrity, were largely unquestioned till the nineteenth century, and in some respects still linger on today (as shown, for example, by recent public concern over the removal and storage of organs of children who have died in hospital[23]). So it is no surprise that Sydenham would also have held these assumptions, and that he had little time for anatomy. Hence he would neither have embraced ideas about the pathological equality of the body, nor about causal equality in physiological terms, and these were necessary to the construction of the other elements of the disease model. His conception only required that equality be extended to the surface manifestations of disease, as an expression of the universal and natural powers of healing possessed by all human beings, but in uniquely different ways. Importantly, mind–body dualism, which was indispensable to the later development of the disease model, was alien to Sydenham's medical views, as to his more conventional contemporaries, and this would not change until the clinical gaze became refocused on internal bodily arrangements.[24]

It has been established then that ideas about bodily equality and mind–body dualism were incorporated into medicine relatively late on, and we will now turn to examining the reasons for this. Toulmin claims that the programme of modernism, which is commonly identified as beginning with the work of Descartes and Galileo in the 1630s, and held out the prospect of continuous political and scientific progress based on rationality, was never actually implemented but followed instead a more partial and zigzag course.[25] However, modernism made even less progress in relation to medicine, particularly in clinical practice which changed very little until the nineteenth century. So in comparison with other areas of life, medicine was stubbornly resistant to reform, and this was at root because it became the locus of social and religious values, which the modernist programme was eschewing. So as other areas of life, most notably the theoretical sciences, progressively abandoned these values, they remained in medicine for much longer, and this had a number of consequences which were of relevance to medicine and society more generally.

As in humoral theory, the body was seen to mirror the wider society, and ideas about the body changed relatively littler before about 1800; this was a factor in ensuring the continuity of the religious and political order. Thus the traditional hierarchical pattern embodied in the church and state was reinforced by the parallel hierarchy enshrined in the notion of bodily inequality. This then had the paradoxical effect of helping to preserve the superior status of the clergy over that of doctors, but at the same time ceded to doctors the potential to undermine the position of the church when medicine eventually adopted scientific rationalism in the nineteenth century. So when the Victorian family doctor, Dr Thorne (Trollope's fictional character described in Chapter 5), challenges the authority of Lady Arabella in the name of modern medicine, he is not only eroding an ancient political system but is also usurping some of the functions previously reserved to the clergy.

Also, the concept of a person which prevailed until the seventeenth century entailed a notion of bodily integrity which involved physical and spiritual unity. This was first challenged by the modernist conception developed by Locke which dissolved this unity by focusing only on physical features of the person. This was another example of the theoretical development of dualism in the seventeenth century. Yet it was the older idea of bodily integrity which continued to inform medical practice until the nineteenth century, and so is a further illustration of how modernist ideas came relatively late to medicine.

The analysis in 'Conceptions of persons and dementia' (Chapter 3) is then about how the condition called dementia came to be reframed by biomedical science in tandem with medicine's acceptance of a modernist conception of the person. The argument which follows involves questioning whether the epistemological and moral complex which emerged from this process is adequate in addressing the issues which are now arising, and what is proposed instead is a reconfiguration of some of the older ideas in the contemporary context. The analysis of a particular case history also shows that the original ideas of physical and spiritual unity have never been eliminated altogether, but rather have become recessive as conversely biomedical science became predominant, following Pickstone's notion of 'coexistence models in which paradigms *run alongside* each other'.[26]

This last point extends the argument about the relationship between modernism and medicine that has been made so far. It suggests not only that medical practice did little to adapt to modernist ideas in the seventeenth and eighteenth centuries, but that even when it did so in the nineteenth and twentieth centuries, it did not forsake older ideas altogether. This applies particularly to general practice, but less so to hospital medicine where they were either reduced to technical and personal components (as described earlier in relation to the two hospital ward rounds) or were marginalised. The persistence of these older ideas is also clear in alternative medicine (*see* Chapter 10), which when considered collectively may be seen as having continued to embrace and develop them. These traditional concepts have then not so much gone away as lost their previous status and gone partially underground. They therefore remain in place in a position to return when conditions are more favourable, and this is what is happening now at different rates and with varying degrees of acceptance in different areas of medicine. This process is perhaps clearest in the current resurgence of alternative medicine, and its rise in status as complementary medicine.

The rationalist ideas that led to the rise of the biomedical model still take precedence, though, and this is demonstrated in two other chapters, each of which addresses the priority given to biological over social factors (the fact that 'biomedical' or 'medical' is often used as a synonym for 'biological' illustrating the strength of that priority). In 'Changing priorities in residential medical and social services' (Chapter 6), it is shown how care labelled as social is downgraded in relation to that deemed medical. Also, in 'Sudden infant deaths: models of health and illness' (Chapter 1), in which three possible contending models – biomedical, social epidemiological and socio-economic – are compared as ways of explaining cot deaths, the pre-eminence given to the biomedical model is clearly shown.

Nevertheless, the debate over the social dimension of medicine has never gone away because it cannot be readily contained within a rationalist discourse, and increasingly is becoming heard in both practical and theoretical contexts. So in relation to the issues concerning medical and social care for the elderly, raised in Chapter 6, it has recently led to a dispute about policy, particularly regarding who should pay for care.[27]

Returning to the example of cot deaths, the social epidemiological model, though it takes second place to the biomedical model, has not been excluded because of its practical utility, and this then opens the way for the more radical questions which the socio-economic model raises. This is illustrated by epidemiological research which was reported shortly after the work republished here first appeared in 1988. It revealed that when babies are put to sleep on their backs the incidence of cot deaths is substantially reduced.[28] This led to a 'back to sleep' campaign in the early 1990s which has been highly successful in cutting the number of cot deaths in Britain as a whole.[29] What is of particular interest in this context is that the reason for undertaking this research did not come about in order to test a new scientific hypothesis, but rather from a pragmatic suggestion that babies might be better off on their backs.

Taking a wider perspective, medicine has witnessed a curious paradox since the late nineteenth century. The predominance of biomedicine, which has led to medicine's ascendancy over the church, has been enabled by the claim that modern scientific medicine can dispense with values and thus deny any definitive place for personal, social and spiritual elements. On the other hand, in the same period medicine has become the repository for dealing with these same values, which were previously mainly the province of the church. This applies in particular to issues of life, birth, death and the nature of the person, which in recent years have become more visible through debates about fertility, genetic engineering and euthanasia.

The ambiguity of medicine's current denial of values at the same time that it has become their key locus may then help to explain why society is witnessing a love–hate relationship with medicine, and many doctors are feeling so ambivalent and uneasy about their role. The public and politicians both love the technical utility of medicine's modern programme, but are at the same time unwilling to face up to its shortcomings because this would require an open acknowledgement of the need to confront these contradictions, and so each side avoids taking its share of responsibility. By allowing medicine and healthcare to adopt a semi-autonomous status, partially sealed away from the rest of society by its apparently value-free technical status, people can feel comforted by the sense that at its deepest and most fundamental level, life is secure, because medicine, at least, provides certainty. For some it is only the prospect of death which disturbs this evasion of reality, but for the majority there is an inchoate yet pervasive sense that all is not well, and this is expressed in a wide range of different ways, e.g. the huge rise in popularity of alternative medicine, and open requests for assisted suicide.

So although this ambiguity has also meant that medicine has been left till last in the switch from rationalist certainties to the puzzling reflections that post-modernism requires, they are increasingly becoming unavoidable. It may then be that this will not only lead to a new medical cosmology (on the lines proposed in Chapter 11), but precisely because medicine has never entirely succumbed to the rationalist impulse of the seventeenth century, the issues raised by medicine will prove valuable in the restructuring of other areas of society as well. The return to reason proposed by Toulmin requires a simultaneous transformation of medicine and society in such a way as to reconnect them. So the return to the healing tradition and the conception of health that will be required in bringing this about applies to both medicine and society.

Values and goals in health and healing

The editor of the *British Medical Journal* described a recent issue as perhaps the most important to have been published for 50 years because of a cluster of papers in which it was claimed that a pill with six ingredients could prevent 80% of heart attacks and strokes.[30] By coincidence the same issue of the journal reported on a government White Paper on genetics, *Our Inheritance, Our Future: realising the potential of genetics in the NHS*:

> An estimated six out of ten people will, by the age of 60, develop a disease that is at least partially genetically determined. The White Paper lays out a future NHS where patients are routinely tested in GP surgeries or local pharmacies for predisposition to common diseases such as heart disease and diabetes. Treatment, lifestyle advice and monitoring will then follow.
>
> In addition, the Human Genetics Commission has been asked to consider the case for screening babies at birth and storing genetic information for future use.[31]

Taken together, this is a graphic illustration of how far the medical and political establishment remains in thrall to the set of values and goals embodied in an unreconstructed biomedical programme. The prospect being held out is of the elimination of disease and disability, to be achieved technically through a combination of drug therapy and genetic surveillance, each to be applied on a population basis. If implemented, such an approach would turn the majority of the population as a whole into 'partial patients' (*see* Chapter 8), and so would bring about the concerns that this raises in a most extreme form.

At first sight it appears that medicine is still being viewed solely as a scientific and technical arena, which despite all the criticisms and debates of recent years has not relinquished the prospect of finding quick biological fixes to life's most serious problems. The hubris of a unipolar Asclepian notion of health and disease, with medicine 'the last and purist bastion of Enlightenment dreams',[32] would seem untarnished. Yet behind this brash front there may be a different impulse, one of medicine preparing the way for the possibility of a more holistic approach to health and well-being. Medicine could then be seen as providing an opportunity for the positive qualities of well-being to be developed by other means. In this way it would seem that the pure Asclepian notion of technical medicine could be supplemented by a Hygeian one of personal and social well-being, but without the latter becoming part of medicine itself.

However, what this assumes is that there are two discrete sets of resources relating to 'medicine' and 'well-being' which can be kept in separate compartments, even when they are being amalgamated within the expanded conception of 'health and well-being'. But this more holistic approach, which fits comfortably with the famous World Health Organization (WHO) definition of health as 'a state of complete physical, mental and social well-being, not merely the absence of disease or infirmity', opens the way for the inclusion of almost anything, and there are two problems with this. First, the original Asclepian idea of medical need as fixed, limited and value free has been replaced by one of medical demand, implying that everything technical that can possibly be done should be done, but as if this notion was still value free. Second, and related to the first point, it fails to deal with the difficulties posed by adding qualitative matters of 'well-being' to quantitative 'medical' matters. The heart of the problem is that the rationalist values of biomedicine have only been partially abandoned, sufficient to ease some of medicine's constrictions, but not to deal adequately with the more holistic concepts of 'health' or 'health and well-being'. So rather than achieving a new and balanced relationship between Asclepius and Hygeia, there is instead an extension and permeation of scientific rationalism to cover Hygeia as well as Asclepius. Thus one absolute conception has been replaced with another and this must be confronted if progress is to be made in finding a different conception without the precision of such clear boundaries.

The underlying reason for the enduring attachment to the apparent certainties of scientific rationalism is captured in the following passage from Hauerwas:

> Sickness challenges our most cherished presumption that we are or at least can be in control of our existence .... In such a context, medicine becomes the mirror image of theoretical theodices sponsored by the Enlightenment because it attempts to save our profoundest hopes that sickness should and can be eliminated. We must assume a strict causal order so that this new emperor can be assured of success. We do not need a community capable of caring for the ill; all we need is an instrumental rationality made powerful by technological sophistication .... Illness is an absurdity in a history formed by the commitment to overcome all evils that potentially we can control .... It is only against this background that we can appreciate the widespread assumption that what we *can* do through the office of science and medicine we *ought* to do.[33]

This argument is further developed by McKenny:

> ... once we accept the limits of medicine in eliminating suffering, we will be in a better position to use technology, as part of a more general commitment to caring, in ways that help more and more people to live better with conditions that cannot be eliminated.[34]

Thus our expectations of medicine and healthcare need to be curtailed in relation to technical methods of curing, whilst at the same time increased in relation to caring and healing. This challenges the widespread assumption that orthodox medical provision must and should carry on expanding, and so incur ever-increasing financial costs. Hence the approach being advocated here would lead to a reversal of these assumptions in developed societies, and focusing on caring and healing rather than curing would also make it inappropriate to conceive of the cost of healthcare solely in monetary terms.

Another paper from the *British Medical Journal* will be described as a way of illustrating what is at stake.[35] It compared the illness experiences of two groups of patients with incurable cancer, one from Scotland and the other from Kenya. Those living in Scotland had access to a range of specialist palliative services, and pain was usually well controlled. The main problem for these patients was in coming to terms with the prospect of death. They showed frustration and anger, had difficulty sharing their distress with family, friends and professionals, only occasionally found comfort in religion, and worried about how carers would cope in future. In contrast, the main problem for the Kenyan patients was the lack of money to purchase services to deal with physical suffering, especially pain. However, they were well supported by their community network, were comforted and inspired by belief in God, and were at peace with themselves and accepting of their impending death.

Although, as the authors of this study note, it is difficult to generalise about developed and developing countries from a single study, the differences are so striking that some lessons are clear. For developed societies, no amount of sophisticated technical management and specialist expertise, however expensive, can compensate for the lack of personal, cultural and spiritual meaning in the face of death. Conversely, for developing societies, a personal, cultural and spiritual acceptance of death cannot compensate for the relief from physical suffering that access to technical services can provide. This does not only apply to death from cancer though; broadly speaking, developed societies have an abundance of physical resources but are relatively short of spiritual ones, whereas developing societies have an abundance of spiritual resources but are relatively short of physical ones. The use of the term 'spiritual' here is not intended to be restricted to religious matters, but nevertheless cannot be contained by being reduced to concepts such as 'personal' and 'cultural' alone.

The important point to be made is that the best way to make improvements is not simply to maximise both the physical and spiritual resources according to which was deficient in each case. Rather, the physical and spiritual resources are not separate and so additive components, but form an interactive whole in the production of health and well-being, which varies according to the culture. Thus the aim of providing what is best through ever-increasing technical and spiritual means is neither coherent in theory, nor desirable as a goal. Developing countries would unquestionably be better off with more and readily available technical medical resources, but if they are not introduced as part of the culture, their overall effect may be damaging. Some cultures remain sufficiently strong and coherent to prevent this happening, e.g. in Swaziland 'Swazi healing easily incorporates biomedicine into the traditional idiom of illness and healing, and, as it is based upon learned knowledge, gives it a place like herbalism next to but also morally inferior to divination'.[36]

Equally, developed countries cannot readily improve their spiritual resources as a matter of public policy or through private provision, although this is where most attention is required. Even the hospice movement, which has made an explicit attempt to address spiritual issues in relation to death from cancer, can only hope to make a limited contribution in this respect because it has been grafted on to the British culture, rather than becoming an integral part of it. It is the physical and spiritual culture as a whole which needs to change, and aiming for sustainability by placing limits on material consumption and technical solutions would be a good place to start in medicine as elsewhere. 'Contrasting perspectives of inequalities in health and in medical care' (Chapter 7) provides a good example of the relevance of such a strategy, where it is shown that 'Scientific rationalism and materialism on their own will not solve the problem of inequalities in medical care any more than those of inequalities in health'. What is required in addition to a moderate level of material wealth is the spiritual dimension which comes from social cohesion, engendered by relatively low differentials in wealth by social class. But there is no definitive prescription; what counts in the end is the cultural appropriateness of the material and spiritual meld.

To give full recognition to these issues will require a new set of goals and values, matched by a more adequate concept of health which can encompass that of healing. Boyd's definition, which he derived from Canguilhem, is helpful:

> ... health is not a matter of getting back from illness, but getting over and perhaps beyond it.
> ... to be healthy is not to correspond with some fixed norm, but to make the most of one's life in whatever circumstances one finds oneself, including those which in terms of some fixed norms may seem severely impaired or unhealthy.[37]

This then does not hold out fixed norms of health which are beyond the reach of all but a few Adonises, or require complete recovery from disease or disability. The focus is less on curing disease and correcting deformity for their own sake, and more on healing in the sense of restoring the conjoined physical and spiritual aspects of the whole person.

Reviving the soul of Western medicine

Hans Jonas describes the continuing effect of dualism as one of draining 'the spiritual elements off the physical realm',[38] and Rudolf Steiner, the founder of Anthroposophical medicine at the beginning of the twentieth century, viewed replacing them as essential for healing, after the rise to dominance of biomedicine which he saw as seriously deficient:

> The modern natural science which is oriented entirely towards the inorganic world can be used as the foundation for technological work, but not for the healing of diseases. For the essence of an illness is to be found at the place where the spiritual and corporeal elements are connected. If one says that natural science is the only possible science, and that it cannot arrive at the spirit because of its boundaries, then one also has to say that any real medicine is impossible.[39]

Thus the revival of Western medicine requires a rejection of dualism and a commitment to reinstating and further developing the role of those spiritual values which have been neglected since the demise of humoral medicine, yet persist in some of the less glamorous areas of orthodox medicine and have remained central to the medical systems of non-Western societies, as well as alternative medicine.

In describing this in terms of the *soul* of Western medicine, it is necessary to discard the ancient conception of a dichotomy between body and soul which was followed by Descartes, and Hacking's pre-Socratic view of the soul is helpful in this regard:

> Philosophers of my stripe speak of the soul not to suggest something eternal, but to invoke character, reflective choice, self-understanding, values that include honesty to others and oneself, and several types of freedom and responsibility .... It stands for the strange mix of aspects of a person that may be, at some time, imaged as inner — a thought not contradicted by Wittgenstein's dictum, that the body is the best picture of the soul.[40]

This concept of the soul invokes more than is usually intended when referring to spiritual matters because it cuts across the traditional boundaries of physical and spiritual realms, and denies the possibility of their separate coherence. The use of the term 'soul' (as with spiritual) should not be thought of as restricted to religion, but at the same time goes beyond what is currently captured by words such as 'personal', 'psychological' and 'emotional'. This more encompassing idea of the soul is less readily graspable and has something of a mythical quality which inspires a sense of wonder, reverence and awe. Midgley claims that it is just this sort of disposition which Western societies need if they are to replace the powerful myths that have been generated by the idolisation of our favourite technologies, e.g. the computer.[41] Elsewhere she discusses an alternative myth, that of Gaia, and observes that because it depends on medical imagery it makes it much easier for scientists (and I would suggest society in general) to see the relevance of global issues.[42] Thus thoughts about the health and healing of sick patients can be more readily transposed to the planet. Reviving the soul of Western medicine is then not only vital to a new medical cosmology, but may also be a source of inspiration in dealing with the global crisis.

References

1   This derives from the classic description of the 'sick role' described in: Parsons T (1951) *The Social System*. Free Press, Glencoe, IL.
2   Jacob JM (1988) *Doctors and Rules*, p. 170. Routledge, London.
3   Quoted in: Downie RS (ed.) (1994) *The Healing Arts*, p. 184. Oxford University Press, Oxford.
4   Saunders J (2001) Validating the facts of experience in medicine. In: M Evans and IG Finlay (eds) *Medical Humanities*, p. 228. BMJ Books, London.
5   Ibid., p. 228.
6   Lown B (1999) *The Lost Art of Healing*. Ballantine, New York.

7 A whole industry has now developed around the production of such guidelines. See, for example: Thematic issue (1999) Advancing the evidence-based healthcare debate. *Journal of Evaluation in Clinical Practice.* **5** (2).

8 Downie RS (1999) The role of literature in medical education. *Journal of Medical Ethics.* **25**: 529–31.

9 Woolf V (1994) On being ill. In: A McNeillie (ed.) *The Essays of Virginia Woolf,* vol. iv, 1925–28, p. 317. The Hogarth Press, London.

10 Ibid., pp. 317–18.

11 Merleau-Ponty M (1962) *Phenomenology of Perception.* (Translated by C Smith.) Routledge and Kegan Paul, London.

12 Leder D (1992) A tale of two bodies: the corpse and the lived body. In: D Leder (ed.) *The Body in Medical Thought and Practice,* p. 28. Kluwer Academic Publishers, Dordrecht.

13 Leder D (1999) Flesh and blood: a proposal supplement to Merleau-Ponty. In: D Welton (ed.) *The Body: classic and contemporary readings,* p. 202. Blackwell, Oxford.

14 Ibid., pp. 204–5.

15 Toulmin S (2001) *Return to Reason,* p. 13. Harvard University Press, Cambridge, MA.

16 Ibid., p. 13.

17 Ibid., p. 80.

18 Cunningham A (1989) Thomas Sydenham: epidemics, experiment and the 'Good Old Cause'. In: R French and A Wear (eds) *The Medical Revolution in the Seventeenth Century,* p. 189. Cambridge University Press, Cambridge.

19 Greaves D (1996) *Mystery in Western Medicine,* p. 30. Avebury, Aldershot.

20 Wear A (2000) *Knowledge and Practice in English Medicine, 1550–1680,* p. 450. Cambridge University Press, Cambridge.

21 Porter D (1999) *Health, Civilization and the State,* p. 57. Routledge, London.

22 Richardson R (1987) *Death, Dissection and the Destitute.* Routledge and Kegan Paul, London.

23 News (2000) 105,000 body parts retained in the UK, census says. *Lancet.* **357**: 365.

24 Foucault M (1973) *The Birth of the Clinic,* p. 146. Tavistock, London. (First published in French, 1963.)

25 Toulmin S, op. cit., p. 79.

26 Pickstone JV (2000) *Ways of Knowing,* p. 42. Manchester University Press, Manchester.

27 Heath I (2002) Long-term care for the elderly. *British Medical Journal.* **324**: 1534–5.

28 See, for example: de Jonge GA, Engelberts AC, Koomen-Liefting AJM *et al.* (1989) Cot death and prone sleeping position in the Netherlands. *British Medical Journal.* **298**: 722.

29 Dwyer T and Ponsonby A (1996) Sudden infant death syndrome: after the 'Back to Sleep' campaign [editorial]. *British Medical Journal.* **313**: 180–1.

30 Editor's choice (2003) The most important *BMJ* for 50 years? *British Medical Journal.* **326**.

31 Godfrey K (2003) Genetics White Paper heralds 'a revolution in healthcare'. *British Medical Journal.* **326**: 1413.

32 Callahan D (1987) *Setting Limits,* p. 60. Georgetown University Press, Washington, DC.

33 Hauerwas S (1990) *Naming the Silences,* pp. 62–3. WB Eerdmans Publishing Co., Michigan.

34 McKenny GP (1997) *To Relieve the Human Condition,* pp. 223–4. State University of New York Press, Albany.

35 Murray SA, Grant E, Grant A *et al.* (2003) Dying from cancer in developed and developing countries: lessons from two qualitative interview studies of patients and their carers. *British Medical Journal.* **326**: 368–71.

36 Reis R (2002) Medical pluralism and the bounding of traditional healing in Swaziland. In: W Ernst (ed.) *Plural Medicine, Tradition and Modernity, 1800–2000,* p. 107. Routledge, London.

37 Boyd KM (2000) Disease, illness, sickness, health, healing and wholeness: exploring some elusive concepts. *Medical Humanities.* **26**: 9–17.

38 Jonas H (1982) Life, death, and the body in the theory of being. In: *The Phenomenon of Life: toward a philosophical biology,* p. 13. University of Chicago Press, Chicago. (First published in 1966.)

39 Quoted in: Laing P (2002) Spirituality, belief and knowledge. In: W Ernst (ed.) *Plural Medicine, Tradition and Modernity, 1800–2000,* p. 165. Routledge, London.

40 Hacking I (1995) *Rewriting the Soul,* p. 6. Princeton University Press, Princeton, NJ.

41 Midgley M (2003) *The Myths We Live By,* pp. 119–21. Routledge, London.

42 Midgley M (2001) *Science and Poetry,* p. 180. Routledge, London.

CHAPTER 1

Sudden infant deaths: models of health and illness

Abstract

The assumptions underlying the traditional biomedical model of health and illness, and criticisms of it, are described. An examination of the historical development of ideas concerning cot (crib) deaths shows how early explanations, which were congruent with this model, came to be discredited. Because subsequent explanations have also been considered unsatisfactory, cot deaths have come to be regarded as medically problematic. The relationship of models of health and illness to cot deaths has therefore been exposed to an unusual degree of scrutiny.

Two possible contending models, social epidemiological and socioeconomic, are identified, and their status *vis-à-vis* the biomedical model is considered. The choice as to which of these models is applied to cot deaths is shown to be not only of theoretical interest but also to have ethical implications for healthcare policy and medical practice.

Introduction

Raphael states that in his view 'the main purpose of philosophy as practised in the Western tradition, is the critical evaluation of assumptions and arguments'.[1] In recent years attention has been drawn to the failures of Western medicine to be critically aware of the underlying assumptions and concepts from which it derives both its logical structure and its legitimacy.[2]

In this chapter some of the general assumptions and arguments concerning models of health and illness will be reviewed. Cot (crib) deaths[3] will then be looked at as a specific topic in order to examine how models of health and illness can be used in determining both the nature of the deaths and the appropriate medical response in attempting to deal with them. Cot deaths have been selected because they have proved persistently resistant to established modes of medical explanation. Many hypotheses have been proposed and some have gained acceptance for a while, but all have been rejected as unsatisfactory. The very nature of the deaths has proved problematic and they therefore provide a challenge to medical assumptions, which has produced more explicit argument and comment in the medical literature than is usual.

From the demonstration that alternative models can be adopted in dealing with cot death, it follows that certain claims are involved in deciding which to choose, even if they are not recognised. The ethical implications of such claims will therefore be explored and their importance shown in relation to practice.

The traditional biomedical model

Wright and Treacher[4] have argued that there are four main assumptions that have traditionally characterised Western medicine.

1   The nature of medicine and medical knowledge poses no difficulties which require debate or argument. Medicine is what doctors and their ancillary workers do and it is taken for granted that medical knowledge is simply transmitted through professional teaching and literature.
2   Modern medical knowledge is distinctive because of two particular features:

  • it is built on the findings of modern science
  • it is effective.

3   The disease entity is a key conceptual component. Diseases are natural objects which exist prior to, and independently of, their isolation or designation by doctors.
4   Social factors – whether much attention is given to them or not – are self-evidently distinct from medicine. Society and medical knowledge are regarded as independent and autonomous zones, by their very nature.

Mishler[5] also identifies four assumptions which he relates to the traditional biomedical model, which he sees similarly as defining the framework of modern medicine:

1   the definition of disease as deviation from normal biological functioning
2   the doctrine of specific aetiology
3   the conception of generic diseases, that is, the universality of a disease taxonomy
4   the scientific neutrality of medicine.

The first three of these are more detailed characteristics of the disease as a discrete entity identified in Wright and Treacher's third assumption. The fourth of Mishler's assumptions, the scientific neutrality of medicine, relates to Wright and Treacher's first assumption, and is the position which underpins all the other assumptions, without which they have no credibility.

A combination of these two sets of assumptions provides the basis for the traditional biomedical or clinical pathological model. What, though, is wrong with it, and what are the arguments against continuing with it unchanged?

The first difficulty is that the traditional model is treated as *the* representation or picture of reality, rather than being understood as *a* representation. This idea is comparatively recent. Historically there have been two polarised conceptions of health and illness, the first concentrating on diseases as entities with specific causes, the second focusing on the sick individual and the inter-relationship between personal characteristics and aspects of the environment. The Hippocratic writings as represented in, for example, *On Airs, Waters, Places*,[6] the medieval notion of humoral pathology and the nineteenth-century theory of miasmata, all relate to the second of these concepts. It has only been since the late nineteenth century that the first has gained such pre-eminence. To settle for it as the only correct and rational pathway implies that medicine is embarked on an inevitable course of scientific progress that cannot be denied. It is merely a question of uncovering nature. But this positivist view of science has long been challenged by historians and philosophers of science, e.g. Kuhn,[7] engaged in the study of physics, chemistry and biology, the very disciplines which medicine lays claim to, as forming the basis of its scientific approach. The fact that scientists are not agreed amongst themselves about the nature of scientific knowledge would seem good reason for doctors also to develop a more sceptical attitude to the foundations of medicine.

One of the features of positivist science is its claim to be value free, and by adopting it medicine purports to be sustained by an internal rationale which is independent of any set of general values. This allows doctors to assert that medical theory and practice are not open to challenge from religious, legal, ethical or other perspectives. It is therefore impossible to encompass insights from a range of different disciplines. So, for example, anthropological theories which postulate that science and medicine can be understood as systems of symbols which societies use to make sense of their existence in the world, e.g. the theories of Mary Douglas[8] and Susan Sontag,[9] are simply discounted.

So far these arguments against the traditional biomedical model have been largely theoretical, but the practical results of adherence to the model have also been called into question in recent years. These doubts have been expressed both from within medicine itself, e.g. by Muir Gray[10] and McKeown,[11] and from a variety of sources outside medicine, e.g. Powles,[12] Doyal and Pennell,[13] and Illich.[14] Whilst the arguments from within medicine do not necessarily imply a direct attack on the traditional scientific approach and may even be used to call for a greater adherence to it, those from outside claim that medicine has been positively damaged by its application (Illich) and that present medical problems will prove resistant to it and are therefore misguided (Powles).

A further argument against the model is the way in which it has structured the power relationship between doctors and patients, giving doctors an unwarranted degree of professional autonomy. According to Jewson,[15] the historical process by which this imbalance in power relationship came about took place over the period 1770–1870. Waddington[16] describes how in the Paris hospitals of the Napoleonic era, the medical focus was directed away from the whole person to particular anatomical organs and pathological lesions. As this process spread to medicine as a whole, the effect was to limit the power of the patient in defining his needs and in being involved in determining his own treatment and care. By the end of the nineteenth century the medical profession had achieved a legitimacy which united it and so freed it from the direct competition of other healthcare workers, who were diminished to the status of fringe practitioners and whose claim could no longer be assessed on an equal footing with that of doctors. Medicine had also acquired the right to regulate its own teaching and conduct, and by implication the manner in which it would work with patients. It is this protected insularity which Freidson describes as the critical flaw:

> It develops and maintains in the profession a self-deceiving view of the objectivity and reliability of its knowledge and of the virtues of its members. Furthermore, it encourages the profession to see itself as the sole possessor of knowledge and virtue, to be somewhat suspicious of the technical and moral capacity of other occupations, and to be at best partronizing and at worst contemptuous of its clientele. Protecting the profession from the demands of interaction on a free and equal basis with those in the world outside, its autonomy leads the profession to so distinguish its own virtues from those outside as to be unable to perceive the need for, let alone undertake, the self-regulation it promises.[17]

These are a number of arguments against the traditional biomedical model. Once they are conceded, the model no longer has an absolute status and it is possible to think in terms of competing models of health and illness. Such models introduce social factors. The problem then raised is whether social facts are a function of attitudes, expectations and rules in a way radically unlike natural facts, and so whether any alternative model of health and illness is congruent with the traditional model. Set in its wider context the question touches on whether the social sciences can be dealt with simply as an extension of natural science or whether they should be viewed in an entirely different manner.[18] These issues will be explored further by considering how possible alternative models might be conceived through an examination of the historical development of ideas relating to cot deaths.

Cot deaths

The task is to explore the way in which certain deaths in the first year of life have been conceived historically and identified as a particular problem. This involves unravelling the details and framework of the explanations which have been investigated as possible solutions.

During the nineteenth century, death in the first year of life was a common event. It occurred at a rate of approximately 150/1000 live births and had probably remained much the same over the previous centuries. What did change was the perception of how death came about. Foucault[19] describes how the notion of clinical death gained acceptance in the early years of the nineteenth century. This implied that death was necessarily accompanied by disease and was no longer to be regarded as natural or inevitable. Illich takes up this theme in describing how 'The general force of nature that had been celebrated as "death" turned into a host of specific causations of clinical demise'.[20]

Such ideas were a precondition to the development of a universal classification of death by cause, which became established in Britain in 1837 following the Registration Act of 1834. This allowed the statistical compilation of mortality rates by cause and in later years the designation of the Infant Mortality Rate (IMR) as an index of public health. So by the end of the nineteenth century the certification of deaths had become an important task, and it meant that doctors were increasingly expected to produce a specific explanation for every death and ideally this should be definable in pathological as well as clinical terms.

The notion of deaths as sudden and unexpected took on a new meaning under these new circumstances, because if death had to have a clinical explanation then it should also be preceded by manifestations of disease. New rules had been established which allowed the possibility of sudden and unexpected death as a residual group which was 'abnormal' and therefore problematic by definition.

Early explanations

Overlaying

Both before and during the nineteenth century it was common for infants to sleep with parents or siblings, so that when death occurred in bed with no obvious evidence of illness, mechanical suffocation from overlaying or smothering provided a ready explanation. One of the earliest reports to challenge this explanation and to imply the existence of a problem came in a letter to the *Lancet* in 1834:

> I have lately been called upon to examine two children, who without having been previously indisposed, were found dead in bed .... In these cases one naturally asks − what was the cause of death? The similarity of the post-mortem appearances would lead one to suppose that the cause must in each case have been the same.
>
> In the first case I was strongly disposed to think, in spite of the evidence of the mother, that the child must have been destroyed by overlaying it; but after the occurrence of the last case, where, from all the testimony that could be obtained it seemed impossible that the child could have been suffocated, as it was lying in bed by itself, and was not obstructed in its breathing by the bed-clothes, I confess that the opinion I had formed was a good deal shaken, and that I became almost entirely at a loss how to account for death in either.[21]

Despite such reports and the fact that the explanation of overlaying rested on a position of considerable uncertainty, it continued to be cited as a common cause of infant death even when new pathological techniques were developed later in the century. So, although doubts about overlaying continued to be expressed, established medical opinion ignored them and overlaying remained an acceptable explanation well into the twentieth century.[22]

This position was not seriously challenged until the late 1930s and 1940s when pathologists and coroners mounted systematic studies based on large series of cases.[23,24] These combined post-mortem evidence with detailed investigation of the social circumstances surrounding the deaths, and they showed conclusively that in the great majority of cases ascribed to mechanical suffocation, there was no positive pathological or circumstantial evidence to support this explanation. By 1950, sudden and unexpected death in infancy had become widely accepted as a medical problem requiring investigation.

Status thymicolymphaticus

Whilst overlaying remained as an accepted cause of infant death throughout the nineteenth century and the first half of the twentieth century, a quite different explanation had come and gone. As early as the seventeenth century it had been suggested that an enlarged thymus gland might be associated with death, and in the latter half of the nineteenth century compression from an enlarged thymus gland was occasionally proposed as the cause of suffocation in children. In 1889 a pathologist, Paltauf, provided a detailed description of a new disease which he termed 'status thymicolymphaticus'.[25] It involved the whole of the lymphoid system, including an enlarged thymus gland, and the condition could lead to sudden collapse and death.

The existence of the disease was quickly accepted and over the next 50 years was greatly elaborated, so that by 1927, Anderson and Cameron, in reviewing 100 cases which they had autopsied, were able to describe three main types of the condition and a wide range of hypotheses which had been advanced to explain the mechanism of death.[26] The condition could occur at any age, but was said particularly to affect children and was frequently invoked following death from anaesthesia for elective surgery. It also provided an alternative explanation to death from overlaying and was cited in the differential diagnosis.

At about this time, though, considerable doubt began to be expressed as to the existence of the condition and a Status Lymphaticus Investigation Committee was set up. It reported in 1931 and concluded that there was 'no evidence that so-called status thymicolymphaticus has an existence as a pathological entity'.[27] What had been previously regarded as pathological was, on more careful comparison with controls, accepted as falling within the range of normal anatomical variation. This conclusion was rapidly endorsed by general medical opinion and 'status thymicolymphaticus' disappeared from use.

This false creation of 'status thymicolymphaticus' should not be seen as just an intriguing historical curiosity. It testifies to the fervent medical belief of the period in the ability of the biomedical model to provide solutions to all medical problems.

The search for new explanations

By 1950, both overlaying and status thymicolymphaticus had been discredited as causes of infant death and were regarded as ephemeral medical myths, created by inadequate investigation and erased by more rigorous scientific examination, enabled by advances in the design of experimental studies and of pathological techniques. Sudden and unexpected death in infancy had emerged as a medical problem to which established medical opinion had no satisfactory answer.

The situation was very different from a hundred years previously though. The IMR had fallen rapidly between 1900 and 1950, in line with the general decline in infectious diseases. Also, the new and more sophisticated scientific technology and methods of research which had been used to disprove previous explanations might also be capable of replacing them with alternative explanations, which had been developed in the interim. However, the results of investigations during the 1950s reached the opposite conclusion, by revealing that the number of deaths in which no adequate explanation could be provided was much larger than had been supposed.[28]

The problem had therefore been established as resistant to medical explanation, and has continued so until the present. During this most recent period the number and range of research studies have grown dramatically throughout the developed world, and led to international conferences in Seattle in 1963 and 1969. This work has been characterised by two distinct lines of enquiry (although they have frequently been incorporated in single research projects): the first biological and pathological, and the second social and epidemiological. The present purpose is to examine how these have been jointly interpreted in reformulating the nature of the problem, in relation to both the object of enquiry (the dependent variable) and its cause or causes (the independent variables).

The main thrust of the biological and pathological studies regarding the dependent variable has been a relentless search, using more and more exacting and sophisticated methods, to establish whether there are biological variables which show differences in those infants who die compared with those who do not. The ability to demonstrate the existence of differences has been conceived as the central and most crucial issue because it would determine whether the deaths constituted a 'real disease entity'. At first the consensus was that no differences could be reliably detected, but by the second international conference in 1969, it was stated that 'sudden infant death syndrome (SIDS) is a real disease, not a vague mysterious killer'.[29] By 1977, this conclusion was endorsed by reference to evidence collected between 1970 and 1975 which showed that '*as a group* these infants are different from normal anatomically, histologically, chemically and even physiologically'.[30]

This change in the status of the problem had also led to a change in nomenclature. During the 1950s and 1960s, the terms most commonly used were cot death in Britain and crib death in North America. By the 1960s these were being replaced by increasingly specific labels, e.g. sudden infant death syndrome (SIDS), and at the 1969 conference it was pointed out that the word syndrome 'has the important virtue of communicating to the medical profession the concept that this is, in fact, a distinct clinico-pathological entity'.[29] No consensus could be reached over a standardised term at this time, but SIDS became generally accepted and has been incorporated in the most recent revision of the *International Classification of Disease (9th)*, giving it the final seal of approval.

During the same period a wide range of theories has been developed proposing a single biological independent variable. The agents suggested have included bacteria, viruses, immune mechanisms, hypersensitivity, trauma and biochemical imbalance, and most recently specific developmental defects of the cardiac and respiratory systems. Logically, it was premature to consider such causal explanations before the existence of a distinct pathological entity had been accepted. So the fact that such hypotheses have been repeatedly brought forward as others have been rejected testifies to the continuing strength of the assumption that death must imply specific disease. It also demonstrates that, within this biological and pathological tradition, the unifactorial causal model involving a single independent variable remains the underlying force in directing much research effort. These studies represent a straightforward extension of the methods of research worked out in the nineteenth century and relate to the traditional biomedical model.

In contrast, the social and epidemiological research which has paralleled this work over the past 30 years has been a new departure. Instead of concentrating on the search for a specific disease, with a single specific cause, the fact of sudden and unexpected death is taken as given and the task is to describe and compare its incidence in different populations and the frequency of its association with social, as well as biological, variables. The question to be asked is 'How often and under what circumstances do possibly preventable deaths occur?'.[31]

This line of enquiry offered the hope of providing the means to preventive action through the statistical definition of high-risk groups. Nevertheless, such

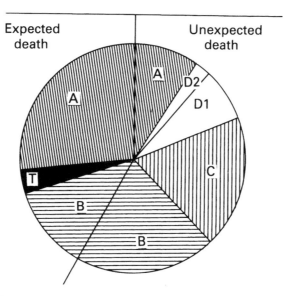

Figure 1.1 Distribution of postperinatal deaths in Sheffield, 1972–73. From: Emery JL (1976) Unexpected death in infancy. In: D Hull (ed.) *Recent Advances in Paediatrics.* Churchill Livingstone, Edinburgh.

studies still require a theoretical framework. Preventable death had been made the dependent variable, but definitions had to be made, of which deaths were to be included, and associated factors had to be selected for consideration. The way in which these were determined implies the theoretical orientation. Emery has been the pioneer in developing this work and his classification of postperinatal deaths, i.e. those occurring between one week and one year of age, is instructive (Figure 1.1).

Group A: Deaths in children with severe diseases of long standing in whom death is almost certainly not preventable, though it may be delayable. Such deaths occurred in children with gross congenital deformities of the central nervous system and the heart. In this group also were children with progressive degenerative diseases.

Group B: Deaths from diseases for which treatments are available. There is an accepted mortality rate in such diseases as meningitis and pneumonia. However, in these, mortality is probably modified depending on the time of treatment.

Group C: Deaths in children in whom the disease found at necropsy would not ordinarily be considered adequate to account for death but would produce symptoms. These deaths include children with virus infections but in whom the cause of death was not obvious and children with tracheitis and gastroenteritis.

Group D: Deaths with no evidence of ordinary disease. These deaths occur in two forms: (1) those where there is evidence that the children have been unwell – they had fatty change in the liver and evidence of an alteration of growth rate in the costochondral junction (D1); (2) those where the child appears to have died in a healthy state (D2).

There was also a small group of malignant tumours (T).

Emery's concern in the possible prevention of all postperinatal deaths is shown by the single division of deaths into 'expected' and 'unexpected'. In this context the latter represent those he considers potentially preventable. His initial conceptua-lisation of how to deal with these deaths, though, involves demonstrating that there is evidence of disease in almost all the 'unexpected' deaths, so that a more rigorous search for cases C and D1 will reduce D2, which he sees as the true incidence of sudden and unexpected death, to a tiny proportion of all the deaths. Then because C and D1 represent accepted and comprehensible disease, strategies can hopefully be developed to deal with them. The focus has switched from the attempt to discover a new disease to deal with the problem deaths, to extending the definitions of known diseases. So although the starting point was all prevent-able deaths, they have been broken down again into their disease components. Therefore reliance has still been placed on diagnosing disease and hence on the biomedical model.

Emery and his colleagues have also developed a second strategy in parallel with this, involving a predictive system for C, D1 and D2 as a single group, which they have used in a preventive programme at Sheffield.[32] It is this strategy which makes use of a social epidemiological model and differs from the biomedical model in two important respects:

- it focuses on a group of sudden and unexpected deaths, rather than disease, as the dependent variable
- it incorporates both social and biological variables in a multifactorial statistical association, rather than a single independent variable.

Once again, though, the focus is not on *all* preventable deaths as a group, but only on a subgroup of them, those considered to be sudden and unexpected by the more conventional definition, i.e. when a recognised disease process is not detected before death.

By not making these twin strategies explicit, Emery is able to give the appearance of having developed a radically new departure in concentrating on possibly preventable deaths. However, the analysis above shows this to be false. Even his social epidemiological model remains firmly anchored to the biomedical model, and he demonstrates ambivalence in pursuing it as other than a practical expedient. This may be seen by examining the way he derived the predictive variables in developing the social epidemiological model. They were taken from data which are routinely available from obstetric and perinatal records, and are therefore presumably thought to be of some medical significance. They offer the possibility of developing a different and legitimate mode of explanation related to the deaths as a group, and to use them as Emery does suggests that he at least partially accepts such alternative explanations, if only by implication. For example, two variables utilised in the Sheffield predictive system are mother's age and intention of breast-feeding. Being a young mother and bottle-feeding appear to be interpreted as part of a poor sociocultural background in which infant deaths are more likely to occur. A web of such relationships could then be understood as representing one level of explanation in that although that web is not directly responsible for the deaths, it forms a backdrop to them.

Mother's age and infant feeding practice would then be labelled 'social' variables, within the social epidemiological model; but they would equally be regarded as 'biological' variables when related to the biomedical model. The implication of Emery's work is that in the final analysis the social epidemiological model and the explanations derived from it are informal and of uncertain status. They therefore remain subservient to the more secure biomedical model.

It is not that Emery is specially worthy of criticism, but merely that he demonstrates that he is wary of straying beyond the traditional limits of scientific medicine, and how conservative those limits continue to be. The underlying ideas that death must imply specific disease, and that discovering disease is the ideal way to determine action, still predominate. The framework of the biomedical models remains the cornerstone of medical explanation for sudden and unexpected death in infancy, and to seek variables which have a causal relationship with deaths C, D1 and D2 as a group is therefore theoretically dubious. It is acceptable to look for statistical associations, but it is less certain whether this denotes causality. The best test of medical progress, in this view, is to reduce and mould all explanations to the biological and pathological, so that although the importance of social explanation may be acknowledged, its significance is diminished.

The social epidemiological model has not superseded the biomedical model and, indeed, has not achieved equal status with it; rather, it represents a contingent model which can be put into practice in the community. Ultimately, it may even be expected to give way to the superior biomedical model, as soon as satisfactory empirical evidence becomes available.

These two alternative models can be clearly discerned by reviewing the medical literature on cot deaths, but there is a third possible model which, though alluded to, is rarely made explicit. This will be referred to as the socio-economic model.

As previously described, the IMR in Britain a century ago was well above 100/1000, and since that time it has shown a fairly continuous decline, right up to the present day. During this period the IMR has been considered the single most reliable indicator of the state of public health and, conversely, poor socio-economic circumstances the underlying causal factor in explaining high IMRs when taken as a whole. As cot deaths occur almost exclusively in the first year of life, it is pertinent to consider whether they are influenced by socio-economic conditions in the same way as other infant deaths. There are two sources of evidence which suggest that they are.

- Studies, such as those in Sheffield, which have closely monitored the incidence of cot deaths over a number of years have shown that as there has been a general reduction in IMR as a whole, cot deaths have also declined. (Care must be taken not to use the general level of notification of SIDS for this purpose because it has risen as SIDS has become more widely accepted as a valid cause of infant death.) This is well demonstrated by noting that the graph of total infant deaths by age does not show an increased proportion of deaths around two to four months, when the incidence of cot deaths is at its highest.[33]
- Surveys carried out in both Britain[34] and North America,[35] which have included assessment by indices of social deprivation, have been consistent in demonstrating an inverse relationship between cot death and socio-economic conditions.

On this evidence there would seem good reason not to focus so specifically on cot deaths, but to regard them as a variant of all those infant deaths which might be lessened through prevention, by positive measures of social and economic improvement. This socio-economic model would therefore embody the following features:

- the dependent variable would not be cot death but all possibly preventable infant deaths
- causation and intervention would be primarily considered at a social, economic and political level, as opposed to an individual level.

The components of the model described above are not congruent with the assumptions of the biomedical model, which represents the standard against which other models are judged, and this may explain why the model does not feature in the medical literature relating to cot deaths. Whilst the social epidemiological model can be viewed as no more than an extension to the biomedical model, which does not replace it and can be regarded as either complementary to it or expendable, once the biomedical model is sufficiently researched, the socio-economic model provides a more radical alternative, and the two cannot be readily integrated. Even to mention socio-economic status when discussing a medical problem may be seen as embarrassing. Bernard Knight, in his book which is addressed to parents as well as professionals, demonstrates his wariness in even broaching the subject:

> It has been found time and time again that there is an undisputable 'social gradient' in the frequency of SIDS, more cases occurring as the social scale is descended. In these egalitarian times, even speaking of social class can be a controversial and delicate matter.[36]

It is not therefore that the socio-economic dimension is ignored altogether, but it has somehow to be sharply distinguished from true medical knowledge. So to allow its importance in relation to a specific medical topic such as cot death is inadmissible. It may be legitimate to analyse IMRs and relate them to socio-economic factors which need to be considered in determining social policy as, for example, in the Black Report,[37] but this is seen as operating in a different realm. The socio-economic model of health and illness is acceptable here, but it cannot also be accommodated within the structure of the biomedical model, so must assume a residual position in medical terms.

This also leaves the scientific status of the socio-economic model in doubt. On the one hand, it might be argued that by using it in detailed empirical research to establish exactly which social and economic variables lead to infant deaths as a group, it could be aligned with natural scientific models. On the other hand, it could equally be argued that attempting to subordinate it to the structures of traditional medical models in this way would be to destroy its very nature, which does not allow such detailed specification and quantification. This uncertainty suggests that the model could be interpreted so as to support either of the views of the relationship between natural and social science, previously referred to. So the exact scientific status of the socio-economic model, though different from the biomedical and social epidemiological models, remains obscure. What is plain, though, is the medical status of these three models. There is a clear ranking in their medical recognition and acceptability and hence the use to which they are put. The biomedical model remains pre-eminent, the social epidemiological model has achieved a secondary position alongside it, whilst the socio-economic model is at best peripheral.

Some ethical implications

Most work relating moral philosophy to medicine has been concerned with analysing the effects of different courses of action in particular medical situations. The relevant facts of the medical situation have to be correctly identified, but they have not themselves been the object of critical scrutiny. In this chapter it is the philosophical interpretation of medical knowledge and explanation which has been the focus, and this opens up to ethical enquiry a much wider range of questions. Two areas will be considered: the question of moral responsibility for the occurrence of the deaths and the determination of resource allocation.

Moral responsibility for death

One of the initial reasons for sponsorship of large-scale enquiries into cot death in the postwar period was the suspicion that the deaths might have been due to infanticide. The question of moral and legal responsibility was therefore central to these investigations. Although none of them produced evidence to suggest infanticide except in rare cases,[38] a legal procedure which involves a police investigation and a coroner's inquest may still be instituted. Where this occurs, as it frequently did in the past, the parents' feelings of guilt are greatly heightened either because blame is positively directed towards them or because the absence of a satisfactory medical explanation leaves them feeling that guilt must somehow attach to themselves.

The three models proposed contain very different implications for the attribution of moral responsibility and therefore have an important bearing on this situation. One of the positive aspects of the biomedical model is that by locating the problem as due to a specific disease, the deaths are seen as natural events for which no blame or responsibility can be attached to the parents. Instead, the responsibility is placed squarely at the door of doctors and medical science. So the parents have a reason for welcoming this model and the introduction of SIDS as an accepted cause of death. It provides a means of obviating distressing legal procedures and of promoting the idea of the parents as victims of a disaster. In Britain, a voluntary society, the Foundation for the Study of Infant Deaths, has been very successful in recent years in campaigning to persuade the public of this view, and in providing support to parents on this basis.

The social epidemiological model has the reverse effect as it stresses the personal aspects of parental responsibility. The programme developed at Sheffield involves intensive visiting of high-risk families by health visitors, who advise mothers about essentially personal habits such as nutrition, personal hygiene and cleanliness. These all require implementation by the mother and although they correspond with the normal work of health visitors, there are important differences. In the specific identification of high-risk families, particular mothers are being selected as specially morally liable, and they may be made to feel negligent simply by having been selected. If despite this attention their child should die, then these mothers are likely to feel even greater guilt and stigma for having not complied sufficiently with the advice they were offered. Part of Knight's reticence about raising social questions was no doubt because of this desire not to stigmatise individuals or groups. But although programmes may be offered on the basis of providing preventive advice and support to families, their nature is determined by the structure of the model and will tend to leave the onus of responsibility for the deaths with the individual parents rather than the health professionals.

The socio-economic model changes the moral responsibility from an individual to a collective level. It implies the need for action by government, both at local and national level, on matters such as improving housing standards, nutritional policy and child benefits. It also recognises that programmes outside medical care are important in improving health, and that health issues involve much more than a series of interactions between individuals or families and healthcare professionals. Nevertheless, the inability to specify exactly how cot deaths are caused at a collective level leaves a puzzling uncertainty as to exactly where moral responsibility lies. It is precisely this nebulous quality of both causation and responsibility which cannot be reconciled with the certainties of the other two models. Parents and doctors may be reassured that a particular cot death was outside their sphere of influence, but their anxieties remain because the socio-economic model offers no concrete reality or tangible structure which they can make sense of in coming to terms with the death.

Resource allocation

In considering resource allocation, ethical debate has focused on different theories of justice in deciding who should receive the limited resources available.[39] The nature of the problem in terms of which model of health and illness is considered appropriate has not usually been questioned. It has been viewed as an internal medical matter and not therefore the province of ethical enquiry. But by demonstrating the possibility of utilising different models, which are not framed by a neutral set of facts, the different modes of intervention which follow are revealed as legitimate matters for ethical analysis.

The choices to be made are between very different lines of action. The biomedical model points to laboratory research as the principal activity, with the possible addition of continuous respiratory monitoring of babies considered at very high risk, either at home or in hospital (the baby alarm system). The social epidemiological model would favour a system of primary care intervention carried out by a structured programme of home visits. The socio-economic model would indicate a public health programme. This would require advice and monitoring from healthcare professionals, but would depend on a political commitment for its implementation.

The effect of these different programmes will not be limited to their impact on cot deaths. Determining which to choose will therefore also reflect a broader commitment to one of the respective branches of medical practice, namely hospital and laboratory medicine (biomedical), preventive aspects of primary care (social epidemiological) and public health (socio-economic). To favour one programme for cot deaths entails favouring one of these types of practice more generally.

What the consideration of single issues, such as cot death, does make clear is that in making such choices it is not just a political decision that is involved, but one that has ethical implications for individual doctors and patients. It is therefore impossible to compartmentalise the issues of resource allocation into different levels of macro-allocation and micro-allocation and assume that the former are exclusively the responsibility of politicians and health service managers and the latter those of doctors and patients. Resource allocation questions must therefore be considered as a whole, and the different levels of allocation be viewed as interactive. Conceptualising them as within different spheres of responsibility is only possible because of the dominance of a particular mode of medical knowledge.

The biomedical model represents the bedrock of that medical knowledge, and the basis of the traditional security of the doctor–patient relationship. The social epidemiological model widens that relationship to include at least the patient's family and potentially others to whom the family relate. It therefore represents an important step away from the tight confines of individual doctor–patient interaction, and as such a threat to insulating that relationship from outside scrutiny. Once the logic of following the path of the social epidemiological model is fully exposed, the door is open to the possibility of extending it further and allowing room for the socio-economic model in medical practice as well as social policy. Emery's concern to underpin the social epidemiological model within the framework of the more secure biomedical model may be seen as reflecting this anxiety. But in the late twentieth century, the structure of what is considered legitimate medical knowledge is gradually being revealed as an appropriate topic for public debate. As this change becomes accepted, the full implications for medical ethics are also made apparent.

Exposure of the presently accepted relationship between the three models of health and illness described gives rise to the opportunity to explore ways in which they might be balanced and integrated differently. It is not simply a question of choosing between the models, but of reflecting on the practical and ethical questions that would be raised in seeking new directions for medical care and social policy.

References

1 Raphael DD (1981) *Moral Philosophy*. Oxford University Press, Oxford.
2 For example: Burns C (1975) Diseases versus healths: some legacies in the philosophies of modern medical science In: HT Englehardt and S Spicker (eds) *Evaluation and Explanation in the Biomedical Sciences*. Reidel, Dordrecht.
3 The term 'cot deaths' is used in the UK and 'crib deaths' in the USA.
4 Wright P and Treacher A (eds) (1982) *The Problem of Medical Knowledge*. Edinburgh University Press, Edinburgh.
5 Mishler EG (1981) *Social Contexts of Health, Illness and Patient Care*. Cambridge University Press, Cambridge.
6 Hippocrates. *On Airs, Waters, Places*. Translated and republished in: (1938) *Medical Classics*. **3**: 19–42.
7 Kuhn TS (1970) *The Structure of Scientific Revolutions* (2nd edition). University of Chicago Press, Chicago, IL.
8 Douglas M (1966) *Purity and Danger: an analysis of concepts of pollution and taboo*. Routledge and Kegan Paul, London.
9 Sontag S (1978) *Illness as Metaphor*. Vintage Books, New York.
10 Muir Gray JA (1979) *Man Against Disease: preventive medicine*. Oxford University Press, Oxford.

11   McKeown T (1976) *The Role of Medicine*. Nuffield Provincial Hospitals Trust, London.

12   Powles J (1971) On the limitations of modern medicine. *Science, Medicine and Man.* **1**: 1–30.

13   Doyal L and Pennell I (1979) *The Political Economy of Health*. Pluto Press, London.

14   Illich I (1977) *Limits to Medicine*. Pelican, London.

15   Jewson ND (1976) The disappearance of the sick man from medical cosmology, 1770–1870. *Sociology*. **10**: 225–44.

16   Waddington I (1973) The role of the hospital in the development of modern medicine: a sociological analysis. *Sociology*. **7**: 211–24.

17   Freidson E (1970) *Profession of Medicine*, p. 370. Dodd, Mead, New York.

18   See, for example: Winch P (1958) *The Idea of a Social Science*. Routledge and Kegan Paul, London.

19   Foucault M (1973) *The Birth of the Clinic*. Tavistock, London.

20   Illich I (1976) *Medical Nemesis*. Pantheon, New York.

21   Fearn SW (1834) Sudden and unexplained death in children. *Lancet*. **1**: 246.

22   For example: Brend WA (1915) *An Inquiry into the Statistics of Death From Violence and Unnatural Causes in the UK*. Griffin, London.

23   Davidson WH (1945) Accidental infant suffocation. *British Medical Journal*. **2**: 251–2.

24   Werne J and Garrow I (1947) Sudden deaths of infants allegedly due to mechanical suffocation. *American Journal of Public Health*. **37**: 675–87.

25   Paltauf A (1889) Ueber die Beziehung des Thymus Zum Plotzlichen Tod. *Wiener Klinische Wochenschrift*. **2**: 876.

26   Anderson J and Cameron JAM (1927) Lymphaticus and sudden death. *Glasgow Medical Journal*. **108**: 129–47.

27   Young M and Turnbull HM (1931) An analysis of data collected by the Status Lymphaticus Investigation Committee. *Journal of Pathology and Bacteriology*. **34**: 213–58.

28   Banks AL (1958) An enquiry into sudden death in infancy. *Monographs and Bulletins of the Ministry of Health*. **17**: 182–91.

29   Bergman AB, Beckwith JB and Ray CG (eds) (1970) *Proceedings of the Second International Conference on Causes of Sudden Death in Infants*. University of Washington Press, Seattle and London.

30   Valdes-Dapena MA (1977) Sudden unexplained infant death 1970 through 1975. *Pathology Annual*. **12** (1): 117–47.

31   Emery JL (1976) Postneonatal mortality in Sheffield. *Proceedings of the Royal Society of Medicine*. **69**: 12–14.

32   Carpenter RG, Gardener A, McWheeney PM *et al.* (1977) Multistage scoring system for identifying infants at risk of unexpected deaths. *Archives of Disease in Childhood*. **52**: 606–12.

33   Knight B (1983) *Sudden Death in Infancy*, pp. 26–7. Faber, London.

34   Working Party for Early Childhood Deaths in Newcastle (1977) Newcastle Survey of Deaths in Early Childhood, 1974/76, with Special Reference to Sudden Unexpected Deaths. *Archives of Disease in Childhood*. **52**: 828–35.

35 Valdes-Dapena MA, Birle LJ, McGovern JF *et al.* (1968) Sudden unexpected deaths in infancy: a statistical analysis of certain socio-economic factors. *Journal of Paediatrics.* **73**: 386–94.

36 Knight B (1983) *Sudden Death in Infancy*, p. 34. Faber, London.

37 Report of a Research Working Group (1980) *Inequalities in Health.* Department of Health and Social Security, London.

38 Editorial (1984) Cot death: the unfounded lurking suspicion. *Lancet.* **2**: 1137.

39 For example: Gillon R (1985) Justice and allocation of medical resources. *British Medical Journal.* **291**: 266–8.

CHAPTER 2

What are heart attacks? Rethinking some aspects of medical knowledge

Abstract

There has been a modern epidemic of heart attacks in the Western world, and this chapter is concerned with this 'new' medical condition and how it arose. Two competing theories are commonly proposed, relating either to conventional accounts of medical science or to social construction. Whilst recognising that aspects of both theories have some validity, it is claimed that neither is wholly adequate. This issue has particular relevance for heart attacks and is explored in some detail, but it also points to some more general conclusions. First, that medical knowledge cannot be separated into 'scientific' and 'social' compartments but is united by its human aspect; and second, that although medical knowledge has a special dimension, when understood in this way, it may also resonate with a more general re-examination of the relationship between scientific and human knowledge.

Introduction

Disorders of the heart have been recognised since ancient times, but the conceptualisation of acute myocardial infarctions – or in lay terms 'heart attacks' – as one aspect of coronary heart disease, characterised by a clinical syndrome, pathology and specific causes, did not occur until the twentieth century. Heart attacks are therefore a modern condition, which has become the most serious life-threatening epidemic of the Western world, rivalled only by cancer.

The question which will be addressed in this chapter concerns the nature of this 'new' disease and how it arose. Two competing theories are commonly proposed, relating either to conventional accounts of medical science or to social construction. Whilst recognising that aspects of both these theories have some validity, it will be claimed that neither is wholly adequate. Only by transcending the entrenched dichotomy between 'scientific' and 'social' explanations can a more comprehensive and satisfactory account be found, and this will require a reassessment of historical and contemporary knowledge about heart attacks, which, although of special relevance to this particular condition, also has implications for medical knowledge more generally.

The background

A typical definition of coronary heart disease in a modern medical textbook is as follows: 'a condition where the heart muscle (myocardium) receives insufficient oxygen because the coronary arteries fail to maintain a sufficient supply of blood.'[1] Two separate but related medical disorders are then recognised as falling under the general heading of coronary heart disease: the clinical condition of angina usually resulting from coronary atheroma; and the more serious condition described in medical terms as an acute myocardial infarction, and in lay terms as a 'heart attack' or 'coronary'. The focus of this chapter will be on the latter, which in medical theory is defined in relation to the three elements which are characteristic of the current Western disease model:

- the clinical syndrome – crushing chest pain radiating to the left arm, shock and breathlessness, frequently followed by collapse and death
- the pathological lesion – coronary atheroma, predisposing to coronary thrombosis, which leads to myocardial infarction
- the causal agents – risk factors, typically high blood pressure, raised blood cholesterol and smoking.

The medical terms coronary heart disease and myocardial infarction were not in existence at the beginning of the twentieth century, and emerged as part of the recognition of 'new' heart conditions which became established clinically in the 1920s and 1930s. The origin of the lay term heart attack is difficult to trace, but presumably appeared as the diagnosis of myocardial infarction gained ground, and later became a familiar part of everyday language.

Since it was first identified the incidence of coronary heart disease has risen dramatically, reaching epidemic proportions in the postwar decades in most Western countries. However, there are large variations between Western countries, and it is relatively uncommon in some developed societies such as Japan.[2] Currently the epidemic is tending to decline, though in many countries such as Britain it remains the single most common cause of death.[3] Coronary heart disease and heart attacks in particular are, more than any other condition, products of twentieth-century Western society. During a period when health in general has been greatly improving, they have had a profound effect, not only on the individuals and families involved, but on society as a whole. Most striking is the dramatic onset of severe pain often followed by sudden death in people who are relatively young and otherwise healthy. Also, even if the victim survives the initial episode, he remains in the shadow of the likelihood of subsequent attacks.

Heart attacks represent a new challenge to medical science and its claims to be able to explain and control disease, as well as a public threat, equivalent perhaps to that of tuberculosis in the nineteenth century. Cancer poses a similar risk to the population, but has been known for many centuries, so although it has become more prominent as a cause of death this century, it is not entirely unfamiliar. Heart attacks, on the other hand, have inaugurated a novel and terrifying form of suffering and death, and as such constitute the most distinctive plague of Western society during the twentieth century. They provide a current example of soteriology, the idea that every age has its characteristic modes of suffering and salvation.[4]

Rival theories

Lawrence writes that:

> Historians and clinicians generally agree that only toward the end of the 1920s did the bedside diagnosis of acute myocardial infarction (sudden death of heart muscle) consequent on coronary thrombosis (clot formation in the heart's arteries) become a regular clinical event. This condition, 'heart attack' as it popularly became known, was soon to be designated one of the leading causes of death in western societies. By 1930 the disease seemed to have a clear-cut character.[5]

He then goes on to question why before the 1920s physicians failed to describe, discover or diagnose the disease, which in later years appeared to be so obvious.

Two main types of theoretical explanation have been given, 'scientific' and 'social', and Lawrence favours the latter, having reviewed some of the historical evidence for the 'scientific' approach which he regards as flawed. The claim that will be made here, though, is that both these types of explanation have deficiencies.

Considering the scientific approach first, two principal biological theories have been advanced, both of which assume that acute myocardial infarctions or heart attacks are ontological entities which have real existence. The first holds that in earlier centuries the condition was present but not diagnosed; the second that the condition was previously latent, emerging in the twentieth century as a result of the 'epidemiological transition'.

The theory involving the failure of diagnosis in earlier eras rests on the argument that scientific medical investigation has evolved only gradually over recent centuries. Hence it was not until the eighteenth century that systematic clinical descriptions led to the delineation and classification of many of the diseases which are recognised today. Thus the first description of the clinical syndrome of angina is attributed to Heberden in 1768, and it remains largely unchanged as the key element in diagnosing the condition. Likewise, detailed systematic pathological examinations were not carried out till the nineteenth century, and so on this account it is not surprising that the pathological changes of myocardial infarction associated with coronary artery occlusion were (according to Leibowitz) first described only in 1880 by the German pathologist Weigert. Leibowitz further claims that in 1919 Herrick correlated myocardial infarction with specific electrocardiogram (ECG) changes (the ECG machine having come into regular use a few years previously), so paving the way for the new medical understanding of coronary heart disease, which became established soon afterwards.[6] This whole process is then seen to be one of discovery, through a gradual uncovering of evidence. Pieces of a jigsaw, which are originally recognised by individual pioneers, are gradually fitted together as part of a picture which already exists but is only discernible when enough of them have been selected and put in their proper place.

The second biological 'scientific' theory involves the notion of the 'epidemiological transition' described by Wilkinson as follows:

> When countries round the corner in the curve relating health to income, they also go through the so-called 'epidemiological transition'. The term is used to demarcate the change from predominantly infectious

causes of death, still common in poor countries, to the degenerative
diseases which have become the predominant cause of death in richer
countries. All the rich developed countries … went through this
transition in their causes of death earlier in the twentieth century.
In contrast to the poorer countries … their death rates are dominated
by cardiovascular diseases and cancers rather than by infections.[7]

The suggestion then is that coronary heart disease and heart attacks did not occur
before the twentieth century, because conditions were such that they did not have
the opportunity to be expressed. The assumption, though, is that they were
nevertheless lurking in man's biological make-up, ready to appear once conditions
became favourable.

   Lawrence condemns these 'scientific' theories (though he only explicitly deals
with the first of them), claiming that they contain epistemological assumptions
which until recently historians have tended to accept uncritically, and he favours
instead the alternative theories of social construction:

> What is required is an explanation of how and why perceptions are
> structured as they are and how and why they change. The establishment
> of coronary thrombosis, I suggest, was a complex, socially sustained
> reclassification procedure. It was not a negative process of remov-
> ing obstacles but a positive restructuring of clinical and pathological
> experience. Further, the features held to be characteristic of the disease
> were not suddenly recognised but were arrived at by a process of
> negotiation and persuasion over a period of time. In other words, there
> was disagreement over whether the disease existed and what consti-
> tuted its significant features.[8]

A Polish physician and philosopher, Ludwik Fleck, was the first person to apply
this type of theoretical approach to medicine, as exemplified by his work on
syphilis, which was first published in German in the 1930s.[9] He argued that
'thought collectives' develop particular 'thought styles', through which every concept and theory, whether scientific or not, is culturally conditioned. In more recent
years many different versions of this type of work, which has become known as
social construction, have been advanced and become well known, especially
through the work of Kuhn and Foucault.[10]

   From this general perspective, it is not a question of diseases existing all along
and either gradually becoming defined as the penetrative power of scientific
method improves or of their surfacing as the burden of infectious diseases recedes.
Rather, it involves a process of social negotiation and construction, summarised by
Wright and Treacher as follows:

> In brief, the distinctive theme of the work which we call social
> constructionist is that it refuses to regard medicine and technical
> medical knowledge as pre-given entities, separate from all other human
> activities. Instead, it is argued, medicine is to be seen as a highly
> specialised domain of social practice and discourse, the limits and
> contents of which are themselves set up by wider – but not separate –
> social practices.[11]

Although this may give the impression that social constructionism allows for the co-mingling of social and technical medical knowledge, this is not in fact the case. Rather, social practices are seen as a wider frame of reference within which 'scientific' knowledge can be interpreted. Thus the expression 'not separate' here means within, and so still divided from, and not integrated with.

Having clarified the contrast between these two theoretical approaches, the 'scientific' and the 'social', it will now be shown that neither of them is adequate in explaining the nature and origin of heart attacks. First, each contains deficiencies when taken on its own terms, and second, there is a more deep-seated ontological and epistemological problem concerning the division of medicine into two spheres, which is reflected here in these two competing theoretical types of explanation.

In relation to the first of these, despite the evolution of the biopsychosocial model of disease, which has extended scientific modes of explanation from biology to include social and psychological factors, a large proportion of the coronary heart disease epidemic remains unexplained despite a huge international research effort.[12] The orthodox explanation for this is that the methods of research and identification of risk factors are not yet sophisticated enough to reveal the complicated mechanisms involved, but that these methods are constantly being improved. It would seem more plausible, though, that the relevant variables are connected in a dynamic way, such that it will never be possible to specify any complete and fixed relationship between them. So if this disease model is regarded as a blueprint for medical research, it is flawed from the start because its basic structural assumptions are faulty.

The social constructionist method also raises its own inbuilt difficulties because different researchers from within the tradition may arrive at very different conclusions, without any definitive means of judging between them. This is particularly apparent in respect to researchers who focus either on an 'internal' or 'external' type of social explanation. In the present instance, 'internal' explanations of coronary heart disease and heart attacks concentrate on their emergence as having arisen from within medicine, as part of the professionalisation of cardiology. Lawrence follows this line of analysis and argues that at the beginning of the twentieth century there were a number of reasons why physicians working in the field of heart disease were anxious to create a separate academic speciality; and for them, 'bringing' coronary heart disease into existence was one important way in which they were able to engage in what was seen to be valid scientific research, so boosting their claims to academic and professional status.[13]

In contrast with this, Bartley adopts a mainly 'external' mode of analysis, focusing on changes within the wider society.[14] In doing so she changes the debate, though, by claiming that the apparent epidemic of heart disease in the twentieth century might better be regarded as part of a longer-term trend in deaths relating to cardiorespiratory disease, which have consistently shown a marked social class gradient. The issue of the emergence of coronary heart disease and heart attacks is then placed in a wider social, historical and ideological context, in which the medical profession and specific disease categories are of far less significance.

The difficulty encountered is which of these types of social analysis to accept, given that the researcher's own methodological stance would seem to influence the form of explanation arrived at, so making a certain degree of circularity inevitable. Hence although both the 'internal' and 'external' types of approach are capable of generating some interesting insights which are intuitively appealing, judging how to weigh them against each other is an inherent problem in this type of social research.[15]

So far the problems discussed have been those that arise from within 'scientific' and 'social' theoretical approaches. However, as indicated, there are also deeper conceptual difficulties which have their origin in the fact that both types of approach ignore different aspects of the experience of heart attacks. Whilst it is impossible to gain satisfactory historical evidence about the pathology of the heart and of biological risk factors such as blood cholesterol,[16] what can be concluded is that the characteristic clinical picture of heart attacks did not occur in earlier centuries because no consistent recognisable accounts are found in either the medical or lay literature. The experience of heart attacks as an unpredictable threat which potentially can strike any time and often without warning is therefore both new and deeply disturbing. The idea of an attack on the heart, striking at the very centre of man's being, conveys a sense of its shocking and symbolic significance. Thus heart attacks have had a profound impact on individuals and families, as well as culturally, yet this is not well captured by current conceptions of medical knowledge, as embodied in either the 'scientific' or 'social' theories of explanation that have been considered.

In 'scientific' terms, risk factors are intended to exclude the personal and cultural values and meanings associated with heart attacks, and so provide an objective account of causation. This is despite the fact that when they are extended to cover psychological and social factors, they inevitably deal with matters of lifestyle, e.g. exercise, diet, drinking and smoking habits, which would seem difficult to divorce from questions of value and meaning. A striking example of the incongruity this can lead to is the causative role ascribed to the behaviour of 'type A' personality types, which was claimed to be factual, although recent statistics reveal otherwise.[17]

Therefore it would seem better interpreted as the 'scientisation' of an underlying belief that heart attacks specially affect competitive middle-class executives. Equally, though, reducing the evidence to social class differentials excludes all personal experiences and beliefs about heart attacks. Such 'social' explanations leave the impression that the material fact of the condition, although it must have some sort of existence to be the subject of description at all, is of relatively little significance. Comments are sometimes made that social constructionism does not seek to deny the biological reality of illness, but such claims, whilst acknowledging the issue, do so only to set it aside.[18]

The human experience of this new and unprecedented form of suffering and death is then excluded by scientific method, and under-described or ignored by social constructionism. Part of the problem arises because some social researchers are themselves attempting to produce value-free knowledge, so distancing themselves from the subjective aspects of the condition, and this will be returned to later. But the more central issue which will be focused on here concerns the entrenched historical separation between the two types of medical explanation and knowledge that have been discussed – 'scientific' and 'social'. In philosophical terms they are examples of two counterpoised positions, realism and nominalism, which were well expressed in relation to disease in a classic paper by King:

> We are faced with the problem whether certain relational patterns, like diseases, 'exist in nature', while other patterns, like a melody or a poem,

we can create arbitrarily by our own skill and ingenuity. The question becomes, does a disease, whatever it is, have real existence, somehow, in its own right, in the same way as the continent of Australia? Such real existence would be independent of its discovery by explorer or investigator. A disease exists whether we know it or not. The contrasting point of view would hold, that a disease is created by the inquiring intellect, carved out by the very process of classification, in the same way that a statue is carved out of a block of marble by the chisel strokes of the sculptor.[19] (p. 200)

This is a graphic description of the two approaches, but it does not suggest how they might be reconciled. The contrast being described here is between one view according to which disease categories match, reflect or mirror the world, and a second in which they are simply imposed upon the world. If both these positions are taken to be inadequate, another way must be sought, and that which is favoured here attempts to avoid these two extremes. The source of the difficulty in adopting this approach seems to lie in the historical tradition which has shaped the way in which medical explanation and knowledge have been formulated in the West. Only by addressing this issue will it be possible to envisage a different and more adequate conception, which transcends the division between them.

A new approach

The two approaches to medical explanation and knowledge, referred to as 'scientific' and 'social', form part of a cluster of ideas which underpin medical thinking as a whole, and fall on two sides of a more general division.

Objective	Subjective
Science	Art
Individual	Social
Technical	Cultural
Body	Mind
Physical	Mental
Disease	Illness
Facts	Values
Quantitative	Qualitative

Although no one term captures all the different aspects represented by these two clusters of ideas, 'objective' and 'subjective' perhaps come closest. Therefore, for the sake of simplicity and convenience, they will be used here as a means of shorthand. There are several ways in which the disjunction between them has been handled in the attempt to maintain that medicine is a unified discipline.

- *Prioritisation.* The prioritisation of either set of ideas attempts to deal with the division between them by subordinating one of them, so appearing to lessen the problems that are raised by diminishing the importance of one side or the other:

- *of 'objective' side.* Boorse is a well-known exponent of this view who, by claiming that health and disease can be defined objectively, and that the concept of illness is reliant on that of disease, aims to show that the 'subjective' component of medicine is marginal.[20] However, this position has been much criticised, most notably by Engelhardt[21]
- *of 'subjective' side.* Those who highlight the 'subjective' side of medicine marginalise the 'objective' side, whilst continuing to envisage it within a separate compartment; and all those who favour social constructionism are committed to this to a greater or lesser degree.

- *Capture.* An alternative strategy to direct prioritisation is the capturing of the 'subjective' by the 'objective' cluster of ideas (although the reverse does not seem to have been proposed). One interpretation of the biopsychosocial model is that it provides for this by dealing with psychological and social factors as if they were equivalent to biological factors, so regarding them as objective, quantifiable and manipulable within risk score calculations. This 'scientisation' of psychological and social factors could then be viewed as an indirect method of prioritisation of the 'objective' component of medicine, through the reduction of the 'subjective' cluster of ideas to an 'objective' one.
- *Integration.* In recent years the problem of the relationship between the 'objective' and 'subjective' sides of medicine has received greater recognition and been given considerable attention, particularly in regard to what is often seen as the inappropriate subordination of the 'subjective' component. In response to this, consideration of narratives has become an important way of focusing on, and highlighting, the personal experience and symbolic meaning of illness.[22] However, taken on its own, this is no more than an attempt to redress the perceived imbalance between the 'objective' and 'subjective' sides of medicine, and a further step is required if they are to be integrated. Good has reviewed the research in this area and encouraged medical anthropologists to develop it further, but ends with the following conclusion:

> The essential qualities of medicine as a symbolic form, an institution, and a moment in our lives − its joining of the natural sciences and the narrative, of the rational and the deeply irrational, and of physiology and soteriology, and its mediation of our experiences of negation and ultimacy − will continue to challenge our formulations.[23]

However, he gives no precise indication of what this might entail, and the following section is an attempt to respond to this challenge by suggesting a hypothesis which is relevant to heart attacks, and also has more general implications for other medical disorders.

In his work on multiple personality disorder, Hacking discusses what he calls the 'looping effect', essentially the complex process of interactions which result when people are given certain labels:

> We tend to behave in ways that are expected of us, especially by authority figures − doctors, for example. Some physicians had multiples among their patients in the 1840s, but this picture of the disorder was very different from the one that is common in the 1990s. The

doctors' vision was different because the patients were different; but the patients were different because the doctors' expectations were different. That is an example of a very general phenomenon: the looping effect of human kinds.[24]

This 'looping effect' provides a means by which ideas and behaviours become part of evolving patterns, because those who are labelled are themselves actively engaged in the process and provide a feedback which influences the social categories involved, which are then open to revision. However, Hacking makes no suggestion that his sophisticated analysis of this effect might be relevant beyond the psychosocial disorders which are the subject of his enquiries, and so does not apply it to physical disorder.

Morris, though, in his book *The Culture of Pain*, takes the issue of the relationship between the 'objective' and 'subjective', as represented by the 'physical' and 'mental' aspects of pain, to be central:

> We live in an era when many people believe — as a basic, unexamined foundation of thought — that pain comes divided into separate types: physical and mental. These two types of pain, so the myth goes, are as different as land and sea. You feel physical pain if your arm breaks, and you feel mental pain if your heart breaks. Between these two different events we seem to imagine a gulf so wide and deep that it might as well be filled by a sea that is impossible to navigate .... one main purpose of this book is to begin to collapse the artificial division we create in accepting a belief that human pain is split by a chasm into uncommunicating categories called physical and mental.[25]

After considering these issues at length, Morris suggests the following analogy:

> We might represent The Myth of Two Pains as two closed fists. Now imagine that the hands are open and the fingers interlaced. Pain, especially chronic pain, calls forth some such interlacing of mind and body. It is physiological, to be sure. But, as Richard A Sternbach was arguing as far back as 1968, the physiology of pain is also powerfully adjusted to broadly cognitive influences such as meaning, emotion and culture.[26]

This raises the possibility of a 'psychophysiological reaction' which, as Morris notes, Sacks had already proposed in his work on migraine. What both these authors are raising through this integration of the physical and mental is something quite different from the more customary notion of 'psychosomatic' illness. This term tends to be used as another means of subordinating the 'subjective' psychological aspect of medicine when it does not appear in a conventional manner by being clearly separated from the physical.[27]

If we now put these insights together and apply them to coronary heart disease and heart attacks, the following hypothesis might be suggested. Doctors and lay people within certain societies continually reconstruct these heart disorders through a 'looping effect', which involves the interaction of physiological and psychosocial elements. This interaction of these many different elements is not simply a more complex mechanical process, though, but such that the physiological aspect has become included in a wider humanistic process. The following quotation from Wartofsky captures something of the general flavour of this:

> ... though there is clearly the biological basis of human beings that is shared with animals, it is the transformation of this biology by social and cultural life that produces the new human species and gives it its distinctive historical character.[28]

And Leder spells this out in more detail by emphasising the need to go beyond the Cartesian model of embodiment:

> Just as the lived body is an intertwining of intentionality and mate-riality, subject and object, so we would arrive at a medicine of the *intertwining.* That is, our notions of disease and treatment would always involve a chiasmatic blending of biological and existential terms, wherein these terms are not seen as ultimately opposed, but mutually implicatory and involved in intricate 'logics' of exchange.[29]

Whilst the individual labelling of patients by doctors is important here, it cannot explain the whole of what is involved. There must also be a cultural climate and expectation which is conducive to, and sustains part of, the epidemic of these heart disorders. This could be thought of as generating a more pervasive 'looping effect', in which the medical and lay perceptions of the whole of the affected society are implicated.

Thus these new heart conditions, in both their medical and lay expressions, arose from a complex of 'objective' and 'subjective' individual and social circum-stances, which are not wholly describable in terms of conventional science. Such a composite of circumstances is potentially unstable and so is likely to unravel at some time in future, but how long it will last is uncertain, so the fate of the current epidemic of heart conditions is unpredictable.

An illustration of how this process might have operated in a very different set of circumstances can be demonstrated by considering the designation and diagnosis of the disease 'idiopathic adrenal atrophy', which, after briefly flourishing in the early years of the twentieth century, was discredited and discarded as a medical mistake. It first became recognised because from 1830 to 1930 most cadavers dissected in the London medical schools were those of paupers, whose lives of poverty, social stigma and hardship seem to have led to a chronic enlargement of their adrenal glands. However, the size of these glands was taken to be normal, and hence by comparison the glands of others in the population (who were only rarely the subjects of dissection) came to be regarded as abnormally small, so giving rise to the designation of the disease of 'idiopathic adrenal atrophy'. Subsequent dissections of a more representative sample of the population unmasked the condition, but at the same time indicated that there could have been a more genuine disease designation, that of 'paupers' adrenal hypertrophy'. The fact that no such diagnosis was ever made demonstrates the power of the medical gaze in withholding as well as formulating disease, but this does not take away from the reality of the paupers' condition, which resulted from the interplay of psychosocial factors and long-term bodily changes (which were known to have affected the thymus as well as the adrenal glands). Paying attention to the dead bodies of paupers for purposes that had nothing to do with their own lives gave rise to a medical mistake. However, by shifting the focus, what emerges is a neglected condition specific to, and symbolic of, the age of incarceration in the workhouse, bearing a unique biological and social imprint in which both aspects are intertwined.

Morris suggests that chronic pain, although far less visible than cancer and acquired immune deficiency syndrome (AIDS), is nevertheless a characteristic malady of our age, in which the physical and mental elements are merged: 'It seems clear that specific historical periods possess not only their characteristic crimes ... but also their defining or representative illnesses'.[30] Perhaps this also applies to 'paupers' adrenal hypertrophy' in an earlier era, even though the condition was not perceived at the time.

In the present age, on the other hand, heart attacks are highly visible, as well as being as characteristic of a historical and cultural period as any of the other conditions considered. What they all have in common is their own unique combination of symbolic, psychosocial and physiological elements. To envisage these as different aspects of these disorders, which can be understood separately, is a misinterpretation because their emergence and recognition are conditional on the interaction and combined effect of all the elements.

Coronary heart disease and heart attacks cannot therefore be conceptualised or explained in either 'scientific' or 'social' terms or more generally as 'objective' or 'subjective' matters. Equally, their emergence in the 1920s and 1930s is not adequately described in terms of either realism or nominalism. Some of the currently recognised pathophysiological and psychosocial elements of coronary heart disease may have existed before this time (although we can never expect to find any satisfactory evidence of this), but they cannot be regarded as part of what later became designated as coronary heart disease or heart attacks because these categories had no existence then, either conceptually or experientially. What is being proposed does not entail a complete reversal of previous theories, though, but rather the bringing together and transformation of what were previously thought to be competing and irreconcilable points of view.

Conclusion

The emergence of an explosive epidemic of coronary heart disease and heart attacks in the twentieth century is in one sense unique, and the hypothesis suggested here is of particular and special relevance to it. In essence these heart conditions arose because a certain set of human responses, at once both physical and psychosocial and framed by a historical and cultural period, precipitated a pattern of recurring events. How long this epidemic will last will then depend on how long the whole complex of inter-related elements persists, but this is not a matter that is open to statistical prediction, even in principle.

As has already been indicated, other dramatic epidemics such as those of cancer and AIDS, as well as quieter ones, for example of chronic pain, are in some respects comparable, though no attempt has been made to explore the similarities and differences between them in detail. Rather, the point to be made is that if the general theoretical issues relating to the specific hypothesis have any validity, then they must have some degree of universal application, being of particular relevance to those other epidemics, but also to the understanding of medical disorders as a whole. Thus the following general conclusions can be abstracted from the particular analysis developed in this chapter.

- Medical knowledge cannot be separated into 'scientific' and 'social' compartments, or more generally 'objective' and 'subjective' clusters of ideas.
- What unites medical knowledge is its human dimension, and this transforms the traditional conception of there being two separate realms.
- This new relationship determines that medical knowledge has a special dimension, which in one sense differentiates it from other areas of knowledge, but may also resonate with a more general re-examination of the relationship between scientific and human knowledge.

References

1   Calnan M (1991) *Preventing Coronary Heart Disease*, p. 1. Routledge, London and New York.
2   Keys A (1980) *Seven Countries*. Harvard University Press, Cambridge, MA and London.
3   Rose G (1992) *The Strategy of Preventive Medicine*, p. 76. Oxford University Press, Oxford.
4   See, for example: Good BJ (1994) *Medicine, Rationality and Experience*, pp. 83–7. Cambridge University Press, Cambridge.
5   Lawrence C (1992) 'Definite and material' coronary thrombosis and cardiologists in the 1920s. In: CE Rosenberg and J Golden (eds) *Framing Disease*, p. 51. Rutgers University Press, New Brunswick, NJ.
6   Leibowitz JO (1970) *The History of Coronary Heart Disease*. Wellcome Institute of the History of Medicine, London.
7   Wilkinson RG (1996) *Unhealthy Societies*, pp. 43–4. Routledge, London.
8   Lawrence C, op. cit., p. 53.
9   Fleck L (1979) *Genesis and Development of a Scientific Fact*. (Translated by Bradley F and Trenn TJ.) University of Chicago Press, Chicago. (Originally published in German in 1935.)
10 For example: Kuhn TS (1962) *The Structure of Scientific Revolutions*. University of Chicago Press, Chicago, IL; and Foucault M (1973) *The Birth of the Clinic*. Tavistock, London, (Originally published in French in 1963.)
11 Wright P and Treacher A (eds) (1982) *The Problem of Medical Knowledge*, p. 10. Edinburgh University Press, Edinburgh.
12 Wilkinson RG, op. cit., p. 64.
13 Lawrence C, op. cit.
14 Bartley M (1985) Coronary heart disease and the public health, 1850–1983. *Sociology of Health and Illness*. **7**: 289–313.
15 A range of such issues relating to qualitative social research is considered in, for example: Hammersley M (1992) *What's Wrong with Ethnography?* Routledge, London and New York.

16 One study did examine the reports of 6000 routine post-mortems carried out at the London Hospital between 1907–8 and 1949, which indicated that there had been a sevenfold increase in coronary heart disease, despite a substantial decrease in advanced coronary atheroma. However, these apparently objective findings must be treated with caution as they span the period when coronary heart disease became established, so that reporting of the condition is likely to have changed; and perhaps this explains what otherwise appear to be these paradoxical findings: Morris JN (1951) Recent history of coronary disease. *Lancet.* **1**: 69–73.

17 The type-A personality and its associated behaviour pattern was originally described by: Friedman M and Rosenman R (1959) Association of specific overt behaviour with blood and cardiovascular findings. *Journal of the American Medical Association.* **12**: 1286–96. Recent research is being focused on seeking an identifiable component of hostility and its underlying physiological mechanism: Whiteman MC, Fowkes FGR and Deary IJ (1997) Hostility and the heart. *British Medical Journal.* **315**: 379–80. This is despite the fact that other studies have cast doubt on the predictive value of type-A personality types. See, for example: Tunstall Pedoe H, Woodward M, Tavendale R *et al.* (1997) Comparison of the prediction by 27 different factors of coronary heart disease and death in men and women of the Scottish Heart Health Study: cohort study. *British Medical Journal.* **315**: 722–9.

18 See earlier comments relating to Wright P and Treacher A, op. cit.

19 King LS (1954) What is disease? *Philosophy of Science.* **21**: 193–203.

20 Boorse C (1975) On the distinction between disease and illness. *Philosophy and Public Affairs.* **5**: 49–68.

21 Engelhardt HT Jr (1982) The roles of values in the discovery of illness, disease and disorders. In: TL Beauchamp and L Walters (eds) *Contemporary Issues in Bioethics* (2nd edition), pp. 73–5. Wadsworth Publishing Company, Belmont, CA.

22 For example: Kleinman A (1988) *The Illness Narratives.* Basic Books, New York.

23 Good BJ (1994) *Medicine, Rationality and Experience*, p. 183. Cambridge University Press, Cambridge.

24 Hacking I (1995) *Rewriting the Soul*, p. 21. Princeton University Press, Princeton, NJ.

25 Morris DB (1991) *The Culture of Pain*, p. 9. University of California Press, Berkeley, CA.

26 Ibid., p. 277.

27 Jonas H (1976) On the power or impotence of subjectivity. In: SF Spicker and HT Engelhardt Jr (eds) *Philosophical Dimensions of the Neuromedical Sciences*, p. 161. Reidel, Dordrecht.

28 Wartofsky M (1992) The social presuppositions of medical knowledge. In: JL Peset and D Gracia (eds) *The Ethics of Diagnosis*, p. 143. Kluwer Academic Publishers, Dordrecht.

29 Leder D (1992) A tale of two bodies: the cartesian corpse and the lived body. In: D Leder (ed.) *The Body in Medical Thought and Practice*, p. 28. Kluwer Academic Publishers, Dordrecht.

30 Morris DB, op. cit., p. 65.

CHAPTER 3

Conceptions of persons and dementia

Abstract

The understanding and management of people with dementia have largely been determined by a particular view of the condition which readily fits with attitudes about their diminished worth. It relates to a mechanistic notion of impaired capacity and an essentialist concept of persons. Some of the contradictions and adverse consequences of this position are explored, and a contrast is then made with a different and more positive approach. This focuses on the continuity of the person as a whole and how it can be sustained by ongoing dynamic relationships. Attention is also drawn to the complexity of interactions between the neurological and psychosocial processes involved, and how, when handled in a constructive way, there is the possibility of enabling 'rementia'. The conceptualisation of dementia and ways of dealing with people who are affected should therefore be redirected to nurturing the person, rather than attending to particular facets of dementia in terms of loss. This analysis is also relevant to other chronic conditions and involves returning to and reinvigorating an older complex of ideas, which combines moral and epistemological dimensions.

Introduction

The notion of impaired capacity has been developed in medicine through the use of a mechanical analogy and this has serious deficiencies. One of these is that it is consonant with, and fosters the acceptance of, a widely held concept of what constitutes a person, which involves fulfilling a set of criteria. This then tends to lead to the view that chronically ill and disabled people have less than the full moral and social status of persons and are therefore less worthy of respect. The purpose of this chapter is to apply these general ideas to a particular condition, dementia, with the intention of both examining some of the implications for dementia itself and also of using this more detailed and practical context to explore some issues of general relevance.

It was only in the twentieth century that dementia became conceptualised as a discrete mental disorder. The manifestations now taken as characteristic of the condition had previously often been regarded as simply an exaggerated variation of the normal ageing process, as suggested by the term senile dementia, or associated with symptoms which would now be classed as belonging with other mental illnesses, such as depression. A typical modern view of dementia states that it 'is an acquired, global impairment of intellect, memory and personality, but without impairment of consciousness'.[1] However, even though this current definition is more precise it still does not represent a single disease entity with a unitary underlying pathology and cause, but continues to be identified clinically in terms of a syndrome. So there are a number of pathologies which are associated with the syndrome, senile dementia/Alzheimer's type (SDAT) and multi-infarct dementia being the most common, with rarer conditions being very diverse and including Huntington's disease, vitamin deficiencies, neurosyphilis and brain tumours. The relationship between these pathologies and the clinical syndrome is inexact, the syndrome sometimes developing with little evidence of pathology and vice versa. Therefore dementia is a much looser clinical entity than would be required for the delineation of a disease, and because its manifestations are very varied, encompassing physical, mental and behavioural elements, its nature is open to a range of different interpretations.

Two questions are raised which are particularly problematic. First, because all the symptoms of dementia when they are mild are so similar to changes which may occur in any old person, how is it possible to define the boundary which distinguishes dementia? Second, which of the features of dementia are to be regarded as crucial and therefore central to the conceptualisation of the nature of the condition?

Impaired capacity

The notion of impaired capacity appears to offer a resolution to the first of these questions. It relies on the idea of a standard pattern and range of normal human functioning which is clearly specifiable. Thus physical, mental or behavioural functioning can be measured in any individual, and any deficit or failure to meet that standard can be related to an equivalent underlying impairment of capacity in the relevant physical or mental structure. This seems to provide a value-free description of impaired capacity to be measured in terms of functioning, which gives an accurate delineation of normal and abnormal functioning, and so of the boundary of cases of dementia. However, there are a number of difficulties with it, even when considered on its own terms.

First of all, what is the appropriate standard of functioning to apply? Should it be universal, or should it compare each person's functioning with their own previous level of performance? Also, should it be assessed differently within different cultures? Second, do the incapacities have to be consistent and progressive; what of those cases where the changes are intermittent or variable? Third, how should a marked impairment in a single dimension be assessed in comparison with mild impairments in several dimensions? Thus should dementia only be diagnosed when a range of manifestations develops, or is one sufficient, and if so, are only certain ones enough on their own?

To answer each of these questions requires the introduction of evaluations. So the notion of impaired capacity once applied in this type of context cannot be value free. The last of the questions also goes beyond the difficulty of defining boundaries to touch on the uncertain nature of the condition itself. The problem here is that the manifestations of dementia may be physical (e.g. incontinence), mental (e.g. memory loss) or behavioural (e.g. aggressiveness). Hence dementia demonstrates features which are partly like physical illness, partly like mental illness and partly like learning disability, and though it is usually classified as a mental illness there is no obvious or logical reason why this should necessarily be so. The variations in reaction to the condition are a further illustration of this point and are described here in some detail.

In the early stages of dementia it is typical for the affected person to be acutely aware of their mental and social deficiencies and to strive to rectify them, often becoming irritated, frightened or embarrassed by being unable to function as previously. This stage of dementia has parallels with physical illness and some forms of mental illness; the person is aware of being ill and may attempt, either by himself or through seeking professional help, to improve the condition. The person is aware of deviating from both a social norm and their own personal norm and is anxious to conform with them. Alternatively, he may make use of complex social skills to conceal the condition, e.g. through humour.

As the dementia progresses, it is typical for the person to lose insight and deny difficulties and so not make any positive effort to improve. Different emotional reactions may then develop. Some people demonstrate disturbing and intractable behavioural problems, such as persistent screaming, crying or aggression. Others become passive and placid in temperament, not initiating anything but accepting guidance from others. At this stage it is not easy to tell what part intellectual disability *per se*, as opposed to psychosocial reaction to that declining ability, plays in determining the person's level of social functioning. The condition can therefore be interpreted in two ways. It may be seen as having parallels with many forms of mental illness, where the person retains some awareness of social norms and although not conforming with them, is unable to do otherwise. Alternatively, it may be seen as having parallels with learning disability, where the person does not have the ability to know that they are not conforming or does not appreciate that such things as social rules even exist.

There are two issues being raised here. First, that there are difficulties in thinking in terms of impaired capacity if there is uncertainty over which features are central to the constitution of the condition. Second, that the assessment of whatever features are selected is itself open to a wide variety of interpretations. So when taken together, these concerns pose serious shortcomings for the notion of impaired capacity in its application to dementia.

An essentialist approach to persons and dementia

Attention will now be turned to a commonly adopted mode of conceptualising persons which has parallels with that relating to impaired capacity. It falls within a tradition which can be traced back to Locke in the seventeenth century, and which makes mental functioning, rationality and self-consciousness central:

> . . . we must consider what *person* stands for; which I think, is a thinking intelligent being, that has reason and reflection, and can consider itself as itself, the same thinking thing, in different times and places; which it

does only by that consciousness which is inseparable from thinking and as it seems to me essential to it; it being impossible for any one to perceive without perceiving that he does perceive.[2]

There are a number of modern developments of this tradition – see, for example, Tooley[3] and Harris[4] which have in common the primacy given to mental functioning, rationality and self-consciousness as the essential features relevant to the designation of persons.

This way of understanding persons views them as fulfilling a set of criteria. It envisages a standard model of persons, such that specified qualities or features must be present for any being to qualify as a person. Hence not all human beings necessarily qualify as persons, although the criteria laid down as being essential in the different formulations of this general approach vary widely. A complete person is viewed as rather like an inanimate mechanism such as a clock, which can only be considered a clock when a number of essential components are present and put together in such a way that the whole functions so as to tell the time. Similarly, to qualify as a person requires that there are certain essential features organised so that they function in a particular way. A shortage of such features or a failure of their functional relationship can now be seen as having a parallel with the notion of impaired capacity.

This approach has an obvious relevance to dementia, especially for those who regard the central feature of the condition as the loss of mental ability. For them it is possible to run the three notions of dementia, impaired capacity and loss of personhood very closely together. It then follows that the diagnosis of dementia may be seen as automatically carrying with it the idea that mental capacity is impaired so as to entail diminishment or loss of personhood. Thus it is not that a person is first diagnosed as having the clinical condition dementia, and then that some people with dementia are judged to be deficient as persons both socially and morally. Rather, those with dementia are regarded as incomplete persons by definition because the relevant clinical, social and moral aspects of the condition are seen as coincident.

A case history illustrates that the way in which dementia is commonly experienced and perceived does not fit well with the description given so far. This suggests a different way of conceptualising the condition itself as well as of persons. Barlow describes the case as follows:

> My father's symptoms began innocently with the loss of memory and the onset of confusion and disorientation; they advanced to the loss of intelligible speech, to gradual withdrawal, and to unresponsiveness to others' efforts at communication; and they culminated in severe habitual anger, hostility, and physical combativeness. Near the end of his life, my father's belligerent gestures of striking out with his arms seemed to be his way of driving the world away, of disconnecting himself from it, of punishing anyone who simply wanted to be with him in some semblance of companionship.[5]

The salient point to be drawn from this case is that it was not the intellectual deterioration of Barlow's father which he found most distressing, but the emotional and behavioural changes of the final stages of the condition. This is a typical response from relatives and friends of sufferers. Therefore the challenge to the interpretation of dementia arising here is that it is not simply one of the loss of certain mental functions, although this aspect should not be diminished, but of a change in emotional and behavioural characteristics. It is not only that the person affected is less able than previously, but that he is markedly different, even to the extent of being hardly recognisable as the same person.

Now if this aspect of dementia is given primacy, the notions of impaired capacity and deficit do not have ready application to it. There are a number of dimensions of mental ability that can be measured and shown to be functioning either more or less well, e.g. memory. However, emotional and behavioural responses cannot be dealt with in this way. For example, a person with a good-natured disposition cannot be said to be functioning more or less well than another person with a bad-tempered disposition. Unlike a clock which can be assessed for its ability to measure time, there is no accepted universal standard by which to measure emotion and behaviour. It is of course commonplace to refer to inappropriate behaviour, but this itself begs the question as to what 'appropriate' means in this context. People exhibit very variable behaviours and there is no straightforward method by which it is possible to say which of them is appropriate in any general sense. Different behavioural responses only make sense in the light of particular circumstances as they affect particular people. So what is possible is to compare changes in the response of an individual at different stages, and this is the principal basis for concern in cases such as that described above. The point, though, is that this is not captured by the idea of loss, as is shown by the fact that the direction of change may not itself be regarded as of particular significance. Thus a change from typically aggressive to typically passive behaviour may be seen as just as serious and disturbing as the reverse. If such changes are extreme and global and affect the person permanently, they are often described in terms of a change of personality.

The question that will be considered next in relation to this is how should such a change of personality be understood with regard to the moral status of the person? If the concept of a person already described, entailing the fulfilment of a set of criteria, is adhered to, the tendency will be either to focus on those aspects of dementia which can be measured in terms of loss or to attempt to deal with behavioural changes in a similar way (or to consider these two aspects jointly). In the latter instance a change of personality may be seen not as a loss of all personality in general, but loss of those features which had previously made up the specific personality of a particular individual. The relevance of different aspects of such loss may then be interpreted in various ways. What is crucial in this approach is that certain types and degrees of such loss are seen as leading to the conclusion that the moral status of the person is also lost; and this raises two important areas of ethical concern.

First, if severe dementia is viewed as leading to the loss of the person affected, there can be no possibility of a further relationship with that person. Returning to the case raised by Barlow, he believed that although his father was finally completely changed in comparison with his former self, nevertheless it was possible to find some meaning in his behaviour that allowed for a sense of continuity. So Barlow relates that:

> Just as I had become aware of the problem of discontinuity through
> my anxieties over my father's illness, recognising the need for a more

continuous, more connected, less contentious, less disrupted existence, so too my troubled spirit finally rediscovered a sense of continuity through my effort to understand our relationship.[6]

However, if no person was considered as continuing to exist there would be no point in searching for such meaning and continuity. It is not a question of whether Barlow's own interpretation is thought to be the correct one, but that there would be no reason for, or point in looking for, any personal meaning. So to view Barlow's father as having been lost as a person extinguishes any possibility of relating his present behaviour and experience to any previous relationships with his family or friends. This must then disrupt any logical basis for the continuation of such feelings as respect or obligation towards him. Barlow's expression of involvement and of ongoing guilt for the perpetuation of his father's uncharacteristic behaviour would therefore be seen as groundless. Now in such distressing cases it may be more comforting to believe that the person who was known has been lost, in that it allows for such disengagement, but the conceptual justification for doing so has been left unchallenged.

The second issue concerns what in practical terms would be morally permissible to carry out on a dementia sufferer who is no longer regarded as a person. Most significantly, it may be considered that such a being no longer has the same right, or strength of right, to life. So in circumstances where his life is threatened he may be allowed to die, e.g. if he contracted pneumonia. This is not to suggest that doctors always have a duty to keep every person alive in all circumstances, but that they have a duty to act in the best interests of their patients, which is usually construed as their having a prima facie duty to preserve life. In dealing with a human being rather than a person this duty may then be modified, perhaps most frequently when resources are scarce by allocating them on the basis of a lower priority; and a similar principle may also be applied to the allocation of resources for the general care of those with dementia who are not considered to be persons.

In each of these circumstances there is a real danger that this becomes the standard response to all those with dementia, not just in the most severe cases not considered to be persons. Some may consider that there is a sound theoretical justification for this if it is applied in an incremental manner, reflecting a gradual loss of the status of persons according to the severity of the condition. For others, it reflects no more than a general slide which has no conceptual foundation. The problem, though, is that conceiving of persons in terms of criteria all too readily leads to both the development and reinforcement of attitudes which tend to categorise all those with dementia as of diminished worth.

Within the general approach which sees the loss of specified criteria as leading to the loss of the person, there is an alternative interpretation to that which has been considered so far, and this is that a new person has arisen to replace the old one. Engelhardt describes this as follows:

> In cases where memory has been greatly impaired and past experiences lost, one may have grounds for holding that the same person is no longer there. The successor person who arises after the links of memory have been broken is perhaps best seen as a new person with some of the personality of the old person.[7]

This position raises at least two problematic issues. The first concerns how this new person could have arisen, and where they are considered to have come from. He has apparently emerged *de novo*, but within the body of a man which has already existed for many years. Without any personal history or development it is puzzling to imagine what such a person could amount to. The second issue which follows from this relates to how the successor person could come to embody some of the personality of the original person. If a personality is truly that of a particular person, it is difficult to envisage how it could be detachable to become part of a new person. Otherwise a personality would be like a mask, or a part in a play, things that can be adopted or discarded at particular times. These issues would seem to provide strong reasons for being sceptical of the notion of one person being replaced by another. What perhaps it represents is an attempt to escape from the unpalatable conclusion that sufferers from conditions such as severe dementia are not persons, but without abandoning the underlying concept of persons and of dementia. Another way of viewing this, though, is to see the inconsistencies that it raises as pointing to fundamental problems with the concepts themselves. The final section of this chapter will therefore be concerned with an alternative to this concept of persons, as well as of dementia.

A different approach to persons and dementia

Ward contrasts the concept of persons previously described with that of a second tradition in which:

> ... personhood is not to be ascribed or assessed in terms of the presence of an actual set of distinctive properties. What is of more fundamental importance is the existence of a substance, *hypostasis* or subject, which begins to be at a discrete point of time, which continues to have a distinctive history, receiving and losing properties continually, and which ends as discretely as it began, perhaps long after its most distinctive properties have ceased to be evident.[8]

He then goes on to distinguish two elements which mark out this tradition from the first:

> One is that entities are seen not merely in terms of the properties which they eventually possess, but in terms of the possession of a nature which is properly realised in certain properties, but which may not be realised because of some impediment, frustration or handicap.
> ... The second element is that human persons are not just particular cases of a general category of persons, or rational agents in the abstract. Humans are particular kinds of persons, embodied in specific forms of sexuality, corporeality and community.[9]

In this tradition the presence of any condition, including dementia, has no direct bearing on the question of personhood, and given that sufferers from severe dementia would previously have been considered persons, the presumption would continue to be that they are persons unless there is some other independent reason for determining that personhood has been lost. It follows that in the absence of such a reason, all people with dementia should be accorded the same rights as other persons, and this is particularly relevant in relation to the doctors' duty to their patients for the preservation of life and in the allocation of resources. It would also have personal implications for the response to sufferers such as Barlow's father. The recognition of his remaining the same person should lead to a striving by relatives, friends and carers to maintain whatever continuity with his former self is still possible, and should this become impossible, to go on caring for him in a manner which respects him as a unique human person.

The importance of this sense of belonging may then go beyond the recognition that a person still exists to a more dynamic understanding in which the person is sustained by being included:

> As the sense of self sustained by internal processing begins to fragment, it is the environment of others that can alone give continuity. As agency breaks down, it needs to be sustained increasingly by the facilitation which others provide. As emotional traumas continue and intensify, a greater degree of support and holding must be provided by others.[10]

This interpretation builds on and expands Ward's notion of personhood. Not only does it emphasise that persons can only arise from, and be understood within, a social context but also, following from this, that loss of personhood is not simply a physically predetermined process, and there is the possibility of nurturing a person so as to preserve their integrity. Similarly, it follows that developing dementia is not simply a matter of inevitable neurological loss, but that social and psychological factors play an integral role in determining the course of the condition, and this casts the prognosis in a more positive and optimistic light. Sustaining the person may therefore help in checking dementia and is the result of the dynamic relationships between those involved, rather than a straightforward parallel which automatically links them together by definition. A moving example of the sustenance and preservation provided by an ongoing relationship in this way is described by John Bayley as his wife, the famous philosopher and novelist Iris Murdoch, is progressively affected by dementia.[11]

John Killick, a teacher and poet, has demonstrated how these ideas can be developed more systematically. He has joined forces with a clinical psychologist, Kate Allan, to show that much of the behaviour of people with dementia, which may appear at first sight to be incomprehensible, can, when carefully interpreted, be seen to reveal their attempts to retain a sense of meaning in their lives.[12] They then go on to advocate that continuing to engage with such people, especially through the use of narrative and the arts, has great potential in sustaining them. These insights are further used to challenge carers not to withdraw from people with dementia, but to learn how to continue interacting with them in imaginative ways.

Such visionary approaches show how this alternative understanding of the concept of a person and its relationship with dementia is crucial in encouraging a different interpretation of the condition. What it suggests is that the causes of dementia are not just physically varied and complex, but socially and psychologically as well, produced by and producing an indeterminate web of causal inter-relationships. When this is added to the uncertainties in the clinical delineation of dementia and the diversity of its manifestations already described, a wide and inclusive conception which takes account of the totality of these causes and effects would seem appropriate. This is not just a case of adding in psychosocial elements to a mechanistic conception, but of an altogether different understanding in which the biological and psychosocial elements are interactive. (Ian Hacking's notion of interactive kinds is useful in this context.[13]) Most commonly this leads at present to a negative spiral in which:

> ... the malignant social psychology surrounding the individual attacks his or her personhood through a dialectical process whereby a gradual neurological impairment interacts with a process of disempowerment, a loss of self-esteem and the stereotyping assumptions of others.[14]

However, given a different environment, there is the potential for this to work in the opposite direction and produce a positive spiral. In this case, personhood is sustained and neurological 'rementia' is possible.[15]

This is not to deny some aspects of loss, and also of change of personality, but no longer in a reductionist manner as tends to occur when the focus is on impaired capacity in terms of structure and function. Attempting an exact specification of the condition then becomes much less important than its overall assessment which will necessarily vary from one individual to another.

Conclusion

A commonly held view of dementia has relied on a mechanistic notion of impaired capacity and an essentialist concept of persons.

Midgley describes how the origins of this standpoint can be traced back to the seventeenth-century pioneers of modern scientific rationalism, who developed the 'atomic' model which they accepted:

> ... not just as a scientific hypothesis but as part of a strong and distinctive ideology. They saw it as a symbolic pattern suggesting meanings affecting much wider areas of life. Morally, for instance, atomism seemed to point the way, not only away from religion, but also away from communal thinking and towards social atomism – that is, towards individualism.[16]

As part of this tradition, in Locke's account the concept of a person was reduced to factual features which were potentially empirically testable, and in modern times have been used in this way. But as Elliott points out, in considering children with severe neurological impairment, the concept of a 'person' is not a technical and therefore a purely factual notion, but is at the same time a moral one.[17] Thus Locke's definition, as with those who have followed him till the present day, is shot through with values which have far-reaching consequences.

In the twentieth century dementia has also become shaped and classified in relation to biomedical ideas, which derive from the same rationalist tradition and so also claim to be value free. A self-reinforcing moral and epistemological complex concerning persons and dementia has then emerged and been highly influential in determining how the condition is viewed and managed.

A contrasting view has been outlined which focuses on the bodily integrity and continuity of persons and ongoing social relationships. In deriving from an understanding that predates the 'atomic' model, it explicitly embodies the role of values. It also continued to inform medical thinking and practice until the twentieth century, and the analysis and arguments made in this chapter are a plea for its revival.

Two important implications for the treatment and care of dementia sufferers follow from this. First, that they should be directed to improving the well-being of each person's life as a whole and not become overly focused on any particular facet of the condition. Second, that the lack or failure of specific treatments to improve different aspects of the condition, which are both commonly encountered, should not detract from the need and the duty to go on providing the best possible individual care of the person.

Dementia is a complex and deeply disturbing condition which raises conceptual and ethical issues in a particular and heightened way. However, similar concerns apply to the whole range of conditions which lead to chronic illness and disability where a comparable analysis may be derived by reference to impaired capacity. One illustration of this is Sacks' description of a young woman called Rebecca, who suffered from both mental and physical disabilities:

> She had done appallingly in the testing — which, in a sense, was designed like all neurological and psychological testing, not merely to uncover, to bring out deficits, but to decompose her into functions and deficits … But the tests had given no inkling of anything *but* the deficits, anything, so to speak, *beyond* her deficits.[18]

Whatever condition we may be considering, restricting our gaze to deficits and impaired capacity both limits our vision in regard to persons and our view of the conditions themselves. A different approach of the sort outlined here changes the perspective on both persons and chronic conditions, and in doing so the manner in which they are related.

References

1   Lishman WA (1987) *Organic Psychiatry* (2nd edition), p. 6. Blackwell, London.
2   Locke J (1924) *An Essay Concerning Human Understanding*, p. 188. (Edited by AS Pringle-Pattison.) Oxford University Press, Oxford.
3   Tooley M (1983) *Abortion and Infanticide*. Clarendon Press, Oxford.
4   Harris J (1985) *The Value of Life*. Routledge and Kegan Paul, London.
5   Barlow AR (1983) Senile dementia: metaphor for our time. *Rhode Island Medical Journal*. **66**: 359–60.
6   Ibid., p. 360.
7   Engelhardt HT Jr (1986) *The Foundations of Bioethics*, pp. 126–7. Oxford University Press, Oxford.
8   Ward K (1986) Persons, kinds and capacities. In: P Byrne (ed.) *Rights and Wrongs in Medicine*, p. 61. King Edward's Hospital Fund for London, London.

9   Ibid.

10 Kitwood T (1993) Towards the reconstruction of an organic mental disorder. In: A Radley (ed.) *Worlds of Illness*, p. 157. Routledge, London.

11 Bayley J (1998) *Iris: a memoir of Iris Murdoch*. Duckworth, London.

12 Killick J and Allan K (2001) *Communication and the Care of People with Dementia*. Open University Press, Buckingham.

13 Hacking I (1999) *The Social Construction of What?*, p. 194. Harvard University Press, Cambridge, MA.

14 Cheston R and Bender M (1999) *Understanding Dementia*, p. 81. Jessica Kingsley Publishers, London.

15 Kitwood T (1997) *Dementia Reconsidered*, pp. 61–4. Open University Press, Buckingham.

16 Midgley M (2001) *Science and Poetry*, p. 60. Routledge, London.

17 Elliott C (2001) Attitudes, soul and persons: children with severe neurological impairment. In: C Elliot (ed.) *Slow Cures and Bad Philosophy*, pp. 91–2. Duke University Press, Durham and London.

18 Sacks O (1986) Rebecca. In: *The Man Who Mistook His Wife for a Hat*, pp. 171–2. Picador, London.

CHAPTER 4

The tradition of the healer

Abstract

The role of archetypal healer can be found in all societies and is a key and unifying element. The qualities and evaluation of what it is to be a good healer are described, showing how the notion of healing, which is wider than that of curing, is also capable of encompassing it. As hospital doctors have become more specialised since the nineteenth century and in Britain have restricted their work to secondary care, the healing tradition within orthodox medicine has been maintained principally by general practitioners. This role continues to be relevant and important, but has been threatened in the twentieth century by the rise and predominance of biomedicine, and most recently the increasing use of clinical guidelines, audit and evidence-based practice. Thus the long-held tradition of general practitioners as healers has been compromised, and primary care is currently in a transitional phase in which their future is uncertain. If general practitioners were to abandon it altogether, though, it is probable that it would be reinstated in a different guise, perhaps through nurse practitioners metamorphosing into a new style of archetypal healer.

Introduction

The notion of healing is very difficult to define because it can be viewed from a variety of perspectives and contains a range of different meanings.[1] However, most societies concur in a general understanding of healing as having as its focus and goal the restoration of wholeness in an all-encompassing sense. This may be expressed within secular medical systems, but originally had its root in spiritual or religious ideas:

> Healing is understood by religion not only as the natural process of tissue regeneration sometimes assisted by medical means, but also as whatever process results in the experience of greater wholeness of the human spirit. Healing in the latter sense need not be religious in form (nature, music or friendship as well as religious rites may be agents of healing), nor accompanied by 'cures' or 'miracles'. These or other signs of hope, when attested, may be seen as traces of a transcendent or encompassing wholeness, in which human wholeness is grounded.[2]

It might then be argued that this comprehensive view of healing is so general in scope that it is something that everybody may be involved in at some time in their life, as both a provider and a receiver. In other words, healing is a universal attribute which does not reside only within the specialist role ascribed to healers. Whilst at one level this seems true, it is also the case that all societies designate certain of their members as specialist healers, who to varying degrees are regarded as having special powers of healing not available to others. There is a huge variety of such specialists both across and within different societies, and many of them occupy a disputed position, being accepted by only a section of their society, e.g. spiritual healers and homeopaths in Britain. Others, though, hold a central and more generally respected position within their particular society, e.g. humoral physicians, shamans and general practitioners, and these healers embody a long tradition of practitioners who form a key and unifying element in the different societies of which they are part. It will be argued that such archetypal healers, who are the main focus of this chapter, have an important and continuing relevance in contemporary society.

The archetypal healer

The rise and predominance of biomedicine have posed a challenge to the continuance of the role of archetypal healers in Western medicine because the principal focus has changed from the restoration of the person as a whole to that of components of the person, most notably bodily organs, and thus *curing* rather than the wider notion of *healing*. Despite this, the role of archetypal healer has survived in Britain and is most clearly represented by the traditional figure of the general practitioner. However, there are serious tensions and it is unclear whether this accustomed position will survive in its present form in future. Indeed, it has already largely disappeared in the United States, although there are attempts at revival.

Ever since Descartes envisaged the body as a machine divided from the mind, so laying the groundwork for a reductionist system of medicine, the importance and status of the doctor as healer have been under threat. Once doctors became hospital specialists who only undertook secondary care and so were separated from primary care and embraced a reductionist approach, they ceased to be healers in the true sense (although this applies less to those who continue to be concerned with the full range of patients' complaints, e.g. paediatricians and geriatricians, as well as those who focus on alleviating suffering, e.g. palliative care doctors). Many general practitioners have also attempted to follow a similar pathway by specifying and delimiting the range of patient complaints they consider appropriate to their concern. However, there has been a strong and continuing body of opinion resisting this trend, so far ensuring that the tradition of the general practitioner as healer, which has developed since Victorian times, has been upheld and fostered, albeit in a modified form. Thus it has been argued that 'The physician healer is not an anachronism but a modern necessity'.[3]

What then lies at the core of this healing tradition which stands in contrast to curing and is common to a wide range of healers from many societies? First, we nearly always speak of healing the *sick*, and this is important in indicating that the process of healing is not only about dealing with the individual but also the social dislocation associated with illness. Thus working with the individual patient, e.g. in casting out evil spirits or laying on of hands, is often accompanied by work with the social group, e.g. the African Ndembu people employ soothsayers to reconcile conflicts in order to deal with what is seen as the underlying social problem.[4] In these cases the specific bodily ailment is seen as a secondary concern which will tend to resolve automatically when the more general problem is successfully dealt with. This does not exclude the use of technical interventions at an individual level, but as a complement to the social intervention. Their function will also be symbolic and the two aspects will be inextricably linked, so that the notion of abstracting a separate technical element from the wider social concern will not be seen as meaningful.

This is a strikingly different aim from that of curing the body or parts of it by technical intervention alone, and two important differences will be noted here. First, a cure can only be regarded as completely successful if the body is restored to its previous state or an accepted norm of structure and function. With chronic disease and disability this is impossible by definition, so these patients can never be cured. However, this does not necessarily mean that they cannot be healed because, from this perspective, restoration is seen to concern a wider cosmic order which may be capable of framing, accepting and giving meaning to bodily disorder. Second, when bodily dysfunction is the focus, the norm is typically related to the bodies of young adults, to which the average older person cannot conform, however hard they may strive to do so. Reaching out to such an ideal must therefore result in failure, but the goal of healing does not demand such unattainable standards. It is even possible that the less than perfect bodies of the elderly may come to symbolise the special wisdom which can only be distilled through age and long experience. The essence of wholeness and healing in these circumstances is then enhanced by bodily features which do not depend on a fixed bodily ideal, but are situated within another set of values.

The more specific contrast in Western medicine between specialist hospital doctors as curers and general practitioners as healers will now be explored. Brody suggests that the physician's power and authority may be divided into three components: aesculapian, deriving from knowledge and technical skills; charismatic, deriving from personal qualities; and social, deriving from the status conferred by society.[5] In following this general scheme, the claim that will be made here is that although specialist hospital doctors and general practitioners both typically embody all three aspects, the importance of each and the relationship between them are different in the two cases. Hospital specialists rely first and foremost on aesculapian power. They possess a degree of scientific knowledge and technical skill greater than any other practitioner (although increasingly in narrow fields of expertise), and it is this that marks out their special status. They may also display personal charisma which adds to their aesculapian power, but this is of secondary importance and separate from their aesculapian power. Their social power derives directly from the widely held recognition of their aesculapian power and is little influenced by charismatic power. For general practitioners, on the other hand, the distinction between aesculapian and charismatic power is less easily maintained because the technical knowledge and skills and more personal knowledge of the doctor interpenetrate one another. Indeed, the limits of each are not readily definable and this suggests that there should be a consonance between them. The general practitioner's social power and status then rest on a complex of aesculapian and charismatic power which is quite different from that of the specialist doctor. This is not simply a combination of the two powers, but has a different character altogether.

This goes to the heart of the difference between a curer and a healer. The curer relies ultimately on a particular technical sense of aesculapian power, whereas the healer relies on the indivisibility of aesculapian and charismatic power, in which the technical only has meaning in relation to the personal and vice versa. In this contrast the healer may encompass the functions of the curer, but the curer cannot encompass those of the healer. In contemporary practice, curing may be compatible with healing if the technical and symbolic aspects are well matched, but the character of biomedicine makes this difficult to achieve.

The qualities and evaluation of good healers

So far, attention has been focused on the special role of archetypal healers, particularly as represented in Britain by general practitioners. Attention will now be turned to the more specific qualities required of individuals in order to make them good healers. One approach to this involves the idea of the wounded healer, which raises a number of relevant issues. Most obviously, it is suggested that those who have suffered serious illness or other tragedies, and who have been able to incorporate the experience to gain greater perspective in their own lives, may draw on this to reach out to others who are suffering. Nouwen describes this in terms of 'hospitality': '. . . The virtue which allows us to break through the narrowness of our own fears and to open our houses to the stranger'.[6] This raises the question of the healer being open to the suffering of others. To be successful, he needs on the one hand to be vulnerable to the hurt of others, but at the same time not to be overwhelmed by it. The healer in many traditional societies achieves this by entering into 'the sham battle of the healing ceremony' whereby he 'substitutes himself for the patient in a successful combat with the disease' and during the process exorcises evil spirits.[7] He is only able to do this, though, because he is seen to be invested with special powers which protect him. He can then consort with the evil forces of the sick and overcome them without being harmed.

It might seem that Western doctors are engaged in a wholly different process if the diagnosis and cure of bodily ills are seen as their only tasks, but by also naming the condition and providing it with personal meaning the general practitioner is involved in a not dissimilar process. It is as if he is wresting it from the patient, reconfiguring it and handing it back to the patient in a more palatable form. As Cassell observes: 'The doctor's explanation connects the unknown and apparently uncontrolled phenomena the patient feels with the remainder of the patient's experience'.[8]

Cecil Helman, who is a medical anthropologist as well as a general practitioner, has provided an anonymised account of one of his patients whom he called Eddie Barnett, and who seemed to correspond with this understanding.[9] He was a man in his late sixties who made repeated surgery visits always with the same complaint of pain and presented himself with a doleful demeanour. He was obsessed with his pain which constantly moved around and changed character. He had been referred for an array of physical tests without anything significant being found, had been treated with a variety of painkilling drugs without lasting benefit and refused all offers of psychological or psychiatric help, claiming that it was the pain that made him depressed and not the other way round.

For a time, Helman felt trapped by Eddie Barnett's never-ending demands and came to regard him, as many other doctors had, as a 'heartsink' patient:

> Consultations with him always left me with a feeling of frustration and of exhaustion. He followed every suggestion that I made with a question, and then another question after that. Asking him for more details about his pain provoked more requests for help, and more after that. He was unsatisfiable, insatiable – like an elderly bearded baby, sucking desperately at an empty breast.[10]

Slowly, though, Helman's views of Eddie Barnett changed as he saw that his condition need not be interpreted in the conventional terms of medical and psychological models, which it signally failed to fit, but, by turning to anthropological accounts relating to spirit possession, could be seen in a wholly different light:

> Gradually, I came to believe that the way Barnett interpreted, and described his symptoms suggested the persistence – in a diluted, Westernised form – of this ancient and pervasive mythology [concerning spirits]. That even in the present day he was, as it were, embodying this belief system, acting out this profound metaphor, though largely at the subconscious level.[11]

Helman's conclusion was that for Eddie Barnett: 'The only regular ritual available to him was his weekly visit to a family doctor. To a secular bespectacled healer in a secularised healing shrine'.[12] It was not that the 'spirit' which appeared in the form of his pain could be exorcised, or that there would be any dramatic change in Eddie Barnett's condition, but that 'the authentic voice of the Pain could at last be heard'.[13] So in accepting the pain as part of his total life experience, Helman came to regard it as the other half of Eddie Barnett. Eddie Barnett then became reconnected with this part of himself and an accommodation became possible in which he could learn to live with his pain in relative harmony, and so be partially healed.

The analysis and description of this case are unusual, but the issues raised are relevant to a wide range of common conditions, which in a similar way are not well served by conventional medical categories and interventions. A notable example is the rising consultation rate for back pain, which colleagues and I have suggested cannot be understood from the perspective of the biomedical model. We concluded that:

> Conditions such as back pain can be simply a component of a person's interpretation or reaction to their situation in the world. The role of the clinician is therefore not necessarily to hunt for disordered pathophysiology, and if none is found to do an awkward dance of collusion with the patient around the notion of psychosomatic illness. Rather, clinicians have an important role as experts in the process of helping patients interpret and make sense of their pain as part of their experience of the world ....[14]

The skill of the doctor then lies in making the appropriate connection which enables the patient to enter into the healing process, and to do this patients need to place themselves in their doctors' hands (sometimes literally). Healing cannot be bestowed by the doctor alone, though, but requires a response from the patient, so countering 'the false illusion that wholeness can be given to one by another'.[15]

One of the failings of Western medicine is in not recognising sufficiently the danger and suffering to which all doctors, and general practitioners in particular, are exposed, if they are fully prepared to become healers in this way. A notable example was Dr Sassall, who was held up by Berger as epitomising the good practitioner,[16] but who went on to commit suicide. There is a fundamental tension here due to the stress on doctors whose everyday role is that of the traditional healer, but who are increasingly judged professionally by the standards of the curer.

Unlike curing, healing cannot be understood entirely in terms of scientific rationalism because it involves a meld of the technical and the personal. A good way of illustrating this is through a consideration of placebos and the placebo effect. From the perspective of biomedicine, there are serious difficulties in coming to terms with the notion of placebos and the placebo effect in relation to curing. On the one hand, the power of placebos and the placebo effect is so great and pervasive that it has to be acknowledged and allowed for, e.g. in the design of clinical trials, but at the same time it is often dismissed as somehow not proper or 'real'. The problem is that the biomedical model tends to exclude anything which cannot be interpreted in a rational technical manner, and because the power of placebos is personal and symbolic but may appear in a technical guise, it is viewed as illegitimate. However, from the wider perspective of healing, placebos appear in a different light:

> ... no longer being seen as a deceitful part of a technical treatment, but as therapeutic symbols whose efficacy is determined by the subjective responses of both doctor and patient in each particular circumstance in which they are prescribed.[17]

Those who subscribe most closely to the biomedical model go further and extend the idea of illegitimate or deceitful practice to the whole of alternative medicine, and thus may describe its only benefits as akin to a placebo effect. However, this characterisation produces a serious dilemma for many practitioners of alternative medicine who regard themselves as healers. Consider, for example, the use of acupuncture. In order to conform with the tenets of biomedicine it may be presented in Western countries as a technical treatment, but to do so is to distort its essence which is grounded in traditional Chinese medicine. To abstract the technique of acupuncture from this wider context is to miss the point of what is involved in healing within the tradition. However, if practitioners do not present it in this way, they are liable to be charged at best with 'merely' using placebos and at worst with acting as charlatans who are cheating their patients. What is required to combat this is a different perspective which recognises that no form of medical practice can be completely described in terms of scientific rationalism, and that this is applicable to Western medicine as it is elsewhere.

The relevance of this for the general practitioner as healer will be explored from several aspects. First, if he is judged by the standards of a curer, he will be subjected to tests of his technical performance and ability without regard for any implications this may have for his role as a healer. In recent years the introduction and increasing use of clinical guidelines, audit and evidence-based practice are already leading general practitioners in this direction, with the intention of ensuring a higher degree of conformity. Whilst the claim is that this will be beneficial in raising clinical standards, it is wholly inappropriate in the context of healing if it removes the general practitioner's discretion and judgement in dealing with individual patients within their social environment, as for example in the case of Eddie Barnett described above. Indeed, the idea of imposing clinical standards without reference to this framework is to prejudge what are to count as benefits. These will appear differently from the perspective of healing, where technical interventions will need to be tailored to, and consonant with, the wider view.

So with the earlier example of acupuncture, it can only be properly evaluated within the structure of traditional Chinese medicine, and when understood by both patient and practitioner in this way is likely to be most effective. This can then be extended to suggest that all technical treatments should be evaluated more broadly as to just how well they fit with the overall healing process, and this entails an acceptance that the technical and personal aspects are so intertwined as to make their separate assessment meaningless.

An insistence on the designation of acceptable biomedical diagnoses is another way of constraining and producing conformity in general practice, which is also increasing, e.g. with the requirement to give disease-specific diagnoses in the coding and certification of sickness and death. This trend then has a general influence on practice because the way in which diagnoses are made determines what is considered appropriate treatment, and so is a further way in which practitioners may be led towards a curing rather than a healing role.

The healer in contemporary practice

Finally, consideration will be given to what might happen to the healing tradition described here if it was abandoned by general practitioners altogether. The pressures on general practitioners to become curers have been accompanied by a trend towards the fragmentation of all medical work, with the proliferation of medical specialties, the increasing specialisation and independence of other healthcare professionals, the growth in popularity of alternative medicine and of various types of 'talking' therapists. Primary care has been strongly influenced by these changes, and the modern general practitioner is usually part of a team of practitioners and carers, organised so that for some their role as healer has already been compromised. The logic of this process could eventually lead to the displacement of the general practitioner from his central role, and the dispersal of his different tasks amongst a range of practitioners. The doctor's role could then be restricted to a specifically technical one, more readily understood as that of a curer. The claim might then be that the healing components could be carried out by others, e.g. counsellors. However, such a fragmentation, though it might produce certain benefits, would by its nature be destructive of the essence of healing as described here. This notion of healing entails a special relationship in which the healer engages with the patient as a totality. This is not to decry or belittle the work done by a range of other carers or practitioners, but to recognise that it cannot have the same quality as that of the archetypal healer. Thus the complete fragmentation of primary care which would lead to the loss of the healer's role would leave a vacuum, and the experience of other societies suggests that there would be a general desire to fill it.

Some proposals have already envisaged nurse practitioners becoming central to primary care, by their being the first point of contact for every patient, dealing with simple conditions and referring on more technically complex ones. A systematic review comparing them with doctors in primary care concluded that on average patients are more satisfied with nurse practitioners, and no differences were found in health outcomes, although consultations were longer and they carried out more investigations.[18] So the evidence to date suggests that nurse practitioners could well fulfil many of the tasks traditionally carried out by general practitioners. However, whether they could take over the position of traditional healer is an open question. At present they do not have the same status or professional autonomy as a primary care physician, nor do they have the same level of technical education and knowledge. All of this could change in future, but were it to do so the nurse practitioner would in effect have given up the nursing role which has previously been defined as secondary to that of doctors. They would have taken on the mantle of traditional healer in their own right, and this would have profound consequences for primary care. The tradition would then be preserved, not though by a nurse so much as a new type of 'general practitioner' or archetypal healer.

Conclusion

The central claim of this chapter has been that it is possible to identify archetypal healers in many societies, and that general practitioners have carried on this tradition in Britain. Also that such healers continue to have an important social role which can be clearly distinguished from the narrower one of curing. Biomedicine poses a threat to this healing tradition, but if general practitioners were to abandon it, it is likely that there would be a desire for some form of reinstatement, perhaps by nurse practitioners metamorphosing into a new style of archetypal healer.

References

1 Pattison S (1990) Healing: a flight from definition. *Contact.* **101**: 7–11.
2 Boyd K (2000) Disease, illness, sickness, health, healing and wholeness: exploring some elusive concepts, p. 16. *Medical Humanities.* **26**: 9–17.
3 Dixon DM, Sweeney KG and Pereira Gray DJ (1999) The physician healer: ancient magic or modern science? *British Journal of General Practice.* **49**: 309–12.
4 Unschult P (1986) The conceptual determination (uberformung) of individual and collective experiences of illness. In: C Currer and M Stacey (eds) *Concepts of Health, Illness and Disease.* Berg, Leamington Spa.
5 Brody H (1992) *The Healer's Power*, pp. 16–27. Yale University Press, New Haven, CT.
6 Nouwen HJM (1972) *The Wounded Healer*, p. 91. Doubleday & Co., New York.
7 Cassell EJ (1978) *The Healer's Art*, p. 139. Penguin, Harmondsworth. (First published by JB Lippincott Co., 1976.)

8   Ibid., p. 107.

9   Helman C (1996) The other half of Eddie Barnett. *London Magazine*. **Oct/ Nov**: 29–38.

10 Ibid., p. 30.

11 Ibid., p. 34.

12 Ibid., p. 34.

13 Ibid., p. 34

14 Butler C, Evans M and Greaves D (1998) *Rising Consultations for Back Pain: a challenge to the philosophical basis of medicine*. Unpublished.

15 Nouwen HJM, op. cit., p. 94.

16 Berger J and Mohr J (1967) *A Fortunate Man*. Allen Lane, London.

17 Greaves D (1996) *Mystery in Western Medicine*, p. 91. Avebury, Aldershot.

18 Horrocks S, Anderson A and Salisbury C (2002) Systematic review of whether nurse practitioners working in primary care can provide equivalent care to doctors. *British Medical Journal*. **324**: 819–23.

CHAPTER 5

The enduring appeal of the Victorian family doctor

Abstract

Medicine was in transition in the middle years of the nineteenth century, and there emerged a new figure, that of the Victorian family doctor. An early fictional representative is Anthony Trollope's Doctor Thorne, and his characteristics and values are analysed and described. A comparison is then made with two further portrayals of general practitioners from later periods (the 1930s and 1960s), showing how an ongoing literary tradition has developed around an idealised model of the Victorian family doctor. A 'stock character' has appeared, interweaving myth and reality, and is of vital importance to the continuing inspiration of general practice.

In the middle years of the nineteenth century, medicine and the medical profession were in transition, with the advent of a new medical model and with doctors acquiring a different professional status. In Britain, the clearest marker of this change was the Medical Act of 1858, which established the General Medical Council as the self-regulatory body of the profession, so giving state recognition to the power of this emerging medical orthodoxy. Three literary portrayals of British general practitioners, taken from the 1850s, 1930s and 1960s respectively, reveal that a stereotypical character delineated at this time continues to persist and can be traced in a variety of cultural forms to this day.

Anthony Trollope's novel *Doctor Thorne* was also published in 1858, and is the third in his series known as the *Chronicles of Barset*.[1] Its predecessors, *The Warden* and *Barchester Towers*, had focused on the church with clergyman as the central figures. *Doctor Thorne* is Trollope's only novel in which a doctor is the principal character and the medical profession is subjected to close scrutiny. Dr Thorne is a country gentleman and practitioner, and Trollope's portrayal of his medical life and struggles at this time is of special interest in understanding the contrast between the old and the new order in medicine and in delineating those features of the 'modern' general practitioner which have been admired and incorporated into an idealised model ever since. The aim of this chapter is, therefore, first to examine the Victorian family doctor as represented by Dr Thorne.[2] Its second objective is to show how literary works in later periods have continued to reflect and perpetuate the image that he projects with nostalgia and respect.

Within Trollope's novel, Thorne's story is paralleled by the wider conflict between the old social system based on birth, rank and inherited wealth and the new one based on merit and personal achievement. So while Thorne is the medical hero, his illegitimate niece, Mary, represents the new social order and is the heroine. Although she does not have the 'right' credentials, she is wooed by and eventually marries the squire's son, who thus rejects the traditional values of his proud family. The birthpangs of modern medicine, seen from the perspective of Thorne, are therefore set within the context of changes affecting society as a whole. The main attention here, though, will be on Dr Thorne and the contrast that Trollope draws between him and Dr Fillgrave, who, although his name marks him out as a villain of the story, is nevertheless a highly respected physician within the old order of the County of Barset.

Thorne and Fillgrave inhabit very different worlds, Thorne living in the rural village of Greshamsbury and working there on his own for all his professional life, whilst Fillgrave lives in the county town of Barchester and practises there with a group of physicians. The two of them become embroiled in a war of words conducted in the general and the medical press. The issues which they consider significant reveal their differences of perspective concerning medicine and the role of their profession.

First is the question of the compounding of medicines, which Thorne practises routinely, but which Fillgrave finds abhorrent:

> And then it was clear that this man [Thorne] had no appreciation of the dignity of a learned profession. He might constantly be seen com-pounding medicines in the shop, at the left hand of his front door; not making experiments philosophically, in materia medica for the benefit of coming ages – which, if he did, he should have done in the seclusion of his study, far from profane eyes – but positively putting together common powders for rural bowels, or spreading vulgar ointments for agricultural ailments.[3]

Compounding medicines was the traditional task of apothecaries, who had orig-inally acted as assistants to physicians. By having apothecaries preparing their prescriptions, physicians had maintained a clear separation between manual and intellectual work. Fillgrave, as a physician, respects this ancient division of labour, so for him compounding medicines is associated with a trade and is both unsuited and demeaning to his learned profession. But Thorne, who is qualified as an apoth-ecary as well as a physician, embodies the two aspects of work and considers the division between them outmoded both professionally and scientifically. In the new medical order, medicines are beginning to be seen as an important part of medical technology and science. Thus preparing them acquires intellectual credibility rather than being viewed as the mere concoction of routine recipes.

A second area of dispute between the two is the question of how to deal with the money derived from practice. Both Thorne and Fillgrave are concerned to demonstrate that professional practice is not primarily about making money, but they disagree over how this concern should be shown. Thus Thorne, who accepts payments in cash directly from his patients, is criticised by the conventional physicians of Barchester as follows:

> ... it would have behoved him, as a physician, had he had the feelings
> of a physician under his hat, to have regarded his own pursuits in a
> purely philosophical spirit, and to have taken any gain which might
> have accrued as an accidental adjunct to his station in life. A physician
> should take his fee without letting his left hand know what his right
> hand was doing; it should be taken without a thought, without a look,
> without a move of the facial muscles; the true physician should hardly
> be aware that the last friendly grasp of the hand had been made
> precious by the touch of gold. Whereas, that fellow Thorne would lug
> out half-a-crown from his breeches pocket and give it in change for a
> ten-shilling piece.[4]

And the importance of these sentiments is summarised later:

> The guinea fee, the principle of *giving* advice and of selling no medicine,
> the great resolve to keep a distinct barrier between the physician and
> the apothecary, and, above all, the hatred of the contamination of a bill,
> were strong in the medical mind of Barsetshire.[5]

As already indicated, it is not that Thorne is mainly concerned with business and
money making. In fact, quite the opposite, as the reader learns when Mary has the
prospect of inheriting a fortune: 'He had always professed – professed at any rate
to himself and to her – that of all the vile objects of a man's ambition, wealth,
wealth merely for its own sake, was the vilest'.[6] Rather, what it again reveals is a
difference in view of the correct relationship between material and intellectual
concerns. Fillgrave feels impelled to uphold what he considers the proper distance
between the learned profession of his practice and his material earnings, while
Thorne's openness in dealing with money demonstrates that his idea of professional authority can readily encompass such dealings whilst making clear to the
world that they are not his central concern.

These divisions are also consistent with another difference between them, their
attitudes towards equality or the 'democratic principle'. Whilst Fillgrave is defer-
ential to those he considers his superiors and condescending to others he considers
his inferiors, Thorne treats everyone as his equal: 'Let him enter what house he
would, he entered it with a conviction, often expressed to himself, that he was
equal as a man to the proprietor, equal as a human being to the proprietress'.[7]
His confidence in the status conferred by his medical knowledge gave him this
feeling of universal authority, as is shown in his dealings with the squire's wife,
Lady Arabella. During one heated exchange between them it is made clear that: 'It
was not the man's vehemence that provoked her so much as his evident
determination to break down the prestige of her rank, and place her on a footing in
no respect superior to his own'.[8] On another occasion, Lady Arabella tries to be
condescending but is unable to keep the upper hand: 'And then the doctor used his
surgical lore, as he well knew how to use it. There was an assured confidence
about him, and an air which seemed to declare that he really knew what he was
doing'.[9] This democratic authority extends then to all patients, whatever their
situation in life, and potentially enables Thorne to accept everyone in his local
community as patients and become acceptable to them. Such a position was not

previously open to any one doctor, and certainly not to Fillgrave. So, for example, Thorne's predecessor: '... though he had been allowed to physic the servants, and sometimes the children at Greshamsbury, had never had the presumption to put himself on a par with his betters'.[10]

The manners of the two doctors and the images they project also reflect the contrasting relationship that they have with their patients. Fillgrave exerts his authority and impresses his patients largely through his presence and appearance, which he adjusts according to the occasion and the person he is dealing with:

> ... the great feature of his face was his mouth. The amount of secret medical knowledge of which he could give assurance by the pressure of those lips was truly wonderful. By his lips, also, he could be most exquisitely courteous, or most sternly forbidding.[11]

Thorne, on the other hand, makes no outward attempt to impress, and hence:

> ... there was not much in his individual manner to recommend him to the favour of ladies. He was brusque, authoritative, given to contra-diction, rough though never dirty in his personal belongings, and inclined to indulge in a sort of quiet raillery, which sometimes was not thoroughly understood.[12]

But Thorne's true worth lies beneath this unrefined exterior. His reputation does not depend on the surface but on something deeper, a combination of medical and personal qualities, including competence, honesty and sympathy, whose power is such as not to require their being paraded. Indeed, it is the inner strength that they give Thorne that allows him the freedom to disregard the need to observe social niceties.

Many of the characteristics of an idealised model of the Victorian family doctor can now be discerned in this portrayal of Thorne. For the first time it was possible for a doctor to be a *general* practitioner, in the sense that he could claim to be acceptable to everyone within a small community, and so, with long experience, develop special knowledge of the complex dynamics of the community as a whole. This is a role which till then had been available only to the parish priest, and, in a world which was becoming increasingly secularised, the new perception of science and technology in medicine provided substance and credibility to the doctor's work not only at an individual level but also in the wider social context. The inner authority of knowledge, expertise and character are what matter here, rather than the outer authority which relied on a fashionable image, striking poses and a distancing from manual and monetary associations. Yet the paradox of this new role is that although new technical knowledge and expertise underpinned the doctor's authority, it was not this for which he was chiefly valued, but rather for his personal and social judgement in interpreting the meaning of health and illness. As Peterson observes:

> The efforts of ordinary medical men to gain recognition based upon their science bore little fruit until their own leadership discovered the social value of their knowledge ... Knowledge, expertise and science all offered an alternative system for understanding and explaining the 'real'

world, no longer defined in transcendental terms but in terms of the body and the material universe. The experts gained stature not because they could always act effectively, but because only they could name, describe and explain.[13]

I turn now to two twentieth-century books that exemplify a literary tradition that has focused on the lives of general practitioners. My interest is particularly in how they relate to the model of the Victorian family doctor already described. The first is the novel *Dr Bradley Remembers* by Francis Brett Young, who was himself a doctor. It was originally published in 1938.[14] Dr Bradley is a solo general practitioner from a Black Country village who, on his final day before retirement at the age of 75 years, falls into a reverie in which he reflects on his 50 years in practice, which began in the 1880s. The elements that make up his character are revealed by the comparisons with other doctors and colleagues he has known during his long career, and it is the contrasts they reveal that will be highlighted here.

John Bradley came from a poor family and began work at the age of 14 as an assistant to a bone-setter who, although not medically qualified, styled himself 'Dr' Mortimore. 'Dr' Mortimore's treatments derived from an earlier era and still included bleeding, cupping and the use of leeches. With hindsight, Bradley has no respect for these methods but still admires 'Dr' Mortimore for his practical experience in diagnosis and his humanity.

John Bradley has a brilliant colleague, Martin Lacey, who is his best friend when they are students and later becomes a surgeon. Whilst he admires Lacey's hard work and devotion to study, their paths diverge when it becomes clear that Lacey regards surgery as superior to general practice and makes his professional career and social ambition his only goals, at the expense of his own personal life. For Bradley, clinical accomplishment, professional advancement, social position and wealth, which Lacey has in abundance, are not enough for his own chosen goal, that of general practice.

Later in Dr Bradley's career, two younger practitioners, Drs Boyle and Macrae, set up a partnership in competition with his solo practice. Bradley has scant regard for either of them due to what he sees as their lack of professional etiquette, especially shown in their willingness to put monetary gain first in their dealings with him and their patients. In this comparison, the attitude towards wealth and how to deal with money emerges once again as of great importance in the definition of the character of the ideal family doctor.

This is reinforced on another occasion when Bradley appoints Dr Harwood as successor to his practice, after deciding not to pursue his 'book-debts' which his patients have failed to pay him over many years. Harwood is prepared to deal with them in an altogether more business-like fashion, which is quite alien to Dr Bradley's ideas. Only after much soul searching is the issue eventually dealt with to Bradley's satisfaction, even though it involves him in considerable financial sacrifice.

Harwood, however, does demonstrate certain other qualities which Bradley respects, most notably his up-to-date clinical knowledge and expertise and his modest manner:

> He knew all about things that the older man had only vaguely heard of: the mysteries of hormones and bio-chemistry and electro-therapeutics,

the miracles of radium. In the science of diagnosis he was acquainted with the use of instruments of precision which made Dr Bradley's methods appear elementary. Yet in spite of this intimidating efficiency and superiority in equipment he appeared neither unfriendly, nor inconsiderate nor even condescending.[15]

However, as Dr Bradley later reveals in expressing his regret at the passing of the apprenticeship system, a knowledge of medical science is not what he believes to be of highest priority in general practice, and, if unaccompanied by other qualities, it might even be considered dangerous:

> Many times, in later years, he had come across men newly qualified and far better equipped in the matter of science (as he was ready to admit) than himself, who found themselves quite at sea in general practice – a calling in which science counts hardly more – perhaps less – than experience in a patient's probable modes of thought, his material sur- roundings, the limitations imposed on him by popular custom, by mysterious social taboos, by local traditions – even by superstition. For the doctor's first business, as he maintained, was a knowledge of human kind: their lives first, next their idiosyncrasies, and last of all that scientific lore which was the only equipment these blundering newly-qualified innocents had.[16]

So even over their understanding of the role of science and clinical knowledge, Bradley and Harwood were in fact somewhat divided.

There is a more immediately obvious distinction between them, though, relat- ing to their dress. Bradley continues to wear clothes of a late Victorian style, and, just as Thorne viewed Fillgrave's dress as outmoded, so Bradley's attire is out- dated in comparison with Harwood's. However, from Bradley's vantage, Harwood 'looked less like a doctor to him than a young North Bromwich manufacturer or business-man'.[17] So although by the 1930s Bradley's clothes and appearance seem somewhat eccentric, they are important to him in signifying his identification with, and admiration for, Victorian values. They indicate that his vision of the ideal general practitioner is closer to Thorne than Fillgrave or Harwood, and this is further reinforced by his assessment of Dr Medhurst, his predecessor in the prac- tice. He would have been contemporary with Thorne, and Bradley comes closest to admiring him unreservedly.

Bradley learnt much from Medhurst, starting originally as his unqualified assist- ant, and he muses for a while on the stature of the mid-Victorians, and weighs up Medhurst's best qualities as follows:

> He practised by means of a native clinical instinct and less by know- ledge than by the acute deductive powers which his small, shrewd, bloodshot eyes had developed by observation. He treated men and women rather than cases and sometimes cured them, as he admitted (and boasted) by bluff.[18]

However, there were also elements of the showman in him, extravagant gestures and striking poses, which Bradley found reminiscent of 'Dr' Mortimore. Further- more, he had a propensity for making lightning diagnoses and using standardised treatments and was selective in his acceptance of scientific advances, refusing for example to believe in germs. These very different characteristics displayed by Medhurst could therefore have been partly drawn from Thorne but partly also from Fillgrave, and it is those which relate to the former which Bradley admires and emulates in his own practice.

Francis Brett Young's intention in all this is quite clear; it is Bradley himself and his personification of an idealised version of the Victorian family doctor that are considered most laudable. By the 1930s, the main threat to the values that Bradley represents no longer come from an earlier order, but from a new generation. However, the main concerns raised – the role of money and of science and technology – are remarkably similar to those advanced by Trollope, though appearing in a difference guise. The dispensing of medicines is now routine, but the fear of business interests being seen to be, or actually becoming, paramount is much the same. Science and technology in medicine are now taken for granted, to the extent that they are seen to pose a threat to the whole enterprise of general practice through the rise of hospital medicine eclipsing its rationale and the imposition of impersonal values. The greatest paradox of Bradley's position is his admiration for the latest technical advances, combined with a denial of their importance as central to general practice. He appears, though, to have no confidence that this paradox can or will be resolved so as to preserve his vision of practice, which he sees as nearly extinguished already.

Dr Bradley Remembers poses a stark warning that the old ideal of general practice may not survive these assaults, and this was echoed in other contemporary novels, such as *Dr Serocold* by Helen Ashton.[19] The character of Matthew, Bradley's son, would seem to symbolise the destruction that general practice is apparently facing. Bradley's dearest wish is for Matthew to follow him into his practice, and he gives his son every assistance to do so. Matthew becomes a medical student but wastes his opportunities, becomes a drug addict, and dies before he qualifies.

It would appear from this portrayal, then, as if general practice, or at least the idealised Victorian model of general practice, had little hope of survival. Yet 30 years later many of the same qualities are celebrated in John Berger's perceptive, fact-based, though fictional, account of a real-life general practitioner in *A Fortunate Man*, first published in 1967.[20] The subject of the study, Dr John Sassall, is a solo practitioner, living and working in a rural village, who is first and foremost a country gentleman. Like Drs Thorne and Bradley, he is not particularly concerned with the business side of his practice, and has acquired a unique position within his local community which sets him apart:

> Sassall has to a large extent liberated himself and the image of himself in the eyes of his patients from the conventions of social etiquette. He has done this by becoming unconventional. Yet the unconventional doctor is a traditional figure.[21]

Once again central importance is given not to the technical side of the doctor's skills, but to more personal aspects:

> How is it that Sassall is acknowledged as a good doctor? By his cures? This would seem to be the answer. But I doubt it. You have to be a startlingly bad doctor and make many mistakes before the results tell

against you. In the eyes of the layman the results always tend to favour
the doctor. No, he is acknowledged as a good doctor because he meets
the deep but unformulated expectation of the sick for a sense of
fraternity. He recognises them. Sometimes he fails – often because he
has missed a critical opportunity and the patient's suppressed resent-
ment becomes too hard to break through – but there is about him the
constant will of a man trying to recognize.[22]

Later, and following from this, the difficult question arises as to how a doctor like
Sassall should be assessed and judged. It would seem that the skills of a surgeon or
a medical scientist can be measured and checked, but that:

It is a very different matter when we imaginatively try to take the
measure of a man doing no more and no less than easing – and
occasionally saving – the lives of a few thousand of our contemporaries. Naturally we count it, in principle, a good thing. But fully to take
the measure of it, we have to come to some conclusion about the value
of these lives to us now.[23]

Now Sassall himself plays a part in sustaining the value of his patients' lives, on an
individual level and also collectively. He has an intimate and privileged knowledge
of the whole community that, when gathered over many years, enables him to
create a special record:

He does more than treat them when they are ill; he is the objective
witness of their lives. They seldom refer to him as a witness. They only
think of him when some practical circumstance brings them together.
He is in no way a final arbiter. That is why I chose the rather humble
word *clerk*: the clerk of their records ...[24]

... His position as 'clerk of the records' not only means that, more
than any other man, he knows the continuing history of the area; it also
attributes to him the power to comprehend and realize for the community. To some extent he thinks and speaks what the community feels
and incoherently knows. To some extent he is the growing force (albeit
very slow) of their self-consciousness.[25]

From this account it would seem that many of the qualities of the idealised
Victorian family doctor have persisted into the 1960s and continue to be the
subject of admiration. As in Bradley's time, though, doubts are expressed as to
how long they can survive. So Sassall's contemporaries in general practice fear and
resent '... the sensed but not fully understood fact that the nineteenth-century
status and categories of the medical profession are becoming obsolete'.[26] How
then are these values, which are associated with a Victorian model of practice and
have endured so long, faring with the approach of a new century? Is it inevitable
that they will be lost in the twenty-first century?
    In attempting to answer these questions three issues will be considered that have
consistently emerged as important in the definition of the role of the Victorian

family doctor, namely, the role of science and technology, the place of money and business, and the continuity of relationships with individual patients, families and communities. The first of these, the role of science and technology, although of fundamental relevance in securing the status of the general practitioner, is also often seen as the greatest potential threat to general practice. The increasing sophistication and complexity of medical science and technology make it impossible for generalists to acquire a comprehensive grasp of it, thus lending support to those who argue for increasing specialisation at the expense of general practice. Such specialisation then tends to lead to a focus on a mechanistic and reductionist concept of disease and away from the whole person and their illness, and this diminishes the importance of the values that have already been described as central to the Victorian model. Yet, for many, this perspective is profoundly mistaken because, if personal and social values are taken as paramount in general practice, the more specialised scientific medicine becomes, the more relevant is the traditional general practice role in setting it in a wider context.

Horobin expresses this well:

> We place the GP in the position of the well-informed citizen who can mediate between the world of science and our own mundane concerns. But we also attribute to him the power to mediate between those same concerns and the hostile forces of disease. He is the weather-god that is not diminished by meteorology.[27]

On this view, increasing science and technology, far from undermining general practice, should serve to strengthen it. Thus one of the principal reasons for the emergence of the idealised Victorian family doctor, the reliance on science and technology, still holds good today. This relates primarily to his status, though, rather than to his technical ability.

This powerful factor has protected the Victorian traditions and values of practice, but the changing perception and place of money and business have increasingly worked against them. In the modern era, though, the issues relate less to appropriate standards of professional behaviour as defined by doctors and more to government strictures and directions determining the manner in which doctors are required to act. The old issue of the profession being concerned that doctors 'put patients before business', or at least seem to do so, still remains, but the new issue concerns the state's requiring doctors to give much greater consideration to money and business, and the extent to which this then compromises their relationships with patients. In the nineteenth century, before the advent of the modern welfare state, this situation could not have arisen, and it has become a pressing prospect only since the 1960s when all the Western nations began seriously to question how to control rising healthcare costs. In Britain, general practitioners are now explicitly required to take account of the funding implications of how they treat their patients. So it is no longer the case that NHS patients can confidently expect their general practitioner to put their clinical interests before monetary considerations, and if this continues it is likely to change the ethos of practice by reversing a central tenet of the Victorian model.

The three doctors who form the focus of this chapter and exhibit the characteristic features of the idealised Victorian family doctor are all in solo practice and live and work for the main part of their professional lives in one village that has a stable population. Continuity of relationships with patients, families and the community is thus ensured, but little of this applies to most general practitioners today. A majority of them currently work in group practices centred in large urban areas rather than villages, and there is a much greater mobility of doctors and practice populations.[28] Hence, in many cases, the possibility of general practitioners acquiring an intimate knowledge of their patients, of families and of a self-contained community is much reduced. Nevertheless, there are still many patients who have remained with one practitioner for many years and practitioners who have stayed in communities long enough to develop a special understanding of them, and this image of general practice built on stable relationships is still widely admired, even though in reality it has become eroded.

What emerges from this is that one element of the original Victorian model of practice, that of the role of science and technology, remains as relevant as ever, whilst the others, though compromised by recent events, have not necessarily lost their appeal. Many general practitioners and patients regard the recent economically driven changes in the NHS unfavourably, precisely because they strike at the roots of the model. Equally, the recreation of the idea of community, as a way of providing the continuity through which certain values can be recaptured, has been a pervasive notion in recent years, both in medicine and other areas of social life. So, although general practice has changed quite markedly, much of the Victorian ideal still persists.

Finally, what of the role of literature in this process? Alasdair MacIntyre describes special kinds of social roles specific to particular cultures which have traditionally been represented by stock *characters* in certain dramatic traditions and are immediately recognisable to the audience.[29] As MacIntyre notes, such characters were found in English medieval morality plays. They were also a feature of the Commedia dell'Arte, the name associated with improvised Italian comedy which was popular from the sixteenth to the early eighteenth centuries. In this tradition, each member of the theatre company had their own character or 'mask', and the basic characteristics of each remained the same.[30] In the seventeenth century, the so-called Theophrastian Character was another literary stereotype, with a set pattern of virtues and vices, derived from the 'Characters' by Aristotle's pupil Theophrastus.[31] So the idea of the stock character has a long tradition. MacIntyre goes on to suggest that:

> ... what is specific to each culture is in large and central part what is specific to its stock of *characters*. So the culture of Victorian England was partially defined by the *characters* of Public School Headmaster, the Explorer and the Engineer ...[32]

To this list we might well have added the General Practitioner who, though his immediate impact may be less obvious, has nevertheless outlasted the others in a long literary tradition which has extended well beyond the Victorian era. Today the stock character's impact is felt chiefly through the visual media, as evidenced in Britain by such popular television series as 'Dr Finlay's Casebook'. Drawn from several of AJ Cronin's novels, it was originally set in rural Scotland in the interwar years, and gained popularity in the 1960s. More recently, Dr Legg has appeared in the BBC's long-running TV soap opera 'EastEnders' which, in contrast to 'Dr Finlay's Casebook', is set in an old and poor area of 1990s' London.

Interestingly, and in line with the earlier analysis, Dr Legg's recent retirement from practice has been portrayed as marking the end of an era.

This chapter has focused on the British context, where the tradition of general practice has remained strong. However, the same stock character can be found in other countries, though perhaps less strongly represented than in Britain. He can still be found in the United States, for example, even though general practice has been in decline until recently. The two fictional characters who most clearly demonstrate the stereotype in the United States are perhaps Dr Paul Christian, who appeared on CBS radio from 1937 to 1953, as well as in films and a novel, and Marcus Welby, the star of 'Marcus Welby, MD', which went out on ABC television from 1969 to 1976. Turow considers that Marcus Welby 'became the embodiment of norms for the American family physician'.[33] What is clear, then, from both the British and American contexts is that the general practitioner as stock character is not just a feature of the novel but has moved seamlessly between the wider range of élite and popular cultural forms that are available in an electronic age.

In one sense, the individual characters are so shaped by the necessary features of the stock character as to be in part caricatures. Also, these features become romanticised and idealised so as to conform to a literary tradition. However, this is only part of the picture because it is the constant reworking and elaboration of the tradition which are partially responsible for defining and maintaining the norms and ideals of behaviour relating to general practice. The fictional characters of Dr Thorne and Dr Bradley therefore represent an interweaving of myth and reality, which are not clearly separable, and which, ultimately, become allegorical. Berger's representation of Dr Sassall, though based on a real doctor, is similar in this respect.

The ultimate importance of the literary tradition that portrays the stock character of the Victorian family doctor is therefore twofold: first, it demonstrates that the role of myth is still alive and, far from being marginal, is vital to the understanding of the deepest questions as of human existence.[34] Second, the stock character continues to inspire and contribute to the spirit and pattern of general practice.

Berger's account of why Dr Sassall is acknowledged as a good doctor includes the following passage:

> It is as though when he talks or listens to a patient, he is also touching them with his hands so as to be less likely to misunderstand; and it is as though, when he is physically examining a patient, they were also conversing.[35]

Such a poetic description elevates the doctor–patient relationship to a plane that might seem far removed from the mundane quality of most actual encounters. Yet this romantic aspect, which constantly re-emerges in literature and other cultural forms, reinforces a common set of deeply held values and provides a comforting image. Such accounts then contribute to a composite picture through which the participants, doctors and patients alike, are enabled to 'learn the lines' with which to become actors in their own ongoing drama. They provide a mechanism whereby the participants are helped to cope with stressful and threatening situations and, so far from being set apart from everyday medical concerns, are central to them.

References

1   The edition referred to in this chapter is: Trollope A (1959) *Doctor Thorne*. Riverside Press, Cambridge, MA. (First published in 1858.)
2   The term 'family doctor' is used to indicate the doctor's concern with family and social aspects of practice, as well as with individuals.
3   Trollope, ibid., p. 30.
4   Trollope, ibid., p. 30.
5   Trollope, ibid., p. 32.
6   Trollope, ibid., p. 120.
7   Trollope, ibid., p. 32.
8   Trollope, ibid., p. 277
9   Trollope, ibid., p. 408.
10 Trollope, ibid., p. 29.
11 Trollope, ibid., p. 127.
12 Trollope, ibid., p. 33.
13 Peterson MJ (1978) *The Medical Profession in Mid-Victorian London*, p. 286. University of California Press, Los Angeles, CA. For a more general analysis of the role of science in medicine, see, for example: Bynum WF (1994) *Science and the Practice of Medicine in the Nineteenth Century*. Cambridge University Press, Cambridge.
14 The Severn edition is referred to in this chapter: Young FB (1940) *Dr Bradley Remembers*. William Heinemann Ltd, London. (First published in 1938.)
15 Young, ibid., p. 30.
16 Young, ibid., p. 116.
17 Young, ibid., p. 30.
18 Young, ibid., pp. 241–2.
19 Ashton H (1930) *Dr Serocold*. Ernest Baum Ltd, London.
20 The edition referred to in this chapter is: Berger J (1968) *A Fortunate Man*. Allen Lane, The Penguin Press, London. (First published in 1967.)
21 Berger, ibid., p. 91.
22 Berger, ibid., pp. 70–1.
23 Berger, ibid., p. 155.
24 Berger, ibid., p. 102–3.
25 Berger, ibid., p. 105. It should be noted, though, that in real life Dr Sassall was later to commit suicide. So his 'fortune' in understanding so much of his adopted community may at the same time have left him isolated and vulnerable. His unique access to such a priceless gift seems, ultimately, to have become an unbearable burden.
26 Berger, ibid., p. 105.
27 Horobin G (1983) Professional mystery: the maintenance of charisma in general medical practice. In: R Dingwall and P Lewis (eds) *The Sociology of the Professions: lawyers, doctors and others*, p. 104. Macmillan, London.
28 There is an interesting comparison here with Dr Fillgrave who also worked in a group practice in a town.
29 MacIntyre A (1985) *After Virtue* (2nd edition), p. 27. Duckworth, London.

30   Hartnoll P and Found P (eds) (1992) *The Concise Oxford Companion to the Theatre*. Oxford University Press, Oxford.

31   See, for example: Craig E (ed.) (1998) Theophrastus. In: *Routledge Encyclopedia of Philosophy*, vol. 9, pp. 337–40. Routledge, London.

32   MacIntyre, ibid., p. 28.

33   Turow J (1989) *Playing Doctor*, p. 109. Oxford University Press, Oxford.

34   This idea is developed in: Good BJ (1994) *Medicine, Rationality and Experience*, p. 180. Cambridge University Press, Cambridge.

35   Berger, ibid., p. 71.

CHAPTER 6

Changing priorities in residential medical and social services

Abstract

During the past 30 years a high proportion of all long-stay hospital beds has been closed. The responsibility for those who would have occupied those beds previously has to a large extent been transferred from health to social services departments, or to family, voluntary and private care. The overall effect has been to prioritise acute medical care, and to expose the public provision and funding of long-term residential care, whether medical or social, to the direct determination of political and economic forces. These policy changes have been introduced under the banner of community care, but are dependent on complex concepts which are morally contentious and often obscure. The purpose of this chapter is to analyse these processes as a prerequisite to devising better policies in future.

Introduction

Since the 1960s a large proportion of all long-stay hospital beds has been closed,[1] the majority having been for the elderly, the mentally ill and the mentally handicapped (presently described as people with learning disabilities or difficulties). The rationale for the alternatives for those who would have occupied those beds previously, which are provided under the policy of community care, is much less clear than before in both theory and practice. The responsibility has to a large extent been transferred from health to social services departments or to family, voluntary and private provision, and the continuing role of medical services is contentious and uncertain. The purpose of this chapter is to examine the implications of these major changes from conceptual and moral perspectives, particularly as they relate to questions of prioritisation.

Historical background

The foundations of the modern welfare state, as expressed for example in the Beveridge Report,[2] envisaged medical and personal social services being financed and provided by the state as a seamless whole, so that those in medical and social need would be assured of care from 'the cradle to the grave'. Yet for those requiring long-term residential care, there was seen from the beginning to be what might be called a 'natural fault-line' between medical care and social care. Whereas the NHS was established on the principle that all in medical need, including those requiring long-stay hospital care, would receive services free at the point of delivery, those in long-stay residential and nursing homes were expected to contribute to the cost of their care in cases where they could afford to do so. It was not the intention, though, that anyone requiring long-term residential social care should be excluded, only that they should be means tested. The continuity of provision between those with medical and social needs was also emphasised by the position of the Medical Officer of Health, whose role within the local authority, when combined with that of Chief Welfare Officer, covered the overall planning and management of residential and nursing homes. This then was the basis on which long-term residential care was provided from 1948 to 1970, with the division between medical and social care being mainly restricted to financial matters.

However, by 1970 major changes were to challenge this position. First, all the functions within the local authorities which had a social element but had previously been fragmented were united within new unified social services departments, so that the Medical Officer of Health no longer had direct responsibility for residential and nursing homes.[3] Thus what had been categorised as a public health function became recategorised as a social one.

Second, at about the same time all health and social service provision came under political scrutiny because the total cost of the services was rising, and this led to serious questioning of the original economic assumptions and administrative arrangements that had been put in place in 1948. A transition was occurring from the early postwar period of the welfare state, during which the nature of service provision was largely stable and taken for granted, with economic and administrative considerations being seen as secondary matters, to the more recent period where there have been substantial service reorganisations, in which economics and a new managerialism have taken precedence. During this later phase, from around 1970 to the present, the over-riding imperative has been a concern with how to limit rising public costs.

A third and related issue was that a number of factors combined to produce an increased consciousness about these matters amongst the public. Most notable was the rising proportion of older people in the population, greater public scepticism as to the disinterestedness of the professions (including medicine), the rebellion of women against confinement to unpaid domestic and other roles in the economy, and technical advances in medical knowledge and practice.

Finally, the policy of running down long-stay hospitals and substituting community care, which was first proposed officially in relation to mental illness by the Royal Commission on Law Relating to Mental Illness and Mental Deficiency in 1957, has been transformed into a general ideological commitment to 'Care in the Community', which has continued to gain ground practically and politically ever since. However, the different groups involved, principally the elderly, the mentally ill and people with learning difficulties, have been affected in somewhat different ways (as will be discussed more fully later), and in the past few years the policy has met with some resistance.

The importance of these changes for this analysis is the way in which the concepts 'medical' and 'social' have been interpreted in relation to them, resulting in a new pattern of residential care which is markedly different from that which existed before.

Two models of residential care services

The traditional model for the provision of residential medical and social services, instituted in 1948, embodied the following assumptions.

* Medical need is determined professionally by reference to absolute and factual scientific and technical criteria; social need is determined by a social and political process which is strongly influenced by professionals in the same way as with medical need.
* Residential medical services should be provided and funded by the state for all those in need of them; residential social services should be provided or made available by the state for all those in need of them, with funding to be determined by means testing, so dividing it into two elements according to the ability of individuals to pay: state funded, and privately and voluntarily funded.

Until about 1970 residential services were, by and large, operated on the basis of this model. The difference in the way in which medical need and social need, and hence the corresponding services, were conceptualised was crucial to the model and so determined the way in which changes were to occur subsequently.

As medical services came under pressure the typical reaction (largely shared by the healthcare professions and the public) was to reassert the original principles of the NHS relating to medical need, and to express regret that the ideals they embodied might no longer be affordable. Thus if reductions in services had to be made they were usually seen as appropriately directed at those areas not central to medicine, for example dentistry and infertility services, or described in terms of the unfortunate necessity for resource allocation. The thrust of these responses is to indicate that in the former case the conditions involved do not 'really' give rise to medical needs, and in the latter that although there may be a medical need it is of low priority. What is not called into question is that medical needs can be defined separately from social needs and that the relevant medical services should ideally be funded by the state.

In contrast, the concept of social need and its relationship with the provision of residential social services has traditionally been seen in a different way. The definition of social need has not been regarded as the exclusive preserve of a single professional group (having originally been seen as principally within the province of medicine but more recently that of social work) or indeed as solely a professional matter at all, because fundamentally it involves a social rather than a technical process. Thus the different status of 'social' as opposed to 'medical' needs raises doubts about who should define the need for residential social care, and the extent of the state's responsibility for funding it. Hence when questions began to be posed about the provision of residential social services they arose against a background of less fixed ideas about what should be provided when compared with medical services, and did not presuppose any set level for the proportion of funding that the state should provide. So debates about such funding are not characterised by considerations of the precise limits of social need or service provision, but are conducted in terms of political negotiations regarding variations in funding rather than of resource allocation, because they are not seen as being measured against a fixed amount of need which ideally should be funded.

These differences in understanding find expression in the different provision and development of government policy for medical and social care since 1970. Long-term residential medical care in hospital has become progressively redefined as not deriving from 'real' medical needs, or only doubtfully so, and thus the state has no obligation to provide or fund it as of right. Two factors have been instrumental in enabling this conceptual shift and ensuring its conversion into changes in policy. The first is that collectively the healthcare professions tend to regard long-term care as a poor relation within medicine as a whole, and this is confirmed by the use of the term 'Cinderella services', applied in relation to geriatrics and mental health services. So when pressed these professions have not mounted any powerful defence of long-stay medical services, especially when they are in competition with acute services. The second is the widespread ideological consensus that has developed over recent years and already been referred to, in favour of a policy of community care in preference to long-term residential medical care for patients of all specialties. Not surprisingly, the outcome has been a sharp reduction in the number of long-stay hospital beds provided.

In recent years the provision of long-term residential places labelled social, and state funding for them, has shown an increase at the same time as long-term medical beds and funding have decreased. However, the pattern has varied in relation to different care groups, mainly because of the way in which the policy of community care has developed. For some former long-stay patients, most notably the mentally handicapped, the change in their designation to people with learning disabilities or difficulties has been accompanied by proposals that ordinary domestic houses rather than residential places of any description are appropriate for most of them. To a lesser degree this is also what has happened with respect to long-stay mentally ill patients; but the elderly have tended to be viewed differently, still being seen as having special needs requiring long-term residential provision, though in homes rather than hospitals. Consequently, it is mainly for this group that there has been a large increase in the number of residential places, although the development of these services has arisen in a haphazard, rather than a carefully planned, fashion and came about as follows.

During the 1980s the number of local authority places in residential homes for the elderly was reduced, but were more than compensated for by places in private and voluntary homes, with the majority of clients being paid for through the social security system.[4] As far as funding was concerned, this represented a switch from one public purse, administered by social services departments, to another, administered by social security offices. What is of particular interest for this analysis is that in determining who was entitled to social security, as opposed to social services funding, there was little, if any, reference to need for social care, the main criterion being ability to pay. The decision as to who was entitled to social security funding was, therefore, principally based on a political and economic calculation which, when it worked out in practice to be far more generous than was originally intended, was equally open to being restricted by direct political intervention, as has tended to occur since the implementation of the community care provisions of the 1990 NHS and Community Care Act in 1993. Thus the professional element in determining the need for social care and its use as a criterion for entitlement to both provision and funding has become increasingly marginalised, and this lack of reference to measurable standards reveals the weakness of social need as a necessary feature in determining levels of care and public funding. This is not to suggest that professional definitions of social need should take automatic priority, but rather that they should always be given serious consideration.

The combined effect of these changes has been that long-stay residential medical care has been sharply reduced by redefining the main care groups involved as either not in need of special residential provision at all, or in need of social rather than medical provision. This has resulted in a different model of residential care provision and some important conceptual differences can be noted when this is compared with the original model.

- Medical need continues to be determined professionally by reference to absolute scientific and technical criteria, but this is no longer seen as appropriate in relation to long-term residential medical care, which has therefore been reduced and in theory could be eliminated altogether. By implication, acute medical provision has been prioritised at the same time.
- Determining how to provide social care has tended to become more a political than a professional process, one result being that the public funding of long-term residential social provision is more readily varied than previously.

New directions

For those who find the contemporary model which prioritises acute medical care over long-term residential care (whether medical or social) troubling, it is necessary to address the issues not only at a moral and political level, but also conceptually. It is important to address these issues conceptually in order both to lend substance to criticisms of that model, and to provide a sound basis from which to develop new and better directions.

The contemporary model of how long-term residential care should be provided rests on one particular but widely held understanding of medical and social knowledge, which is nevertheless rarely made explicit in debates about health and social policy. It is well expressed by Wulff,[5] who makes the distinction between what he sees as scientific and humanistic medicine, by which he divides disease into those which are 'traditional', for example acute appendicitis, and those which are 'modern', for example hemiplegia giving rise to aphasia in an old person. He considers that scientific knowledge is only involved in the former and so is making a positivist differentiation between medicine which is value free (mainly acute conditions) and that which is value laden (mainly chronic conditions). Such a position may then lead to the acute scientific part of medicine being seen as necessarily defined by doctors, and representing the central and unequivocal core of healthcare which there is an imperative for the state to provide. By contrast the chronic humanistic part of medicine has an uncertain status, being seen as more appropriately categorised as social than medical, so that state involvement in the care of these conditions is properly determined according to prevailing political and economic circumstances. What follows is that the fault-line between concepts of what is medical and social still exists, but has been relocated.

Two aspects of this approach to medical knowledge are unsatisfactory and require revision; first, the assumption of an absolute separation between scientific and humanistic medical knowledge; and second, that scientific medical knowledge is factual and thus to be defined by doctors, whereas humanistic medical knowledge is value laden and so part of social knowledge to be determined politically. A different view, which would dispense with both of these features, would involve a new understanding of the relationship between scientific medical knowledge and social knowledge as not clearly separable, but rather part of a continuum permeated throughout by both facts and values. There would not then be an exclusive scientific medical sphere to be defined by doctors, nor an exclusive social sphere to be defined politically, but instead the whole of the new combined medical and social realm would be open to a different admixture of professional and political determination. It is not that the former boundaries of medical and social categories would disappear altogether, but they would be less sharp. Thus what is considered medical and so also medical need would acquire a less exact definition, and conversely that considered social and social need would gain a more definite outline.

The present purpose is not to explore the detail of how this might be accomplished, but rather to draw attention to the changes that it would entail in the way in which the state determined its duties in the provision and funding of residential medical and social care. The three main elements of the two models – acute medical care, long-term residential medical care and long-term residential social care – would all need to be considered on a more equal footing. Acute medical care would lose its previous status, common to both models, whereby it was almost exclusively defined by doctors and received virtually automatic priority, whilst all long-term residential care would also change its status but in the opposite direction, being less open to direct political determination and becoming included in a wider debate about prioritisation across the whole of medical and social services.

Conclusion

Although this analysis has mainly been concerned with the provision of residential care, it is of relevance to all aspects of the relationship between medical and social services. It has shown that policy changes do not result from the unmediated interplay of professional and political debates, but are dependent on complex concepts which are morally contentious and which are not usually made explicit. The processes involved are thus obscured, and in this example the social inequality arising from continuing to favour acute medical care can all too readily be ignored or even go unnoticed. Uncovering these issues is then an important prerequisite in devising better policies for the future.

This new understanding would also allow the ideological debate about community care to be disentangled from the issue of public funding of services. The contemporary model is politically convenient in that it permits community care to be equated with social care or self-care which is ideally seen as non-residential, and so appears to hold out the prospect of a service which is more acceptable and cheaper than traditional institutional care. However, by challenging this model, what would count as appropriate care would no longer have to be argued for as a cost-cutting alternative to medical care, so how community care should be provided and funded could be viewed more openly and with greater dispassion. The question being raised would then be how best to categorise, meet and fund different types of need without being tied to unquestioned historical assumptions: this would allow the place of long-term residential care and other potentially costly care options to be reconsidered on their merits, without the question of whether they are considered medical or social being of primary importance.

References

1   Since the 1960s the total number of hospital beds in England for the combined specialties of geriatrics, psychiatry and mental handicap or learning disability has been reduced to less than half. *Health and Personal Social Services Statistics for England* [published annually]. HMSO, London.
2   Beveridge Report (1942) *Social Insurance and Allied Services*. HMSO, London.
3   The Seebohm Committee on Personal Social Services, which reported in 1968, was followed by the Social Services Act of 1970, which established unified social services departments within local government.
4   Between 1984 and 1994 the number of elderly residents in local authority homes fell by nearly a half, whilst those in voluntary and private homes more than doubled. *Health and Personal Social Services Statistics for England* [published annually]. HMSO, London.
5   Wulff HR (1990) Function and value of medical knowledge in modern diseases. In: HAMJ Ten Have, GJK Kimsma and SF Spicker (eds) *The Growth of Medical Knowledge*, pp. 75–86. Kluwer Academic Publishers, Dordrecht.

CHAPTER 7

Contrasting perspectives of inequalities in health and in medical care

Abstract

The background to considerations of inequalities in health and in medical care is first traced to the eighteenth century. It is then shown that with the rise of biomedicine in the nineteenth century, concerns about inequalities in health took second place to those relating to inequalities in medical care and have done so ever since. From that time a succession of different strategies have been adopted in attempting to deal with the tensions arising from these two inter-related issues, and with the creation of the National Health Service (NHS) there was a general consensus that they had been resolved by a process of reconciliation.

However, by the 1970s the tensions re-emerged when it became evident that improving medical care had little influence on the overall level of the population's health, and by the 1980s inequalities in wealth were shown to be the main cause of inequalities in health. Initially this was viewed in material terms, but more recent evidence has suggested that social cohesion is an important additional factor. What is needed is a joint approach to tackling inequalities in health and in medical care, which takes account of both these elements, and will involve a rebalancing of Hygeian and Asclepian notions of health.

Introduction

Condorcet (1743–94), a French philosopher of the Enlightenment, 'believed that society was made up of homogeneous individuals all born equal under the law'.[1] Such ideas fuelled the French Revolution and led to the production of a citizen's charter of health for all its people. However, as Dorothy Porter comments, 'Democratic rhetoric on health citizenship failed to translate into reality in any late Enlightenment state',[2] and this included France. No doubt there were in part sound practical reasons for this, but it was also because conceptual understandings of health and illness, which in the eighteenth century were still influenced largely by humoral ideas (involving the maintenance of a balance in the body between the four humors: blood, phlegm, black bile and yellow bile), were not consonant with the notion of equality. The Enlightenment commitment was then to political and economic equality, but did not encompass biological equality. Thus it was only gradually in the first half of the nineteenth century that equality in bodily health emerged as a new conceptual notion, as part of the emerging biomedical theory which paralleled the decline of humoralism. The central feature of biomedical theory is that it focuses on a mechanistic understanding of the body as the only true and scientific account of medical knowledge:

> Perhaps for the first time in history, measurable value was being placed on the health of each and every citizen in a society. But, at the same time, how health was to be arrived at, recognised, and, more important, what it was *for*, were being construed in terms of medical intervention. This might be said to be an account of health characteristic of modern industrial societies.[3]

What this suggests is that by this time a number of new assumptions about equality, relating to both political and medical ideas, had evolved in tandem. These were part of a wider shift in ideas relating to what is now understood as modernity, and in relation to medicine and healthcare conveyed the following notions:

- that *equality in health* is both meaningful in practice and a desirable goal, so that by implication *inequalities in health* are undesirable
- that *equality in medical care* (or, more strictly, equity) is both meaningful in practice and a desirable goal, so that by implication *inequalities in medical care* are undesirable
- that *equality in both health and medical care* are becoming seen as public responsibilities.

Equality and inequalities in health and in medical care

During the eighteenth century and in earlier times, illness was regarded as a deviation from an individual's own natural state, so that the illness of any one person was not regarded as exactly equivalent to that of any other. By the late nineteenth century, illness (and disease even more so) had come to be regarded as a deviation from a normal state, in which the condition of each person with the same medical disorder was seen to be the same, and this understanding still prevails today. Hence the idea of equality and inequality of health, illness and disease is embedded in this theoretical notion of a normal state. This shift in understanding between the eighteenth and nineteenth centuries can be seen as part of wider changes occurring in Britain, and relating to the development of what is now understood as emerging ideas of modernity, which were fuelled by the Enlightenment.

In the eighteenth century and earlier, health and illness were also conceptualised as being different for different social groups. An illustration of this can be found in recent comparisons that have been made of the heights of military recruits in Britain at age 14 years, for which there are continuous records for the past 200 years. These show that in 1800, those who came from wealthy families and were to become officers were, on average, seven to eight inches taller than those from poorer families who were recruited to the ranks.[4] Indeed, the average difference was so great that there would have been very little overlap in height between the two groups. Now the general assumption at the time was that officers were not just socially but also physically superior, and this was a natural state that it was not possible to alter. So, on this understanding, the idea of physical equality between those of higher and lower social standing would have been incoherent.[5] However, such notions changed radically in the nineteenth century, although they did not disappear altogether. For example, in the late nineteenth century and early twentieth century, eugenics became a widely held ideology that was reliant on the assumption that the characteristics of different racial and social groups were not only culturally but biologically fixed. Earlier in the nineteenth century, though, the idea of such immutable bodily types, some of whom were naturally superior, had been largely overturned as a prerequisite to the establishment and implementation of goals relating to equality of bodily health and illness.

In the eighteenth century there were no universally established standards of medical care, and hence there was a great variety of provision without any notion that a particular form of care was clearly superior for everyone. Porter and Porter argue that there was a pluralist medical scene, characterised by almost complete freedom to practise, which presented genuine alternatives to sufferers. Thus there was a medical market-place limited largely by the ability to pay. In this climate, resorting to 'regular' practitioners, 'quacks', lay healers or self-medication were commonly regarded as being much on a level and so a matter of personal preference in each situation that arose. Even consultations with animal doctors were not uncommon.[6] However, by the late nineteenth century, all these ideas had been overturned, and this was also dependent on the gradual shift in allegiance from humoral to biomedical conceptions of health, illness and disease, which was accompanied by changes in both the profession of medicine and society more generally.

This transformation is eloquently demonstrated by Anthony Trollope in his novel *Dr Thorne*, which was first published in 1858.[7] This was the same year in which the General Medical Council came into being in Britain, so placing a government seal of approval on the emerging orthodoxy of biomedicine. The novel was therefore being written in an important period of transition for medicine, when ideas of equality and inequality in health and in medical care were fast gaining ground, but were still highly contentious. The characters in the story inhabit two ideologically separate worlds, some of them respecting the norms and values of a passing epoch, whilst the others reject them and look to the future. The hero, Dr Thorne, is portrayed as a family doctor who is firmly wedded to the new era, and derives his professional authority from the claims to universal jurisdiction of the new medical science and technology. Thus in the rural village of Greshamsbury he treats everyone as an equal, regardless of their social standing, much to the consternation of Lady Arabella. She, as a staunch member of the opposite camp, has more traditional views, and until Dr Thorne's arrival had only consulted with physicians from the neighbouring town.

This part of the narrative, which centres on the exchange between them, is mirrored by that involving Dr Thorne's illegitimate niece, Mary, who as the heroine is courted by, and eventually marries, Lady Arabella's son. The prospect of such a match fills Lady Arabella with horror, whereas Dr Thorne regards Mary as the equal of any aristocrat. What divides them is whether the biological and social uncertainty arising from her illegitimate birth is to count. For Lady Arabella they are everything, but for Dr Thorne very little. So the two strands of the story are complementary, and reinforce one another in drawing the contrast between the old and new ideas about equality.

The arguments advanced so far mainly concern the meaningfulness of notions of equality in health and in medical care for all citizens, rather than their desirability as a goal to be pursued. No attempt will be made to analyse the historical reason for their becoming seen as desirable by society in general, but the fact that this was so can be inferred from their increasing incorporation into health policy as the nineteenth century progressed. This also entailed a growing acceptance of public responsibility, which is in marked contrast with the late seventeenth century and eighteenth century, when the idea of national health as a public concern involved only a general notion of the health of the whole population in relation to the economic well-being of the country. The health and medical care of individuals were then seen as primarily a private responsibility, in which it would have been improper for public policy to intrude. The differences in perception involved the abstract health of a social body in the eighteenth century, compared with the concrete health of an individual biological body in more modern times.

Increasing state and public intervention

How, though, did this transition to greater public involvement come about? There were many important elements, but one which was most significant in Britain was the emergence of the early public health movement in the 1830s. This was because it was underpinned by Benthamite utilitarianism (as interpreted by Chadwick and his followers), which was reliant on the strict equality of all people. Bentham claimed to be able to compute 'the greatest happiness of the greatest number', and this depended on the egalitarian notion embodied in his felicific calculus.[8] So the practical developments in public health in the period from about 1830 to 1860 are an early instantiation of ideas of equality in relation to health. However, they mainly concerned sanitary engineering, which was implemented at a collective level, and was politically divorced from mainstream medicine, despite the involvement of a number of prominent medical practitioners such as Dr Southwood Smith. Hence at this stage public health did not engage with the individual biological body, but was an interim phase between the humoralism of the eighteenth century and its associated physiological conception of disease, and biomedicine of the later nineteenth century and its ontological conception of disease. The difference between physiological and ontological conceptions of disease concerns two opposing viewpoints. The former sees 'the origins of disease in an imbalance between the forces of nature within and outside the sick person', whereas the latter 'understands diseases to be *entities*, things that invade and are localized in parts of the body'.[9]

Nevertheless, the ontological conception of disease, which was to become central to biomedicine, was developing alongside the public health movement. This can be seen in the operation of the Registrar General's Office for England and Wales, which was established in 1836 for the national collection and statistical calculations of births and deaths by age and cause. It marked the transition from the idea of death as a natural event accompanied by illness, to that of death as a pathological event caused by disease. Of particular relevance for the subsequent medicalisation of public health was the development of the Infant Mortality Rate (IMR), relating to deaths occurring in the first year of life.

Since the late nineteenth century, it has become regarded as the most useful measure in comparing the health of whole societies, as well as subgroups within them, most notably by social class. It is the statistic above all others which has become universally acknowledged in epidemiology and public health. As such, it has acquired an ontological status of its own, comparable in public health to that of disease in clinical medicine. So it is not surprising that although the raw data for the calculation of IMRs had been available for many years,[10] it did not come into existence as a distinct entity with its familiar modern connotations until the 1870s. As Armstrong observes:

> In 1857 the number of deaths under the age of one year were provided for the whole country and in subsequent years an annual breakdown of infant deaths by various causes was published, but it was not until 1877 that infant deaths were specifically reported as the infant mortality rate .... It was of course possible, retrospectively, to calculate the infant mortality rate (IMR) for the years preceding 1875 so that changes in the rate in both earlier and subsequent years could be identified and compared. Yet this contemporary (and modern) emphasis on the content of the statistic should not detract from the historical significance of its form.[11]

So the use of statistics in this way only developed slowly, in parallel with the emerging assumptions that lay at the root of biomedicine and clinical practice, and both were dependent on, as well as encouraging, ideas of equality in health and in medical care.

Whilst public health was evolving, there were also developments in the public provision of medical care in the first half of the nineteenth century, but these were mainly restricted to those who were not seen to be equal to the population in general, but by their nature different and marginal. For example, the insane were increasingly provided for within county asylums, under the Acts of 1808 and 1845, although, as with public institutions more generally, these were originally optional, and universal provision did not come till later. This contrasts with the utilitarian (and hence also egalitarian) principle which informed the Poor Law Amendment Act of 1834. It determined that the inmates of the workhouses were not to be in any way advantaged in relation to the working poor of the general population, and this included their provision of medical care. Thus in a strict sense the indigent and the working poor were being regarded as equals, despite the reality that a large proportion of paupers were unequal in being chronically ill and disabled and so deserving of additional care. It is significant, though, that this was not officially recognised until 1867 when the Metropolitan Poor Act allowed for the provision of Poor Law infirmaries alongside, but separate from, the workhouses, which shows how the Benthamite idea of strict equality did not give way to the modern notion of equity – equal care for those with equal needs[12] – until the 1860s.

Once again, it can be seen how a political notion of equality only became modified later to attain its modern meaning under the growing influence of biomedicine. The original political assumption was that individuals are principally responsible for their own welfare, including their health, whereas later it was acknowledged that the chronically sick and disabled are incapable of taking responsibility for their own health, and so will be unfairly disadvantaged if dealt with strictly as equals. By the 1860s, this gave legitimacy to the improved public provision of medical care, based on the new understanding that people may be politically equal but medically different, a more complex idea which would have been impossible in an earlier period.

By about 1870, then, the assumptions and values associated with biomedicine had become predominant in both clinical medicine and public health, and were congruent with a range of other new ideas. Most notably for this chapter, these included those concerning inequalities in health and in medical care, and were being interpreted in a manner which still continues today. They had also become matters of public concern. However, despite an awareness since this time of systematic inequalities in health, the politicians, the medical profession and the public have consistently paid more attention to developing public policies for reducing inequalities in medical care than in health. The next section of this chapter will therefore be concerned with describing a variety of different ways in which this has come about, and examining the reasons for it.

Strategies for dealing with inequalities in health and in medical care in the modern period

Redefinition

Public health became medicalised between the 1850s and 1870s, and several interlocking elements were involved in its transformation. There was first a change in theoretical orientation from miasmatism to contagionism, which has parallels with the transition from humoralism to biomedicine. Miasmatism holds that ill health is caused by noxious emanations arising from polluted environments, whereas contagionism presumes that there is a direct causal relationship between each particular disease and a specific factor or factors associated with it. Second was a change in professional control, from an overt association with politics and economics to that of mainstream medicine. Finally, there was also a change in the orientation of public health, from sanitary engineering to the surveillance of health and disease of populations.

So by the end of the nineteenth century, public health had become recognised as the third arm within a tripartite medical structure, with an apparently clear division of public responsibility between care for health of the population (public health) and medical care (hospital medicine and general practice). This would suggest that public health should have as a central focus the emerging concerns about inequalities in health. Although to some extent this was true and has remained so ever since, public health began to further redefine its role from this time, away from issues of health and towards medical care. This came about in two important ways. First, it became involved with the management of publicly provided medical care, and as such care grew, this role grew with it. This then came to be a major part of the Medical Officer of Health's expanding empire, reaching its height between 1929 and 1948, when the management of Poor Law infirmaries was added to his brief. Second, from the early years of the twentieth century, there were significant developments in public services relating to personal preventive care (for example, maternal and child health services and the school health service), and these were also included within public health's remit.

The problem for public health as a professional institution was that its incorporation into mainstream medicine involved a compromise which made it very difficult for the health of the population, rather than medical care, to remain its principal concern. Even to speak of the 'medicalisation' of public health is to imply that medicine is not properly about the social and political issues, which were the concerns of its early founders and are necessarily raised in considering questions of inequalities in health. Rather, it is taken for granted that being seen as part of medicine entails an acceptance of the very assumptions and values of biomedicine, particularly value-free knowledge, and a focus on disease in individuals, and this militates against any wider conception of or concern with health. So, not surprisingly, public health doctors have always had an ambiguous relationship with mainstream medicine. If health is their main focus they are not readily acceptable, but to compete for patients is intolerable to clinicians, as well as a denial of the separate role and identity of public health. The additional roles of management and personal prevention that public health adopted can be seen as an attempt to avoid these difficulties, by both reducing the emphasis on health and being complementary to, rather than competing with, clinical medicine. This allowed public health to identify more clearly with biomedicine, but in doing so inevitably diminished its profile and authority in relation to inequalities in health. At the same time, through its management role, it increasingly came to be identified with concerns about inequalities in medical care.

Another aspect of these redefinitions of role was the attempt by public health doctors to raise their traditionally low status within medicine as a whole. However, this was largely unsuccessful, with these manoeuvrings serving chiefly to re-emphasise the dominance of clinical medicine. This failure to command status within medicine has then served to reduce the impact of the work on inequalities in health that public health has continued to produce.

Suppression

In the interwar years, the main concern of those involved with health and medical care was how best to organise and deliver medical services for the population as a whole. In retrospect, this can be seen as a period of public policy debate which culminated in the setting up of the NHS in 1948, and issues of inequality in medical care were central to this debate.

In contrast, those concerns that were frequently raised during the Depression of the 1930s about the nation's health, and especially about inequalities in health, were consistently denied by the government, and Webster has argued that:

> Notwithstanding their solid features, founded on the fine Victorian tradition of public health reporting, the inter-war Annual Reports [of Government] bear the unmistakable imprint of complacency. These reports were essentially reports of progress, and nothing was allowed

to detract from this image. There was no absence of criticism or of appeals for greater effort, but never were deficiencies in the record systematically explored. Thus the Reports risked becoming a means whereby a body of unquestionably accurate data was manipulated by the medical bureaucracy to defend the status quo.[13]

What was principally obscured, as Webster goes on to show, was that although average IMRs for England and Wales did not worsen in the interwar years, the long-term downward trend was adversely affected. Also, this average rate concealed very large variations between geographical regions, areas and districts, and these were closely correlated with economic and social conditions. But this evidence of inequalities in health associated with poverty and unemployment was consistently ignored.

Much of the raw data from which these government reports were derived came from the annual reports of medical officers of health, which were compiled for every local authority as a statutory obligation, and the detail in them often contradicted this rosy picture. What is notable, though, is that the medical officers of health did not counter this message in any significant way. There was a notable case of frank suppression by government,[14] but more importantly public health did not have the power or will to mount a convincing challenge. Medical officers of health were both distracted with their burgeoning management role and reluctant to become engaged in an overtly political struggle which would have called into question the credibility of public health as a medical and scientifically objective discipline.

Reconciliation

Implicit in the creation of the NHS was a very widely held notion that by providing the best available care for all medical needs, not only would care for each individual patient be maximised, but the health of the population and also inequalities in health would improve automatically. It was therefore assumed that given that the sanitary reforms of the nineteenth century were in place, further improvements in health were largely a function of improvements in medical care. This then allowed for a reconciliation between the goals of correcting inequalities in medical care and in health, without having to pay attention to the latter. Thus, as Lawrence notes, the Ministry of Health, which was established in 1919, 'was not a ministry of health at all, it was a ministry of clinical medicine',[15] mainly concerned with improving and developing medical care. This principally meant medical treatment, but was also to be complemented by personal preventive medicine which the first Chief Medical Officer to the Ministry, Sir George Newman, described in 1931 as deriving from the knowledge, provided by laboratory scientists, clinicians and epidemiologists, which if followed would lead to a healthy life.[16]

So clinical science was seen as pointing to the future not only for medical care, but also for public policy on health, and at the same time the older notions of health and public health's role in promoting it were being sidelined. A significant expression of this thinking can be seen in the way in which Bevan devised the structure of the NHS. He decided to organise medical care on a national basis because he was concerned to rectify historic inequalities of provision between different geographical areas, but left public health within the control of local authorities and so to the vagaries of local interpretation and funding. This suggests that Bevan was also influenced by the thesis of reconciliation and so, believing that the NHS would deal simultaneously with inequalities in health and in medical care, saw no need to bring public health activities under central control.

A further implication of this reasoning was that public responsibility for both health and medical care was increased to a degree never seen previously. Conversely, private responsibility was reduced to no more than a personal duty to follow medical orders, with regard to both treatment and prevention. The prevalence and strength of this understanding at the time are well illustrated by Talcott Parsons's original description of the 'sick role' in 1951,[17] and the positivist manner in which it was interpreted, as a fixed concept within the social order. He described how he thought social stability was maintained through the interaction of doctors and patients. He suggested that when individuals became accepted as patients by doctors, they gained two benefits (being exempt from their normal social role and not being held responsible for their illness), but at the same time were expected to fulfil two obligations (wanting to get well and co-operating with medical advice in attempting to do so).

Re-emergence

For some 20 years after the NHS was set up in 1948, questions about inequalities in health and in medical care did not feature prominently on the political agenda. There was a considerable degree of political consensus during this postwar period, particularly concerning the NHS, about which there was a general feeling of national pride and satisfaction. However, by the 1960s this spell of relative calm had come to an end, with all aspects of life, including medicine and the NHS, undergoing re-examination. The reconciliation thesis, described in the last section, began to be seriously questioned, so reopening issues about inequalities in both health and in medical care.

Despite the beliefs of Bevan and the other founders of the NHS, inequality in the provision of medical care continued to persist in the 1950s and 1960s, and two developments will be described which illustrate the way the issue resurfaced politically. The first relates to Tudor Hart's famous characterisation of the 'inverse care law', which was published in 1971, and held that those with most medical needs tend on average to receive the least medical care.[18] This is both because of a maldistribution of services in relation to need, and also because those with greater needs, who are mainly in the lower social classes, are less able to access services. The second development concerns the poor standard and level of services in long-stay hospitals for the chronically sick, when compared with services for the acutely ill. This came to attention following a series of scandals in such hospitals, the first being that at Ely Hospital, the report on which was made public in 1969.[19] These services for the chronically ill became known as the 'Cinderella' services.

In subsequent years, attempts were made by government to address both these issues. For example, in the 1970s a Resources Allocation Working Party (RAWP)[20] was set up which applied a formula aimed at bringing about the geographical redistribution of resources in relation to medical need, and so, taken overall, from richer to poorer areas of the country. Also, the 'Cinderella' services were designated as priority services as part of a policy commitment to redirect funding positively for their improvement.

At the same time, work that had been going on for some years on the health of the population and inequalities in health also received recognition. McKeown's thesis, developed in a book entitled *The Role of Medicine*, gained particular prominence. It was first published in 1976, and in an expanded version in 1979.[21] It claimed that the historical increase in population in Britain resulting from improvement in health had principally been the result of improvements in socio-economic conditions, mediated largely via better nutrition. Public health interventions were considered of secondary importance and, most significantly, it was maintained that medical care had hardly influenced the health of the population at all. Whilst some aspects of McKeown's thesis have been challenged,[22] the relatively small effect that medical services have on population health is now generally accepted. Therefore, however much medical care and its distribution in relation to need is improved, this cannot be expected to bring about major improvements in health or reductions of inequalities in health. Thus, in theory at least, the reconciliation thesis had been overturned. It might then have been thought that the scene was set for a renewal and redirection of public policy in relation to inequalities in health, that did not rely on medical care. However, with an incoming Conservative government in 1979, this was not to be.

Denial

In 1980, the Black Report on *Inequalities in Health*,[23] which had been commissioned by a Labour government in 1977, was completed and presented to the new Conservative government. It brought together a great deal of evidence and concluded that socio-economic factors were the main determinants of inequalities in health. The initial government response was to sideline the report by making available only a very limited number of copies with the least publicity possible. However, this measure backfired, leading to it becoming more celebrated than it might otherwise have been, and to the appearance of a paperback version in 1982.[24] The government's response should not be interpreted as simply a straightforward attempt at suppression, though, as the following passage from the Secretary of State's foreword to the report shows:

> It will come as a disappointment to many that over long periods since the inception of the NHS there is generally little sign of health inequalities in Britain actually diminishing and, in some cases, they may be increasing. It will be seen that the Group has reached the view that the causes of health inequalities are so deep rooted that only a major and wide-ranging programme of public expenditure is capable of altering the pattern. I must make it clear that additional expenditure on the scale which could result from the report's recommendations – the amount involved could be upward of £2 billion a year – is quite unrealistic in present or any foreseeable economic circumstances, quite apart from any judgement that may be formed of the effectiveness of such expenditure in dealing with the problems identified.[25]

What this suggests is an awareness of the failure of the reconciliation thesis, and a redefinition of the government's responsibility by way of response. Essentially, medical care (mainly provided by the NHS) was being seen as a continuing public responsibility, but health was in future to be regarded as largely a private responsibility. This was a very significant retreat from the earlier political consensus, and is clearly demonstrated in the development of health policy in the 1980s. Most notable was the evolution of health promotion, and its displacement of the previous concept of health education. Ideas about health education had been derived from the understanding that government had a responsibility both to supply information and to make available the appropriate means for people to live healthy lives. The individual's responsibility was then mainly to comply with the advice given. Health promotion, on the other hand, involves the restriction of government responsibility to making information available to people in order that they can make their own choices and so take responsibility for them. Hence the Conservative government, in their response to the Black Report, can be seen to be starting to articulate a new ideological position, in which inequalities in health may be unfortunate, but are no longer viewed as a public responsibility.

Contradiction

A Labour government took office in 1997 with the declared intention of re-establishing a public commitment and responsibility for inequalities in health, as well as continuing the traditional commitment to reducing inequalities in medical care through renewed attention to the NHS. It therefore commissioned the Acheson Report, which was published in 1998,[26] and was essentially an updating of the Black Report, echoing its main findings. It revealed that the gap in health inequalities had not only persisted in the 1980s and 1990s but had widened, and it was considered that differences in material circumstances were the major cause.

The problem for the government in responding to this was that it uncovered a contradiction at the heart of its strategy for health policy development, which started in the customary way with a pledge to provide more money for the NHS. Crucially, though, it was proposed that this should not come from increased taxation, but from the creation of more national wealth. This was in line with a general policy aimed at improving public services from economic growth. However, the engine for such growth was dependent on market competition, which was an extension of the earlier Conservative policy of the 1980s and 1990s. Now, it was just these policies which had already led to a widening of inequalities in wealth, and which the Acheson Report had identified as the main cause of the increases in inequalities in health. It would seem then that Labour's policy for reducing inequalities in medical care, by more careful targeting of those with the greatest medical need,[27] would inevitably lead to continuing or even growing differentials in inequalities in health, if financed through economic growth derived from market competition. So by placing the primary emphasis on improving medical care through material growth, the government's commitment to improving health, and especially inequalities in health, would seem to be compromised. Once again, reducing inequalities in health appears to have been given a higher public priority, but this is likely to prove empty in practice.

New theoretical insights have recently emerged concerning the relationship between inequalities in wealth and inequalities in health, and have been demonstrated by Wilkinson to hold across many societies.[28] Of particular relevance for this chapter has been the reappraisal of the long-held assumption that material factors are the principal cause of inequalities in health, and that increasing wealth equates directly with better health. The new evidence suggests that whilst a certain basic level of material wealth is clearly essential to health, once this is exceeded other factors are also important. This has been shown by the fact that above this level, those countries with relatively small inequalities in wealth are healthier than those where the converse is true. The reasons for this are the subject of ongoing debate, and a great deal of theoretical work remains to be done. However, what is not in doubt is that a different type of explanation is required:

> A theory is needed which unifies the causes of the health inequalities related to social hierarchy with the effects of income inequality on national mortality rates. At its centre are likely to be factors affecting how hierarchical the hierarchy is, the depths of material insecurity and social exclusion which societies tolerate, and the direct and indirect psychosocial affects of social stratification.
>   One reason why greater income equality is associated with better health seems to be that it tends to improve social cohesion and reduce the social divisions. Qualitative and quantitative evidence suggest that more egalitarian societies are more cohesive.[29] (p. 593)

What seems clear from this is that current government policy is likely to lead to less social cohesion, as it did in the 1980s and early 1990s, and this will have a negative impact on health. Whatever other policies the government puts in place in an attempt to improve inequalities in health will then tend to be undermined whilst inequalities in wealth persist or widen. So until there is a recognition of this contradiction and a willingness to make more radical changes, reductions in inequalities in health will not have been given genuine priority.

What is required is a new understanding of the relationship between wealth and health, which is reflected in a different conception of the goals of policies for health and medical care and the relationship between them. Without this, a focus on inequalities in medical care, and a particular way of tackling them, will continue in reality to displace concerns about inequalities in health.

Conclusion

Addressing inequalities in health has always taken second place to considerations of inequalities in medical care, ever since they both entered the policy arena in the nineteenth century. Redressing this will continue to be problematic whilst the ideological values relating to material wealth, a positivist conception of science and individualism persist, both generally and particularly as they are expressed in biomedicine. There is a resonance between the dominant interpretation of material factors as the principal and direct cause of the health of populations and the centrality of an ontological account of disease within medicine and healthcare. Refocusing on inequalities in health will therefore require simultaneous attention to both these issues, and this will entail the inclusion of psychosocial factors, interpreted subjectively, to be integrated with material factors, so as to produce a fresh understanding of how they influence health.

In doing this, the conceptualisation of health will itself become modified towards a more Hygeian notion of health as wholeness, and away from the current Asclepian notion that views health negatively as the absence of disease and disability. This is not, though, a wholesale rejection of either the role of material factors in relation to health or of Asclepian accounts of health. Rather, it is a plea for a transformation which involves a rebalancing of concepts of health and a reinterpretation of how best to provide medical care. Scientific rationalism and materialism on their own will not resolve the problem of inequalities in medical care any more than those of inequalities in health, and only by redefining them in a way which is more symmetrical will it be possible to develop viable and enduring solutions.

References

1   Porter D (1999) *Health, Civilization and the State*, p. 66. Routledge, London.
2   Ibid., p. 57.
3   Lawrence C (1994) *Medicine in the Making of Modern Britain, 1700–1920*, p. 62. Routledge, London.
4   Floud R, Wachter K and Gregory A (1990) *Height, Health and History*. Cambridge University Press, Cambridge.
5   It has been suggested that the terms 'higher' (or upper) and 'lower' class may originally have been a literal description of the differences in height involved.
6   An account is given of a Mr Wakefield who in 1658 turned to the local 'Horse-Smithe' for advice and treatment in: Porter D and Porter R (1989) *Patient's Progress*, p. 29. Polity Press, Cambridge.
7   Trollope A (1959) *Dr Thorne*. Riverside Press, Cambridge, MA. (First published in 1858.)
8   These ideas were developed in: Bentham J (1879) *An Introduction to the Principles of Morals and Legislation*. Clarendon Press, Oxford. (First printed in 1780 and published in 1789 and as a new edition in 1823.)
9   Cassell EJ (1991) *The Nature of Suffering and the Goals of Medicine*, p. 4. Oxford University Press, Oxford and New York.
10 Before national registration was introduced, births, marriages and deaths had been recorded locally in parish registers for several centuries.
11 Armstrong D (1986) The invention of infant mortality. *Sociology of Health and Illness*. **8**: 211–32.
12 This idea derives from Aristotle's formal principle of justice or equality (in the *Nicomachean Ethics*), according to which equals should be treated equally and unequals unequally in proportion to relevant inequalities.
13 Webster C (1982) Healthy or hungry thirties? *History Workshop Journal*. **13**: 110–29.
14 McGonigle GCM and Kirby J (1936) *Poverty and Public Health*. Gollancz, London.
15 Lawrence C (1994) *Medicine in the Making of Modern Britain*, p. 82. Routledge, London.
16 Newman G (1931) *Health and Social Evaluation*. George Allen and Unwin, London.

17 Parsons T (1951) *The Social System.* Free Press, Glencoe, IL.

18 Tudor Hart J (1971) The inverse care law. *Lancet.* **1**: 405–12.

19 *Report of the Committee of Inquiry into Allegations of Ill-Treatment of Patients and Other Irregularities at the Ely Hospital, Cardiff* (1969). Cmnd. 3975. HMSO, London.

20 DHSS (1976) *Report of the Resources Allocation Working Party: sharing resources for health in England.* HMSO, London.

21 McKeown T (1979) *The Role of Medicine.* Blackwell, Oxford.

22 One challenge to McKeown's thesis is based on the grounds that the public health movement has had a significant influence on the nation's health. See, for example: Szreter S (1988) The importance of social interaction in Britain's mortality decline c. 1850–1914: a reinterpretation of the role of public health. *Social History of Medicine.* **1**: 1–37. Another important question is whether pursuing prevention rather than cure is necessarily a good thing. See, for example: Skrabanek P (1994) *The Death of Humane Medicine.* The Social Affairs Unit, London.

23 DHSS (1980) Unpublished report of a research working group: *Inequalities in Health.*

24 Townsend P and Davidson N (eds) (1982) *Inequalities in Health: the Black Report.* Penguin, Harmondsworth.

25 DHSS (1980) *Inequalities in Health,* foreword.

26 Acheson D (1998) *Independent Inquiry into Inequalities in Health.* HMSO, London.

27 This can be seen in the government's support for evidence-based practice, and the setting up of the National Institute for Clinical Excellence (NICE).

28 Wilkinson RG (1996) *Unhealthy Societies.* Routledge, London.

29 Wilkinson RG (1997) Health inequalities: relative or absolute material standards? *British Medical Journal.* **314**: 591–5.

CHAPTER 8

The creation of partial patients

Abstract

The emergence and growth of surveillance medicine in the twentieth century has led to the creation of a new social category and role, that of 'partial patient'. It relates to people who do not feel ill or see themselves as disabled either most or all of the time, but who have been informed medically that they have or may have a disease or other medical condition, or are at risk of acquiring such a disease or medical condition because of certain personal characteristics. Seven different types of 'partial patient' are distinguished.

A number of conceptual and ethical issues which arise in regard to this new role are considered, relating to the continuing trend in growth of programmes of screening for, and personal prevention of, disease and disability, as well as more subtle influences on medicine more generally, which arise through changes in its norms of theory and practice. It is suggested that, because 'partial patients' are neither clearly ill nor clearly well, they occupy a role which is inherently ambiguous and stressful. The main ethical issues then arise because medicine fails to recognise this, and both perceives and manages 'partial patients' in much the same way as more traditional patients who feel themselves to be ill or disabled.

The conclusion drawn from this analysis is that rather than continuing to plan and implement more and more programmes which create 'partial patients', a different approach to their evaluation is required, which acknowledges that in attempting to relieve one type of suffering, medicine is at the same time bound to create another type of suffering. A more critical reflection is also required on the wider influence of surveillance medicine on medicine as a whole.

Introduction

Armstrong describes the rise of a new mode of medical practice that he calls 'surveillance medicine' in the following terms: 'Despite the obvious triumph of a medical theory and practice grounded in the hospital, a new medicine based on the surveillance of normal populations can be identified as emerging in the twentieth century'.[1] Surveillance medicine gives rise to a novel and underexplored aspect of the long-standing tension between the different goals of clinical medicine and public health.

The claim that will be made in this chapter is that this new style of medicine has brought into existence a new social category which will be called that of 'partial patient'. This category relates to people who do not feel themselves to be ill or disabled either most or all of the time but who have been informed medically that because of certain personal characteristics, they have or may have a disease or other medical condition or are at risk of acquiring such a disease or medical condition.

Several types of 'partial patient' can be distinguished. These will be described, together with examples of each. Typically, such people are monitored medically on a long-term basis, and may be receiving long-term treatment as well.

Although medical conditions that might be thought to fit the category of partial patient were described in previous centuries (e.g. epilepsy), it will be proposed that a conceptual difference has emerged in the twentieth century which suggests otherwise. Therefore the notion of 'partial patient' represents a new configuration of ideas that has not yet been clearly delineated, and those who fit the category enter a new social role that has not been fully described and evaluated. The importance of this new role is not only conceptual but raises ethical issues in relation to clinical care and health policy that are becoming increasingly important as more and more programmes are instituted that have the potential to create 'partial patients'. Hence both the conceptual and ethical aspects will be explored here.

Types of partial patient

Seven types of partial patient will be distinguished. The first three listed below are perhaps the most readily apparent because they relate to people who have never felt themselves to be ill or considered that they had a medical problem before the question was raised through medical investigation. All these cases arise from different types of screening and personal prevention of disease and may be differentiated on the grounds of patients who have:

- precursors of, or risk factors for, medical conditions, e.g. human immunodeficiency virus (HIV) infection; a genetic family history (such as Huntington's disease); raised serum cholesterol as a risk factor for coronary heart disease
- early symptomless medical conditions, e.g. carcinoma of the cervix *in situ*
- established symptomless medical conditions, e.g. essential hypertension.

The three following types of cases concern patients who have recognised medical conditions that have caused them to be ill in the past, but are currently not making them feel unwell for most or all of the time. Patients falling within this group may be distinguished as having:

- a medical condition that may recur, e.g. cancer, which has been successfully treated, but for which total eradication cannot be certain
- a medical condition in remission or in a latent phase, e.g. tuberculosis and syphilis in certain stages
- a medical condition under control, e.g. diabetes and angina when treated and stable.

The final type of case is that involving people who seek medical help for a particular symptom and then become enmeshed in what Sobel has called a cascade of referrals and investigations, potentially unending because none definitely establishes or excludes the presence of a medical condition.[2]

The concept of the partial patient

Two conceptual changes have occurred without which the emergence of surveillance medicine and hence of the partial patient would not have been possible. The first relates to certain logical consequences of the acceptance of the biomedical model of disease in the second half of the nineteenth century; the second concerns the gradual shift in medical norms, from the beginning of the twentieth century, which encompass a statistical approach. Taken together, these changes enabled medicine to extend its scope both to a concern with entire populations and to people who, although diagnosed as having a medical condition, do not feel themselves to be unwell.

Considering these changes in turn, the biomedical model, as originally developed in relation to infectious diseases, contained three elements organised in a hierarchy: the clinical syndrome, the pathological lesion and the specific causal agent – with the clinical syndrome subordinated to the other two elements.[3] In addition, the clinical syndrome does not consist of a straightforward account of the patient's problems as presented to the doctor, but is the doctor's selection from, and interpretation of, that account within the framework already established by the other elements of the disease model. So in the clinical encounter, the process of searching for a diagnosis will lead inevitably to a separation of the patient's subjective account of illness from the doctor's formulation of disease. There must always have been some difference in perspective between doctors and patients, but biomedical theory not only produced a much greater separation but also one that is qualitatively different. For the first time, the doctor could diagnose disease in the absence of the lowest-ranking element, the clinical syndrome. Now the patient's account was no longer essential. Clinicians have an adage, 'treat the patient, not the laboratory', which those who are wise continue to follow, but the need to state the counsel probably reveals how commonly it is ignored.

Whereas in the first half of the nineteenth century medicine had been characterised by the link between the clinical syndrome and localised pathology (often referred to as 'hospital medicine'), in the second half of the century a third element, the specific causal agent, was added. In combination with localised pathology, the causal agent became so powerful as to eclipse all previous assumptions concerning the indispensability of the patient's complaint on which the clinical syndrome is based. The linkage of a causal agent and pathology proved irresistibly attractive because that link seemed to place medical science on an entirely objective basis for the first time. The practical implementation of this theoretical possibility was crucial in the development of screening for disease and personal prevention. The separation of illness dependent on the patient's subjective account from disease dependent on the doctor's apparently objective account, and the legitimacy of no longer requiring the presence of illness, enabled the scope of medicine to enlarge and to seek out disease in apparently healthy populations as well as in those who present themselves to the doctor.

The second conceptual change involved a further phase that entailed a reconfiguration of medical norms and developed in two distinct but related ways. One depended on the first conceptual change, and further extended medicine's remit to include not only those apparently healthy people with disease but also those at risk of developing a disease. This accomplishment came about early in the twentieth century, in parallel with the 'epidemiological transition' that marked the decline of infectious disease and the rise of non-communicable, degenerative disease as the principal cause of morbidity and mortality, and occurred at about the same time in all the developed countries of the West.[4] With this new epidemiological pattern, the traditional unifactorial model of disease gave way to the multifactorial model. This change entailed the substitution of the specific causal agent by a number of causal risk factors, understanding of whose relative importance and relationships depended on the use of techniques of statistical probability.

The importance of this development in relation to screening and personal prevention was twofold. It dispensed with the 'all or nothing' qualitative notion of cause and replaced it with a quantitative gradation, in which a risk score for particular diseases could be applied to whole populations. Now there was the potential for every citizen to become the subject of medical attention, there being a gradient of concern from patients with identifiable disease through patients at high risk, medium risk and low risk of developing certain diseases in the future. In addition, because risk factors were less directly linked with pathology than the specific causal agent, the relationship between cause and pathology was partially uncoupled. This loosening then enabled a further reinforcement of the priority given to the causal element, so that within the multifactorial model it became possible to envisage dispensing with the need to observe not only the clinical syndrome but also the pathological lesion to define an individual as a 'patient'. Thus individuals at high risk came to be interpreted as having a latent medical condition, even though there was only a probability that they would ever develop symptoms or pathological change.[5] Risk factors alone may then be used to suggest that an otherwise healthy person is medically abnormal and that monitoring and intervention are appropriate.

The other element that had an important role in bringing about this second conceptual change began to gain acceptance slightly earlier than the emergence of the multifactorial model and concerned the new perspective of growth and development in child health that became increasingly important from about 1900. The focus here was not on disease but rather on the physical and psychological development of the child, and relied on the assessment of all children in terms of statistical norms. As Armstrong points out (in relation to height and weight growth charts whose use became universal in all schools in Britain after the setting up of the school health service in 1907), within this new frame of reference 'Abnormality was a relative phenomenon'. A child was abnormal with reference to other children, and even then only by degrees.[6] The notion of what constituted a normal child was therefore extended to include ideas that had no relationship with disease, but applied to children who were at one end of a statistical range in relation to certain variables that were disvalued.

The common element in these related developments was the introduction of statistical methods to produce a quantitative approach that requires the measurement and assessment of whole groups of the population as the basis on which to make judgements about normality and abnormality.

Hospital medicine and surveillance medicine

All of these conceptual changes are clearly inter-related both historically and logically. They represent a major and highly significant development in the twentieth century, that of surveillance medicine, which arose as an addition to, rather than a replacement of, the hospital medicine characteristic of the nineteenth century. A direct consequence of surveillance medicine is that the stage was now set for the entrance of the partial patient, and the extension of publicly funded healthcare in the twentieth century. These developments, when combined with the ever-increasing range and availability of technical tests, have ensured the designation of more and more types and total numbers of partial patients and this trend seems set to continue.

The overall effect of this process, which has brought with it the new social role and status of partial patients, can now be seen to have implications not only for surveillance medicine but also for hospital medicine, as can be demonstrated in Table 8.1 (which relates to competent adults).

Table 8.1

		Personal perspective (relating to patient)	
		Ill	*Well*
Medical perspective	Abnormal	A	B
(relating to doctor)	Normal	C	D

The most obvious change between hospital medicine and surveillance medicine relates to those represented by B. In hospital medicine, patients who have not complained of illness do not become subjects of medical attention and so cannot be found to have a medical condition. Now those represented by D, though not directly affected by surveillance medicine, must also come under medical scrutiny in order that B and D can be distinguished.

The status of those represented by A and C might be thought to remain unchanged because they continue to be subjects of hospital medicine. However, they are also affected in a subtler way because the multifactorial disease model is more complex and more open to interpretation than the unifactorial model. This model allows medicine to make a more sophisticated discrimination between A and C, thus rendering the patient's subjective account even less relevant than previously. Just as surveillance medicine ensures that a person's claim to be well no longer determines medicine's response, so the patient's claim to be ill becomes further disregarded in the new hospital medicine of the twentieth century. The medical norms determining the lines of separation between A and C have then been partially redrawn through a reconfiguration of the biomedical model that has simultaneously reinforced the authority of a technical perception of medicine.

An important consequence of this redefinition of medical norms is that patients in category C come to be viewed as 'medically problematic' and the physical symptoms of which they complain come to be labelled 'psychosomatic'. In this instance, patients who define themselves as ill are being denied the status of being 'real' patients and so occupy an ambiguous position in which they are often held in contempt by doctors. These patients are in fact the mirror image of the partial patient in category B. While those represented by B feel themselves to be well but are designated as medically abnormal, those represented by C feel themselves to be ill but are designated as medically normal. B and C are linked by the conceptual changes that in each case have been interpreted in such a way as to prioritise the medical at the expense of the personal. This result demonstrates that surveillance medicine was not just added to hospital medicine, but that hospital medicine was substantially changed too. Hence the conceptual innovations introduced in the twentieth century have affected the norms of medicine as a whole.

Introduction to ethical and social issues

The concerns to be raised in this section are not intended to advocate that the screening and personal prevention procedures now in routine use should be abandoned wholesale, for to do so would seem to imply the possibility that simply setting the clock back would resolve the difficulties — clearly not an option. What will be attempted is to examine more carefully the underlying assumptions and consequences of the long-term and continuing trend that is creating more and more partial patients. Re-evaluation and modification of some current procedures will be entailed, as well as a more critical appraisal of future proposals.

Illich is the most trenchant critic of the whole process of the medicalisation of life. He describes what he calls 'cultural iatrogenesis' as representing the third level of medical nemesis (superimposed on clinical and social iatrogenesis):

> This cultural iatrogenesis is the ultimate backlash of hygienic progress and consists in the paralysis of healthy responses to suffering, impairment, and death. It occurs when people accept health management designed on the engineering model, when they conspire in a attempt to produce, as if it were a commodity, something called 'better health'.[7]

His concern is with what he sees as tacit collusion between doctors and laymen that leads to the creation of patients who, by becoming dependent on medicine, relinquish responsibility for their lives. He proposes that this process involves agreement between doctors and potential patients about the designation of disease, in contrast to the present concern with partial patients, where the doctor perceives there to be a medical problem though the layperson has no medical complaint — a situation likely to lead to ambiguity and tension between them. If the patient accepts the doctor's opinion, he will be halfway to being regarded as a patient; equally, if he rejects the opinion he will still be implicated, simply by having been involved. So both cases involve the creation of partial patients, patients who are neither ill nor well but who occupy an uncomfortable and ill-defined status somewhere in between.

Medicine's response, however, tends to deny any special problem, apart from the need to ensure compliance with the medical perspective. For doctors, partial patients are essentially the same as other patients who, if they disagree with the medical view, need to be persuaded to conform. The assumption underlying this position is that medicine is unequivocally beneficial if the profession can screen for, and treat or prevent, medical conditions or prevent recurrence, even if only on a statistical basis. Any problems screened patients have are then seen as unfortunate side-effects to be managed in the best possible way, but are not regarded as a challenge to the medical view. The main focus of what follows will therefore be on a range of issues that confront this medical assumption.

Medical labelling

The commonest way to create partial patients is through screening individuals, either undertaken by special programmes or 'opportunistically', i.e. when patients are already consulting a doctor for another purpose. A cardinal principle in determining whether to screen for disease is the assessment of costs and benefits but, as already indicated, the general tendency for medicine is to focus on the benefits and ignore the costs. (I refer here to personal rather than financial considerations.) Two aspects will be considered. First, attention is usually paid mainly to patients who have a positive result, discounting the possibility that patients found to be negative may be detrimentally affected by the programme. Second, any adverse effects on those found to be positive tend to be overlooked or downplayed. Only the second of these considerations involves the creation of partial patients and so, although the first is of great importance, it will not be considered further.

Patients found to be positive at screening become socially transformed in the process of making a diagnosis. These patients have been medically labelled, and the seriousness of this labelling has long been recognised in relation to mental illness, especially when treatment involves patients who are subjected to long-term regimens of total institutionalisation, as Goffman describes in his classic work *Asylums*.[8] In these cases, patients may adapt so completely to the labels assigned them that the whole of their behaviour and demeanour is visibly altered in a stereotyped way. With physical illness such dramatic changes are not usually apparent, but the consequences may nevertheless be very serious because, once labelled, people are viewed differently by others and they come to perceive themselves as different.

False positives

The concern with labelling applies not only to those with disease but also to patients falsely diagnosed as having disease. These patients may either be advised to have treatment or to undergo a series of further investigations before they are finally found to be free of disease. Assuming that in both cases such people feel well, both must be regarded as types of partial patient. They are affected slightly differently but are of no less concern than those who actually have a disease. The comparative lack of studies of patients with false-positive results is itself an indication of the medical bias in attention given to personal benefits rather than to costs, although an editorial in the *British Medical Journal* reviewed such evidence as exists and drew attention to the need to remedy the situation:

People receiving false positive results have been shown in three different screening programmes (for congenital hypothyroidism, breast cancer, and Down's syndrome) to suffer high levels of anxiety which do not resolve immediately when subsequent testing shows no signs of disease.[9]

Statistical probabilities

The conditions referred to so far all concern 'qualitative' disease processes, which are present or absent unequivocally. Further problems arise where 'quantitative' disease processes or risk factors are being considered on the basis of statistical probabilities. The reason is that in most programmes, if left to their own devices, the majority of those identified as positive will never become ill from the condition being considered. Also, the number of people implicated as diseased or as having risk factors for disease and so warranting intervention is likely to be both very large and highly variable according to the level at which cut-off points are defined. Screening for coronary heart disease and hypertension is perhaps the most notable example in terms of both the scale of screening programmes and the seriousness of the condition. The tendency here has been to diagnose and treat hypertension more, rather than less, frequently on the basis of technological optimism.[10] The editorial referred to above indicates the sorts of issues that may arise:

> People found in workplace screening programmes to be hypertensive have increased sickness absence, increased anxiety, and reduced self-perceived health status, regardless of whether their hypertension warranted treatment. Several studies on the effectiveness of cholesterol testing have shown a paradoxical effect: a reduction in deaths from heart disease but a small increase in total mortality. It has been suggested that men who know that they are at increased risk of dying of heart disease may be more inclined to take other risks. Some of these adverse psychological effects probably also have an impact on the family and friends of the individual who has been screened.[11]

Clinical encounters and personal screening

Much of the reason why these problems are neglected lies in the failure by promoters of screening to distinguish between what is properly involved in the clinical encounter when a patient has sought the doctor's help and in a screening procedure in which the doctor approaches people who have no medical complaint, e.g. at a health fair where people off the street are invited to participate. In the former case the implicit contract is that the doctor will do only what is likely to prove of benefit to the patient, having weighed the costs and benefits for each individual. In the latter case it may seem, by analogy, that each person is also being offered something likely to prove of benefit, but in most programmes this benefit cannot come to the majority of people screened. However, this result is not usually clear to those involved because the personal costs and benefits may seem to be weighed just as they were in the traditional clinical encounter and because the onus on doctors is to act only when the overall equation is to the benefit of each patient. But screening does not work on this basis because analysis of personal costs and benefits relates to statistical groups, not to individuals, and the situation is made worse in practice because the personal costs are so commonly discounted.

Disclosure of information

Another problem may arise when the results of screening are considered positive but are judged not to be of serious significance. Should the person to whom they relate be informed? If the doctor is open about this diagnosis, he will in the process of disclosure have created a partial patient, but concealing the results is paternalistic and may lead to other problems in the future. For example, Doyal considered the case of a woman screened for cervical cancer and found to have early pathological changes for which she would normally be required to have a further checkup after six months. He raises the question of what the doctor should say to the patient.[12] To tell her that the smear is not normal is likely to cause her considerable anxiety, but if he tells her that the smear is normal he will have betrayed her trust by lying and will also be in difficulty explaining the need for follow-up.

The attribution of responsibility

So far, a range of specific issues has been considered in relation to the creation of partial patients. There is also a more pervasive concern about how screening programmes are usually designed to identify particular characteristics of individuals and so take for granted the appropriateness of a narrow focus on the traditional medical model of disease. Guttmacher *et al.* recognise the importance of this issue, which they raise in relation to screening for hypertension:

> ... favoring a medical approach to prevention reflects a bias that extends beyond hypertension. It channels attention and action away from altering the social factors that generate risks to physical and mental well-being and toward socially acceptable techniques of medical control. This sort of diversion has the double disadvantage of leaving the root of the problem untouched and of rendering a greater number of people dependent on the health care system. For all the value that lies in the detection and amelioration of hypertension, the medical model of prevention shows the limitations of our ways of confronting the social dimensions of health problems.[13]

Clarke also considers the dangers in relation to genetic screening and 'geneticisation':

> Attention to social and environmental as well as genetic factors is required for a balanced account of human disease, which in turn is needed for the effective and equitable provision of health care. Although developments in genetic technology may lead to benefits in gene therapy or rational drug design, the application of genetic technologies to individualised health screening is quite different. Geneticisation exaggerates

personal responsibility for health, denigrates the collective solutions to health problems that may be the only hope for those with few resources, and favours corporate profits over the collective and equitable provision of health care around the world.[14]

Now attention has been drawn to one of the most important issues, i.e. attribution of responsibility. Because a social and environmental approach to prevention does not identify individuals and thereby creates partial patients, the individual is not made to feel responsible for complying with treatment or altering behaviour. Rather, the social group must find ways to deal with the situation collectively.

Other issues

Attention will now be briefly turned to patients who already have an identified medical condition that is under clinical control or in remission but may recur. These people are already partial patients by definition. Hence the question whether they should have been brought into being does not arise. However, many of the problems already considered in relation to the creation of partial patients apply equally here; given their existence, the main question is how to mitigate these problems. The most important first step is for healthcare professionals to accept that patients under long-term surveillance and/or on treatment for medical conditions who nevertheless feel well all or most of the time are different from traditional patients and thus should be treated accordingly. Appropriate treatment involves adopting an attitude quite dissimilar from that applicable to sick patients, and also requires recognition that many medical routines, such as being treated alongside sick patients in hospital clinics, may be inappropriate.

The final type identified as a partial patient concerns people who are the subject of a cascade of referrals and investigations, without conclusive evidence of disease ever being established. The typing arises largely from the medical ideology expressed in Scheff's decision rule that 'judging a sick person well is more to be avoided than judging a well person sick',[15] combined with a fundamental belief in the efficacy of technical intervention.[16] The number of these cases will therefore be significantly reduced only through a change in medical values and orientation which challenges the imperative in favour of diagnosis and technical intervention.

Conclusion

The emergence and growth of surveillance medicine in the twentieth century have led not only to screening for, and personal prevention of, disease but have also influenced medicine as a whole, giving rise to a new social category and role for which the term 'partial patient' seems most apt. Individuals designated as partial patients may react in different ways, accepting, partly accepting or rejecting the medical label they have been given. In practice, most are likely to accept the label because few people believe they have any choice in the matter. However they respond, they cannot escape the moral and social consequences because they have entered a social role that is medically sanctioned. Once designated as partial patients, their lives will never again be quite the same.

Important features of this new social role are ambiguity, tension and distress. Patients who are implicated inhabit a twilight world, neither clearly ill nor clearly well but somewhere in between. On the one hand medicine marks them out as abnormal, yet for all or most of the time they feel well and essentially normal. Medicine's claim is to be merely helping to prevent and control medical disorder; any personal costs are unfortunate side-effects, no different in kind from those encountered in the more traditional modes of medical practice. What this position fails to acknowledge, though, is that the ubiquitous influence of surveillance medicine has introduced new norms to medical practice, such that the role of partial patient raises altogether different considerations. Most importantly, the new role is inherently stressful. Hence in the name of alleviating one type of suffering, medicine is simultaneously creating other forms of suffering. One is the inevitable corollary of the other.

This acknowledgement does not mean that the whole series of situations in which partial patients are presently being created should necessarily be reversed, even assuming this were possible. The point is that more serious consideration needs to be given to the general direction being taken. Study will require a wholly different approach in evaluating whether to introduce further new programmes of screening and personal prevention as well as a more critical reflection on the wider implications for medicine as a whole.

References

1   Armstrong D (1995) The rise of surveillance medicine. *Sociology of Health and Illness*. **17**: 393–404.
2   Sobel R (1996) The physician as a pathogen. *Journal of Medical Humanities*. **17**: 45–50.
3   Greaves D (1996) *Mystery in Western Medicine*, pp. 52–4. Avebury, Aldershot.
4   Wilkinson RG (1996) *Unhealthy Societies*, pp. 43–7. Routledge, London.
5   Skrabanek P (1994) *The Death of Humane Medicine*. Social Affairs Unit, London.
6   Armstrong D, op. cit., pp. 396–7.
7   Illich I (1984) The epidemics of modern medicine. In: N Black, D Boswell, A Gray *et al.* (eds) *Health and Disease: a reader*, pp. 156–62. Open University Press, Milton Keynes.
8   Goffman E (1961) *Asylums*. Anchor Books, New York.
9   Stewart-Brown S and Farmer A (1997) Screening could seriously damage your health. *British Medical Journal*. **314**: 533.
10 Guttmacher S, Teitelman M, Chapin G *et al.* (1981) Ethics and preventive medicine: the case of borderline hypertension. *Hastings Center Report*. **11** (1): 12–20.
11 Stewart-Brown S and Farmer A, op. cit.
12 Doyal L (1988) The ethics of paternalism and preventive screening. *The Practitioner*. **232**: 820–3.
13 Guttmacher *et al.*, op. cit., p. 19.

CHAPTER 9

The nature and role of medical humanities

Abstract

This chapter considers two contrasting approaches. The first equates medical humanities with the medical arts as a set of subjects which can be set against as well as complement medical sciences, and this is probably the view most commonly taken of the nature of medical humanities. The second approach focuses on the human as relevant to the whole of medicine and so cuts across the traditional formulation of Western medicine as comprising separate realms of art and science, with the human aspects restricted mainly, if not exclusively, to the former. Thus it cannot readily be captured within the familiar categories of medical arts and sciences, or medicine as art and science.

The former restricts the medical humanities to an engagement of medicine with liberal arts, so linking together a range of subjects, variously defined, to match that of medical science. However, it is without any unifying conception, other than the contrast made with science. Its principal aim is therefore usually seen as being to provide a 'balance' to medical science, rather than having any direct influence on it. The latter provides an innovative and unified approach which transcends the present structure of medicine as a divided discipline, so both allowing for a reappraisal of medical theory and knowledge, whilst at the same time enabling practitioners to develop a more rounded and humane attitude to their practice.

This second view of medical humanities is regarded as preferable because it challenges the division of medicine into separate realms of art and science, which is at the heart of many of its current difficulties, and thus holds out the prospect of developing new ways of resolving them. To avoid confusion, though, the first approach might be better called the 'medical arts', with the term 'medical humanities' being reserved for the second more general approach.

This wider conception of medical humanities raises deeper questions concerning assumptions which are usually taken for granted and are of relevance to the whole of medicine. Promoting medical humanities then requires not just an addition to the curriculum, but a permeation and change of orientation of the culture of medicine, which will transform not only clinical practice but also the theoretical basis and social structures of medicine and healthcare.

Teaching the medical arts is fully compatible with developing medical humanities in this way, but their purposes are different. The medical arts are essentially an ornament to medicine, whilst the medical humanities are an integral part of it. The medical arts are aimed at humanising practitioners, medical humanities is aimed at humanising medicine.

Introduction

The idea that the study of medicine and healthcare requires a broad approach embracing what would now be regarded as both the arts and science began in antiquity and has lost favour only since the ascendancy of biomedical science in the past two centuries. However, since the 1960s, the assumptions underlying the authority of modern scientific medicine have themselves begun to be questioned and this has been manifest in a number of different ways, e.g. the emergence of the anti-psychiatry movement which raised questions about the proper boundaries and expertise of medicine; the inability of science and technology to deal effectively with many chronic and disabling conditions, despite escalating levels of public expenditure on healthcare; and an awareness of the personal insensitivity of much of modern medicine and its failure to take account of the patient's perspective.

The response in terms of the education of healthcare professionals has been much slower to develop in Britain than in the United States, where courses in ethics first emerged in the 1960s and in medical humanities in the 1970s. In Britain, medical ethics has only recently been accepted as a compulsory element of the core curriculum for medical students and the wider notion of medical humanities has not yet gained recognition. It would therefore seem appropriate to address some very basic questions concerning the nature of medical humanities and its role in medicine and healthcare.

The nature of medical humanities

The perception since the 1960s of there being a 'crisis' in Western medicine has led either explicitly or implicitly to a range of different responses, which are underpinned by varying notions of the nature of medicine, and so also of medical humanities.

- *Medicine as a science.* Viewed from this perspective, what is required is the further and more sophisticated development of science and technology. This is often combined with the claim that the problems identified have been overstated, reinforcing the idea that they are potentially soluble without any fundamental change of course. This, then, is a conservative position which sees a continuing reliance on a largely unchanged biomedical paradigm as all that is required, leaving no role, or at most a marginal one, for subjects which are not scientific.
- *Medicine as an art.* In an editorial entitled 'Why arts courses for medical curricula?', Calman and Downie suggest that medicine is properly understood as an art which encompasses science and technology.[1] This perspective does not

seek to deny the role of science and technology in medicine, but rather to frame it within a wider conception. The mode of the arts is therefore what is ultimately seen to count, rather than that of traditional medical science. Thus the place of science and technology is subordinated to that of the arts and medicine is viewed as having the character of an art.

- *Medicine and the arts as a counterbalance to medicine as science.* Throughout the twentieth century, concerns have been expressed that science and technology have been an ever-increasing and overdominant influence on medicine and that what is required is a renewal of interest in the art of medicine as counterbalance to this trend. It is this position which has probably gained most allegiance in recent years in the definition and development of medical humanities, with medical humanities being equated with medical arts as subjects which can appropriately be counterposed to a range of other subjects described under the heading of medical sciences.

Within this general understanding, though, a variety of different approaches have been followed. The first is simply to provide a list of subjects which are commonly understood as falling under the rubric of the 'Humanities' and then apply them to medicine. Though at first this may appear straightforward and uncontentious, it is not so because how the list is derived will depend on assumptions about what properly constitutes the 'Humanities', and this is open to a number of different interpretations.

1   Any subject which is not considered a natural science.
2   Any subject which is not considered a natural or a social science.
3   Any subject, or part of a subject, which does not rely on a quantitative method-ology, so that the social sciences may be partially included. This produces a list which tends to be more restrictive than in (1), but less restrictive than in (2), although there is still room for considerable differences of view.[2]
4   Subjects concerned with the uniqueness of individuals rather than general-isation.

These different interpretations all rely on an essentially similar approach which sees medicine as having two separate aspects, those of an art and a science, the main difference between them being where the line that divides them is drawn. They therefore all depend on the idea of there being discrete realms of arts and sciences which are clearly separable, with humanities being regarded as equivalent to arts.

There are two problems with this, however. One is that the medical arts or humanities are regarded as what is left over after the medical sciences have been defined, so that if the medical sciences become revised and redefined so as to be more inclusive, they will gradually expand and take over areas which were pre-viously the territory of the medical humanities. The second difficulty is with the impression that the role of the medical humanities is principally to provide a counterweight to biomedical science, in such a way as to humanise the medical enterprise but without producing any fundamental challenge to it. This is because the traditional separation between the medical sciences and medical humanities is maintained, and for this to be overcome an altogether different and more radical approach is required.

A different conception of medicine and medical humanities

The central problems associated with the three positions identified so far are that they make either the art of medicine or the science of medicine paramount or, in acknowledging the importance of both, provide a sharp separation between them. A more satisfactory position needs to address both these issues and the final position suggested here attempts to do so.

It involves returning to the meaning of the word humanities, rather than assuming that either the 'art of medicine' or 'the arts' in relation to medicine are necessarily interchangeable with medical humanities. Engelhardt has suggested that the central goal of the humanities is:

> ... to provide an understanding of the human condition through a disciplined examination of the ideas, values and images that frame the significance of the human world and guide human practices ...[3]

What this does is to focus attention on the humanities as providing an understanding of the human condition and the values associated with the word 'human'. Such values cannot then be restricted to any traditional boundaries of particular subjects or methods and are equally applicable to both arts and science subjects. Newell and Gabrielson express this as follows:

> The key word in the term *human*-ities is 'human'. The humanities share in common this focus on the human – the human being in the human condition – the cultural and creative expressions, values, outlooks, attitudes and lifestyles of *homo sapiens*. Any discipline which has this focus is a humanities discipline and any time other disciplines focus in this way they are humanistic. Thus archaeology, history, comparative religion, and even the so-called hard sciences are rightfully said to be engaged in humanities pursuits in contexts in which they are able to focus in this way.[4]

So the medical humanities are defined in terms of a humanistic perspective and this embodies a mode of enquiry which is typical of philosophy in particular, but can also be discerned in every subject in its relationship with medicine. For example, in the 1960s, Carr described the need for historians to develop a philosophy of history, by which he meant a critically reflective outlook towards taking facts for granted, which he suggests was conspicuously absent in the nineteenth century:

> This was the age of innocence, and historians walked in the Garden of Eden, without a scrap of philosophy to cover them, naked and unashamed before the god of history.
>
> Since then, we have known Sin and experienced a Fall; and those historians who today pretend to dispense with a philosophy of history are merely trying, vainly and self-consciously, like members of a nudist colony, to recreate the Garden of Eden in their garden suburb.[5]

This need for a 'philosophical outlook' is now widely recognised as being universally applicable to the sciences as well as the arts. As an illustration of this, Oliver Sacks' reflections on his practice are notable examples of such an outlook being applied without distinction between art and science, so that his 'philosophical' observations about the scientific aspects of neurology form an integral part of his work.[6] Thus any attempt to exclude this component would be not only artificial but fatal to his whole enterprise. What this requires, though, is a distinction between the use of the word 'philosophy' in connection with a general approach of relevance to any subject and philosophy as a particular subject. It is the former which is being referred to here.[7]

It is then the desire to foster a humanistic perspective using such a philosophical approach which provides an underlying unity within a great diversity of disciplines. Regarded in this way, the subject of medical humanities has two characteristic features. First, it takes human values, both personal and social, as the focus of interest and as applicable to both the arts and the sciences; and second, it is informed by a method appropriate to all those disciplines which are of relevance to medicine. In fact, these two aspects represent two facets of the same issue. It is the irreducibly human nature of medicine which determines both that no aspect of medicine can be divorced from it and also that a philosophical approach is required if it is to be adequately represented.

A further reason for conceptualising medical humanities in this way is that the overall effect of recognising that a humanistic perspective touches on all subjects as they relate to medicine should be to enhance and enrich the insights which each of them would be able to generate and develop on its own. This is not intended to detract from the fact that each subject has its own unique contribution and that the more varied the disciplines included, the greater the potential insights that may be achieved by virtue of their additive input. Rather, it is to acknowledge both the possibility of a potentiating effect and also that the larger the number of subjects involved, the greater the need for a common theme and purpose which transcends the individual subjects and so gives coherence to the notion of medical humanities.

The strengths of this conceptualisation of medical humanities are that it recaptures something of the ancient idea that art and science in medicine are inextricably linked, whilst acknowledging that modern science and technology have become the dominant aspect of contemporary medicine and are of a different kind and order from that of antiquity. Yet it also recognises that however sophisticated and powerful science and technology have become, they remain properly the subject of a wider unifying perspective that is humanistic. Indeed, as Lewis Mumford appreciated, it is only by developing such a perspective that humanity can hope to confront the problems that science and technology pose:

> If we are to save technology itself from the aberrations of its present leaders and putative gods, we must in both our thinking and our action come back to the human center; for it is there that all significant transformations begin and terminate.[8]

What will be required if this is taken on board is a willingness to envisage a medical restructuring of both the art and science of medicine. Indeed, medical humanities cannot be adequately understood within the more traditional framework of medicine as science counterbalanced by the arts.

On consideration of these four approaches to the nature of medicine and of medical humanities, the first two may readily be discarded – those in which either art or science predominates. The other two approaches contrast in several ways and deserve more serious consideration. The first equates medical humanities with the medical arts as subjects which can both be set against and complement medical sciences, and this is probably the view most commonly taken of the nature of medical humanities.

The second approach focuses on the human as relevant to the whole of medicine and so cuts across the traditional formulation of Western medicine as comprising separate realms of art and science, with the human aspects restricted mainly, if not exclusively, to the former. Thus it cannot readily be captured within the familiar categories of medical arts and sciences or medicine as art and science.

The contrast between these two views can be brought out by describing them respectively as referring to *the* 'medical humanities', on the one hand, and 'medical humanities', on the other. To avoid confusion, though, the former, narrower view might be better called the 'medical arts' with the term 'medical humanities' being reserved for the latter, more general conception. The 'medical arts' are then restricted to an engagement of medicine with the liberal arts, so linking together a range of subjects, variously defined, to match that of medical science. However, this is without any unifying conception, other than the contrast made with science. The principal aim is therefore usually seen as being to provide a 'balance' to medical science, rather than having any direct influence on it. 'Medical humanities', on the other hand, provides an innovative and unified approach which transcends the present structure of medicine as a divided discipline, so allowing for a reappraisal of medical theory and knowledge whilst at the same time enabling practitioners to develop a more rounded and humane attitude to their practice.

This second view is regarded as preferable for two reasons. First, because it challenges the division of medicine into separate realms of art and science, which is at the heart of many of its current difficulties, and thus holds out the prospect of developing new ways of resolving them. Second, because it is compatible with the narrower view of 'medical arts', which can be readily subsumed under the wider conception of 'medical humanities'.

The role of the medical arts and medical humanities

There are a number of possible reasons for studying and making use of both the medical arts and medical humanities as defined above and some of them will be considered here under three main headings.

Recreation, relaxation and therapy

It is often suggested that because the education and training of healthcare professionals are so heavily dominated by medical science and technology, they should be balanced by a degree of exposure to the arts. Some introduction to, and familiarity with, literature, for example, is then extolled either as a good in its own right or for its ability to provide entertainment and relaxation. A further extension of this argument is that because healthcare professionals are placed in situations of exceptional stress, teaching them the arts may prove a helpful strategy in dealing with it. In essence, this is a kind of therapy, which has also been a recent subject of interest for patients, especially the mentally ill.

In all these cases, it is clear that it is the medical arts which are being referred to rather than medical humanities.

Professional education and development

The same starting point as above may also be used to make a different case: that studying the arts will improve the practice of professionals and the quality of patient care. Again, the emphasis has often been on teaching the medical arts rather than medical humanities. However, some authors take the argument further by stressing that they expect such teaching to have a direct impact on clinical practice. Pellegrino, for example, makes the point as follows:

> Rarely are the humanities in medicine assessed for what they are – neither educational flourishes nor panaceas but indispensable studies whose everyday use is as important for the quality of clinical decisions as the basic sciences are now presumed to be.[9]

This then suggests an awareness of the need to develop and teach medical humanities rather than just the medical arts.

The social role of medicine

The reasons for developing and studying the medical arts and medical humanities given above are concerned with the effect of such study on individuals, either professionals or patients or both. There are, however, further reasons relating to the role of medicine as an institution within society and two aspects will be considered here.

First, medicine is necessarily shaped by the society of which it is a part, but it also plays an important role in shaping society's norms and values. Over the past 30 years or so, the previously shared consensus about the proper nature and role of Western medicine has begun to be questioned and a debate has developed about the whole future of medicine and healthcare. As a central focus has been on the way in which the orthodox medical model has subordinated human values to technology and science (or, more correctly, scientism), the interpretation of the medical humanities which sees them as involving not just the arts but a humanistic perspective is of key importance in taking this debate forward.

This not only concerns the role of human values in medicine but it also reflects wider changes within society, and in this context it may have a very special, even unique, role. Renée Fox, who has analysed the modern development of bioethics in the United States, which has emerged in parallel with this debate and as one expression of it, suggests that besides its declared purpose, bioethics also functions as an acceptable focus in which the most significant and profound aspects of people's lives can be brought into the open, in a society which has lost many of the traditional means of exploring them.[10] She is also critical of the way in which bioethics had tended to concentrate on a narrow range of issues and employs a restrictive philosophical method, and the more eclectic medical humanities approach should counter this trend and so enrich this process.[11]

Conclusion

A number of reasons have been considered for developing and promoting the study of the medical arts and medical humanities. Although it is the medical arts which are being referred to in relation to recreation, relaxation and therapy, and medical humanities when considering the wider social role of medicine, there appears to be some uncertainty about which is appropriate in respect of professional education and development, and in this instance they are not always clearly distinguished. This may then give the appearance that the medical arts and medical humanities, as earlier defined, are not properly separable but simply two aspects of the same discipline. While they may and often do overlap, the argument that their role and purpose are very different will be maintained.

It is often assumed that if all healthcare professionals received a liberal arts education in addition to their current healthcare training, this would be bound to lead to their becoming more rounded and humane practitioners. However, this is not necessarily the case, because if medical science and technology continue to be perceived as the central focus which remains untouched by the medical arts, the core values and methods of clinical practice will remain largely unchanged. The medical arts may well encourage some practitioners to treat patients as people, in addition to treating their diseases, but will have no impact on the conceptualisation of the latter. For others, it may have little or no impact at all because while the underlying message of the centrality of science remains pre-eminent, other concerns are readily ignored.

In contrast with this, the medical humanities perspective raises deeper questions concerning assumptions which are usually taken for granted and are of relevance to the whole of medicine. Promoting medical humanities, then, requires not just an addition to the curriculum but a permeation and change of orientation of the culture of medicine, which will transform not only clinical practice but also the theoretical basis and social structures of medicine and healthcare. Although formal education has an important part to play in this, unless it becomes part of this much wider process, its influence will be relatively marginal.

Teaching the medical arts is fully compatible with developing medical humanities in this way, but their purposes are different. The medical arts are essentially an ornament to medicine, whilst the medical humanities are an integral part of it. The medical arts are aimed at humanising practitioners, medical humanities is aimed at humanising medicine.

References

1 Calman K and Downie R (1996) Why arts courses for medical curricula? *Lancet.* **347**: 1499–500.
2 For example, Pellegrino inclines to this view, but tends to focus rather narrowly on ethics, philosophy, history, law and theology: Pellegrino ED (1979) *Humanism and the Physician*, p. 4. University of Tennessee Press, Knoxville.

3   Engelhardt HT Jr (1986) *The Foundations of Bioethics*, p. 11. Oxford University Press, Oxford.

4   Newell JD and Gabrielson IW (eds) (1987) *Medicine Looks at the Humanities*, p. xvii. University Press of America, London.

5   Carr EH (1964) *What is History?*, p. 20. Penguin, Harmondsworth. (First published by Macmillan, 1961.)

6   For example: Sacks O (1986) *A Leg to Stand On*. Picador, London. (First published by Duckworth, 1984.)

7   If the terms 'philosophy' and 'philosophical' used in this way cause confusion, they are better dropped. It is the idea being conveyed, rather than the words, which is important.

8   Mumford L (1970) *The Myth of the Machine, the Pentagon of Power*, p. 420. Harcourt, Brace, Jovanovich, New York.

9   Pellegrino ED, op. cit., p. 3.

10   Fox R (1997) *The Evolution of American Bioethics*. Paper given to the Welsh Section of the British Sociological Association Medical Sociology Group in Swansea on 1 May 1997.

11   In contrast, Kopelman argues that bioethics and humanities have much in common and should be regarded as part of the same general field of study: Kopelman LM (1998) Bioethics and humanities: what make us one field? *Journal of Medicine and Philosophy*. **23**: 356–68.

CHAPTER 10

Biomedical, humoral and alternative systems of medicine

Abstract

This chapter begins with a description of the historical rise of biomedicine and the parallel decline of humoral medicine, and goes on to compare their strengths and weaknesses. It is then shown that alternative medicine has conceptual links with humoral medicine, and because it is defined in relation to biomedicine, its status depends on the view that is taken of biomedical orthodoxy.

It is argued that the inherent and fatal flaw of biomedicine is its denial of pluralism, which is expressed in an overemphasis on Asclepius at the expense of Hygeia. It is therefore claimed that it cannot survive, and that over the next century, will be replaced by a new medical cosmology, which will allow the Asclepian and Hygeian poles of medicine to be better balanced and integrated. It is not, though, that biomedicine will be replaced by a different unitary system, but that it will be transformed within a more comprehensive and plural framework which has its roots in humoralism, and be capable of reassessing and absorbing lessons from both biomedicine and alternative medicine.

Introduction

In 'The Madness of King George', a film made in the 1990s, which paid careful attention to the historic detail of the late eighteenth century, King George III of England was shown being attended by a host of his personal physicians. In one scene they were shown observing, smelling and even tasting the King's urine. A contemporary audience might well have misinterpreted this as an attempt at diagnosing a specific disease, such as porphyria, which in recent years has been proposed as a possible cause of the King's madness. What the King's physicians were actually doing, though, was seeking evidence of a general constitutional change, due to an imbalance in the humours, which would be reflected in the bodily fluids, such as the urine.

Our familiarity with and acceptance of biomedicine, at the expense of humoral theory, is now so complete as to make this medical scene incomprehensible, unless it is explained to us. By the late nineteenth century, one hundred years on from this time, the transition from humoral medicine to biomedicine was complete, and a film which faithfully reproduced this period would present a modern audience with no such problems.

The question then which will be addressed in this chapter is how medicine might look a century on from now. Will it be a further extension and development of biomedicine, and so be readily understandable from our present vantage, or as different and alien as humoral medicine is today?

Because humoralism, which is the generic name for all systems of humoral medicine, is now so unfamiliar, I will first quote Nutton's helpful definition:

> Humoralism is a system of medicine that considers illness to be the result of some disturbance in the natural balance of the humours, within the body as a whole or within one particular part. It stresses the unity of the body, and the strong interaction between mental and physical processes.[1]

I will begin then with a description of the historical rise of biomedicine and the parallel decline of humoral medicine and, after comparing the two systems, indicate some of the strengths and weaknesses of each of them. I will go on to show how alternative medicine has come to be interpreted in relation to biomedicine, and point to some similarities between humoral medicine and alternative medicine. Finally, I will argue for the recognition and re-evaluation of those features which are common to humoral and alternative medicine as of central importance to the development of any new system of medicine.

All systems of medicine encompass two polar aspects – Asclepian and Hygeian – which Dubos described in *Mirage of Health* as follows:

> The myths of Hygeia and Asclepius symbolise the never-ending oscillation between two different points of view in medicine. For the worshippers of Hygeia, health is the natural order of things, a positive attribute to which men are entitled if they govern their lives wisely. According to them, the most important function of medicine is to discover and teach the natural laws which will ensure a man a healthy mind in a healthy body. More sceptical or wiser in the ways of the world, the followers of Asclepius believe that the chief role of the physicians is to treat disease, to restore health by correcting any imperfection caused by the accidents of birth or of life.[2]

The focus of this chapter will be on the contrast between humoralism, in which it will be argued these two aspects can potentially be both balanced and integrated, and the modern tradition of biomedicine, which is unique in the extent to which it has emphasised the Asclepian aspect at the expense of the Hygeian. This has been informed by, and has also promoted, technical rationalism at the expense of the personal and cultural aspects of medicine and healthcare. At the same time it has led to a particular conception of alternative medicine as including all those systems and practices that do not fit within the presuppositions of biomedicine. So it is no surprise that much of alternative medicine has conceptual links with humoral medicine. This is not a question of equating humoral and alternative medicine with Hygeia and biomedicine with Asclepius, but of determining how a new relationship can be forged between Hygeian and Asclepian concepts.

The rise of biomedicine and parallel decline of humoral medicine

Biomedicine only became accepted as orthodox by doctors, the public and the state in the second half of the nineteenth century. However, its roots go back much further. First, to Ancient Greek medicine, and especially the collection of ideas known as the Hippocratic corpus, and second, to the philosophical and scientific ideas which emerged in the seventeenth century.

A number of developments from this later period were of particular importance to medicine, including the foundations of the empirical sciences (Bacon); mind–body dualism and the mechanical understanding of the body (Descartes); the circulation of the blood (Harvey) and the systematic application of empirical method to clinical practices (Sydenham).

However, it was not until the end of the eighteenth century that these ideas began to have a general influence on the whole of medical practice. Foucault describes the switch in clinical gaze, which he claims occurred first in the Paris hospitals in about 1800, as of central significance.[3] It led to the correlation of external symptoms with internal pathological lesions, and so to a new understanding of disease as an objective entity. Jewson elaborates on how these ideas were developed further in the move away from the bedside medicine of the eighteenth century to hospital medicine in the nineteenth century. He describes four significant innovations which enabled this process: structural nosology (disease classification), localised pathology, physical examination focused on internal pathology and statistical analysis.[4]

By the middle of the nineteenth century these ideas had permeated the whole of medical theory and practice, including mental as well as physical disorder. So a new consensus had gradually emerged that biomedicine represented orthodoxy, and this received the final stamp of state authority in the provisions of the Medical Act of 1858. At the same time it marked the end of official recognition of humoral medicine, and the designation of all medical systems and practices which did not fit with the tenets of biomedicine as 'alternative'.

Humoral medicine had held sway for many centuries before this dramatic rise of biomedicine, and the roots of both of them can be traced to the Hippocratic tradition. However, it was not until the second century AD that Galen systematised the Ancient Greek heritage of humoral medicine and laid the basis for the influential tradition that became known as Galenism. This revised humoral system then dominated medical thinking in the Western world for 1400 years until about 1600, and only declined gradually over the next two centuries in parallel with the rise in influence of biomedicine. Neve describes this development as follows:

> Before the rise to power of this model [biomedical], in the period from roughly 1700, the cultures of the world, including the West, display what might be rather grandly called 'transactional' medical systems of belief. Bodies, for example, are healthy if they balance the elements at

work within them, if they can inhabit the right harmony between diet, environment and super-natural agency and the internal influences, for example, humours, at work within bodies. The external and the internal, if balanced, produce health .... the essential point is that interactionist, processional ebbs and flows constitute the pre-biomedical idea, and that part of the history of Western medicine is the journey away from this world, one that earlier had been shared with non-European cultures.[5]

A comparison of humoral and biomedical systems

As we have seen, in the history of Western societies, humoral and biomedical systems are intimately linked, but because their theoretical assumptions are so divergent they are largely incompatible and so exclusive and competitive. Thus biomedicine did not gain the ascendancy over humoral medicine without a struggle. This was particularly apparent in the early years of the nineteenth century. Rosser Matthews describes how there were starkly contrasting views in France, and the central question was whether the professional legitimacy of physicians should continue to depend on the old idea of the humanitarian healer or the new one of empirical medical scientist reliant on 'numerical method'. He then compares how the former depends on a humanitarian narrative where 'The case history constituted step-by-step accounts of the suffering of a particular human being; it was designed to make real the pain of others and to offer a logic of specific intervention'.[6] In contrast, the theoretical orientation of the empirical medical scientist is to map the case history on to pathological and causal elements in the construction of disease, so that the patient's own narrative tends to disappear or be displaced from what is seen as the central core of medicine.

This contrast between the humanitarian healer and empirical medical scientist lies at the heart of the differences between humoral medicine and biomedicine, and can be distinguished by the features shown in Table 10.1.

Both these systems, humoral and biomedical, have strengths and weaknesses, but the strengths of biomedicine are restricted to one narrow dimension, its technical capability, and this has led to two unfortunate consequences. First, it has detracted from and downgraded the strengths of the humoral system, and second, when viewed in historical perspective, the technical utility of biomedicine can be seen to have serious disadvantages of its own as well as the more obvious benefits.

Some of the advantages of humoral medicine were its ability to reflect each individual's adjustment to life as a whole, and over time; and the central place it provided for the patient's story, which led to a sharing of patient and professional responsibility and so avoided undue patient dependency; this also entailed a unique explanation for each individual's illness which united both mental and physical elements.

Biomedicine, on the other hand, by focusing on generalisable causes of disease and the technical possibilities for intervention which follow from this, has had many striking successes. However, this approach embodies a serious conceptual flaw. Although a theoretical model of diseases as unified objective entities has provided the basis for biomedical research, it is an abstraction from the reality of

Table 10.1

Humoral	Biomedical
health and illness reflect nature	disease is separate from nature
health and illness represent harmony and balance as a whole – incorporating mental and physical elements	health concerns the identification and elimination of disease – separating mental and physical elements
the focus is on the course and prognosis of illness	the focus is on the present and the diagnosis of disease
management involves the restoration of balance – a combination of the technical and cultural	management primarily involves the technical elimination of disease
the emphasis is on the uniqueness of the sick individual	the emphasis is on the universal features of disease
lay and professional theories mesh	professional theories dominate

the patient's condition. So the technical interventions which follow provide no more than an approximation to what is best for each patient. In more straight-forward conditions, such as acute infections, this may be of comparatively little importance, but elsewhere, especially with chronic conditions, it means that the treatments proposed are often seriously deficient, and may become a burden to the patient rather than a blessing.

Now the point to emphasise here is that this is a conceptual problem which is inbuilt in the biomedical project. It may of course be that further biomedical research will somewhat improve these situations, but by its nature it cannot overcome them. The reason for this is that biomedicine has consciously excluded the personal and cultural, or subjective, aspect of medicine as the principal means to its technical advance. Yet more subtle and responsive technical improvements can only come through the inclusion of this subjective dimension, and this is not something that can be incorporated as an additional component. What is required is a conceptual reconfiguration which allows for integration, but the ultimate weakness of biomedicine is that it is incapable of such a transformation.

Humoral medicine is in principle less restricted. Although traditionally it embodies personal and cultural elements at the expense of technical developments, there is no theoretical reason why its underlying presuppositions should prevent the development of technical innovations. What distinguishes it from biomedicine is the way such developments would be viewed. First, the judgement as to what constituted technical advances could never be divorced from subjective evalua-tions. An interplay of subjective and objective elements would therefore be key to both diagnosis and treatment, and would no longer be described in technical terms alone. Such an understanding would also necessarily admit an element of uncer-tainty to every medical encounter because subjectivity encompasses both patient and provider. Although it might be possible to devise more nuanced diagnoses and treatments than are presently available, these could never be specified with absolute precision. In fact, it is the recognition of the impossibility of doing so which is the source of this reconceptualisation.

Humoral medicine may then provide a helpful starting point as to how better systems could be developed, and as many systems of alternative medicine have features which are similar to those of humoral medicine, they may be another source of inspiration.

Alternative medicine

It was an inevitable consequence of the orthodox status achieved by biomedicine in the second half of the nineteenth century that all other systems of medicine were, in contrast, designated unorthodox and relegated to a lower status as alternative. However, alternative medicine is not a unified system comparable to biomedicine. This is because it embraces a wide range of medical systems, as well as a large and disparate variety of medical practices, techniques and therapies which don't necessarily relate to any system of medicine. So alternative medicine comprises a rag-bag which is in no way comparable with the single system of biomedicine. The point is made clear by considering some of the better known alternative systems, practices, techniques and therapies (those which are clearly whole systems being listed first):

- Chinese traditional medicine and acupuncture
- Indian traditional systems of medicine, e.g. Ayurveda
- homeopathy
- osteopathy and chiropractic
- anthroposophical medicine
- herbalism
- faith healing and spiritual healing
- creative and sensory therapies, e.g. art therapy and aromatherapy
- hypnotherapy
- mind/body therapies, e.g. meditation and yoga
- naturopathy
- Alexander technique.

The question then is whether the members of this group have anything in common, and, in attempting to answer this, two sets of comments will be made. First, about alternative medicine as a whole, and second, about well-established systems of alternative medicine.

The high watermark of biomedical orthodoxy was from the beginning of the twentieth century until the 1960s. Not surprisingly, this was mirrored by an overall decline in the popularity of alternative medicine during this period. However, in Britain this marginalisation of alternative medicine was primarily based on 'exclusion' as opposed to 'subordination' or 'limitation',[7] which meant it was not so much actively suppressed, but rather excluded from state funding and left to private enterprise (the notable exception being homeopathy). Thus since the 1960s when the orthodox status of biomedicine has increasingly been the subject of debate, alternative medicine has not only been an integral part of that debate, but has burgeoned and flourished in practice without being subject to structural constraints. This growth has then been so dramatic that the total number of alternative practitioners in both Britain and the United States currently outstrips that of general medical practitioners by a considerable margin.[8]

Despite this, what alternative medicine has lacked is the official stamp of approval from the medical profession and the state, and in Britain, with the recent exceptions of osteopathy and chiropractic,[9] has been consistently resisted by both these institutions. Saks views this spectacular rise of alternative medicine as a whole as part of wider societal change which in embracing self-help activities has formed a counter-culture, which contrasts with the established culture which underpins biomedical orthodoxy and its resonances with modernity:

> The notion of 'modernity' here is variously associated with grand theories, large-scale bureaucratic forms, regulation and surveillance, materialistic values, the notion of rational progress, complex bodies of objective knowledge, and the central role of the expert .... In contrast, the self-help element of the counter-culture has stronger affinities with the concept of 'postmodernity', based on fragmentation, local determination, a plurality of cultures, tolerance of diversity, multiple discourses, the denial of absolute knowledge, and the centrality of consumer choice.[10]

So we now have a situation where the counter-culture of alternative medicine represents a potentially serious challenge to biomedical orthodoxy, and how this challenge is regarded and managed may be seen as an indicator of the whole future of medicine and healthcare. Before considering this further, I first want to distinguish between established systems of alternative medicine and alternative practices, techniques and therapies. Although there is not a clear line separating these in all cases, the point in making the distinction is that established systems pose a challenge to biomedicine as a system, in a way which does not apply to practices, techniques and therapies when they themselves are not considered as part of a more comprehensive system. It is therefore systems of alternative medicine which will be the focus here, and especially those which are well established and have stood the test of time. This then avoids consideration of the plethora of new practices which have mushroomed since the recent surge of popularity in alternative medicine, many of which are likely to prove no more than whims of fashion.

Reflecting then not on alternative medicine as a whole, but on well-established systems of alternative medicine, three different stances in relation to biomedical orthodoxy are commonly observed at the present time, depending on whether it is viewed as:

- unproblematic
- having limited problems
- having serious problems.

These will be considered in turn.

Orthodox medicine is considered unproblematic

When, in its application to medicine, the positivist scientific method is accepted unquestioningly, it has '... allowed medicine to go beyond the claim to be the *most successful* medicine to the claim to be the *only valid* medicine'.[11] This leads to a distinction being made between scientific and pseudo-scientific realms of knowledge as a basis on which to demarcate orthodox from unorthodox medicine.[12] The latter is then often labelled 'marginal' or 'fringe' as a way of indicating that it is not just less successful and inferior to orthodox medicine, but has no rightful place. The intention then is that it should be gradually eliminated by the further application of scientific method and rational argument.

From this perspective, alternative medicine is bogus medicine. Recategorisation is possible, but only if a practice, technique or therapy has either not been assessed by science previously or has been incorrectly assessed. A good example of this is acupuncture, which has been re-evaluated in recent years,[13] and many orthodox practitioners are now happy to accept it as having a sound scientific basis. However, this raises the question of whether reductionist scientific methods are appropriate in the assessment of such a technique which has been abstracted from the context of Chinese traditional medicine from which it derives.

Orthodox medicine is considered to have limited problems

Biomedical orthodoxy has been widely criticised since the 1960s for its focus on technical, at the expense of personal and social, elements, and these two aspects are often seen as being relevant to acute and chronic diseases, respectively, although the division between them is by no means an absolute one. The changes required to deal with this difficulty are then usually conceptualised in terms of moving from a biomedical model to a biopsychosocial one (described as biopsychosocial paradigm A in Chapter 11). From this vantage, alternative medicine becomes relabelled as 'complementary' medicine because it is seen as encompassing the personal and social (or psychosocial) aspects of chronic illness, which are poorly served by biomedicine's technical programme as it has been geared mainly to acute physical diseases. At the present time this view probably has the widest following amongst healthcare professionals, the public and politicians, and as such represents the new orthodoxy, in contrast to the old orthodoxy of the biomedical model. However, the increasing popularity of the term 'complementary' suggests that there is a continuing acceptance of the conceptual division between the biotechnical and psychosocial aspects of both medical knowledge and practice, and the problems that this raises remain unresolved.

It implies that there are two medical domains which are theoretically separable: that of acute physical disease to be dealt with by technical means, and that of chronic social and psychological illness. Also, that whilst biomedicine can appropriately take charge of the former, an alliance of biopsychosocial medicine (with the accent on psychosocial) and complementary medicine is required for the latter. The positivist science of the original biomedical orthodoxy is still determining the relationship, though, and as far as alternative medicine is concerned, ensures that it will be allied with the psychosocial element of the biopsychosocial model. Thus any technical utility it possesses will ultimately be captured and redefined as biomedical, whilst what remains will be regarded as 'subjective' because, like the psychosocial element of the biopsychosocial model, it is only open to qualitative as opposed to quantitative evaluation.

So the conversion of alternative medicine to complementary medicine maintains the dualism between medicine's 'biotechnical' and 'psychosocial' aspects, and whilst on the one hand this gives greater recognition to the latter, on the other it continues to entrench many of the same conceptual problems as before in the new orthodoxy. Most serious is the failure to confront the relationship between these two aspects. At the present time this perpetuates the hierarchy between orthodox and complementary medicine, which is most obviously manifest in the reluctance of the state to pay for complementary medicine. Whilst there are signs that this imbalance is gradually changing, this in itself would not necessarily lead to any change in the dualistic nature of the relationship because it is only confronted by those who see orthodox medicine as facing serious problems.

Orthodox medicine is considered to have serious problems

Chiropractic is one amongst a number of well-established systems of alternative medicine, and will be used as a focus for the arguments in this section because Coulter has subjected it to a detailed conceptual analysis, the outline of which is applicable to many other systems of alternative medicine, e.g. homeopathy and osteopathy. He argues that chiropractic derives from several distinct philosophical sources, and I have drawn on his schema to provide the following list of features which are of general relevance to many systems of alternative medicine:[14]

- *vitalism* – by which '... all living organisms are sustained by a vital force that is both different from and greater than physical and chemical forces'
- *holism* – especially in its opposition to reductionism
- *naturalism* – which facilitates a paradigm that is drugless and non-surgical, and encourages the use of techniques which use the hands, or natural remedies and minimal interventions
- *therapeutic conservatism* – based on the notion that the best care is the least care that is necessary
- *humanism* – especially that aspect which emphasises a co-operative relationship with patients
- *a philosophy of health* – which focuses on the *uniqueness of the individual's illness* and regards diseases as symptoms of the failure of the body's natural defence system, and on a *healthy lifestyle*.

Coulter then goes on to specify how such a conceptual framework is applied to chiropractic in practice and suggests the following seven stages of a typical encounter, which also are not restricted to chiropractic but apply to systems of alternative medicine more generally:[15]

1 the initial contact between professional and patient is lengthy, and is a process of 'sounding out'

2   the diagnosis is tentative
3   the explanation provided is in terms that patients sense they understand
4   the treatment plan is ongoing and an extension of the diagnosis, which is changed according to the response of the patient (as is the diagnosis)
5   the treatment is highly personal and variable, and pain is worked on as an integral part of the illness
6   evaluation is an integral part of the treatment
7   termination of the case is usually formal and negotiated.

The conceptual and practical features of alternative systems of medicine, spelt out above, make up the elements of the counter-culture already referred to, and this has a rationale which is opposed point by point to that of biomedicine. It forms a complete and integrated set of ideas and practices, or paradigm, which contrasts in every aspect with the paradigm of biomedicine. Therefore, by their nature, the two paradigms are not readily compatible and so cannot be simply added together to form a new unity. When seen in this light, alternative medicine clashes with, rather than complements, biomedicine, and the only reason this is not usually acknowledged is because the new biopsychosocial orthodoxy embraces and legitimises it. Even Coulter appears to endorse this new orthodoxy when he proposes that a further feature of chiropractic is critical rationalism, by means of which he claims that scientific methods can be applied to holistic practice.[16]

This gets to the crux of the issue because if, as appears to be the case, he is referring to the reductionist methods of biomedical science, then by definition there is no possibility of applying them to holistic practice without their undermining the essence of that practice. However, there is a different interpretation, which involves transforming these methods so as to take account of the two polarities represented by biomedicine and alternative medicine. From the standpoint of those who see that both the old and the new orthodoxy have serious problems, this inevitably follows, but it entails nothing less than the redefinition of the whole of what constitutes medical science as the necessary grounding for a new medical cosmology (cf. Chapter 11). The further question – what such a new medical cosmology and its associated science would look like – may then be approached through considering the relationship between humoral medicine and alternative medicine.

Humoral medicine and alternative medicine

If the features of humoral medicine (shown in Table 10.1, *see* p. 139) are compared with those of alternative medicine listed in the previous section, it will be seen that they are highly compatible in both their theoretical and practical aspects. The reason for this would seem to be that alternative medicine is in large measure a continuation of the tradition and constellation of ideas that have informed humoralism, but expressed in a new guise. Partly this is a straightforward perpetuation of certain aspects of systems of medicine which are humoral, e.g. classical Chinese and Indian systems of medicine; and partly of systems which arose historically in parallel with biomedicine, largely in resistance to its emerging dominance, e.g. homeopathy, osteopathy, chiropractic and anthroposophy. These systems, although diverse in their detail, draw much of their inspiration from ideas which have their roots in humoralism. Equally, those alternative therapies such as reflexology and iridology which have emerged and become highly popular in recent years hark back to the empirical tradition of the eighteenth century, which was also conceived within the overall framework of humoralism.

Thus humoral medicine and alternative medicine belong to the same over-arching tradition which, when taken in its global context, is predominant both historically and geographically. Hence when taken as representing a common set of ideas, they provide a joint resource of enduring provenance on which to draw in the process of discerning how a new conception of medicine might be constructed. This will require a greater recognition of Hygeian concepts, whilst also taking account of the technical advantages of the Asclepian ones. Taken together, humoral and alternative medicine provide a good starting point because they have the potential to encompass both aspects. Some of the features which emerge and would be of relevance to any new conceptual scheme are as follows.

- Humoral systems are *plural*. This determines that, in contrast to biomedicine, they have no single absolute structure and so no clear boundaries. The implication for the future is that rather than the unitary system of biomedicine and additional heterodoxy of alternative medicine, what is needed is a pluralistic structure. It could be argued that we are already heading in this direction, having reached an interim stage represented by the new orthodoxy of bio-psychosocial medicine, which encompasses alternative medicine. Another view, though, is that the heterodox and counter-culture of alternative medicine represents a fatal challenge to the scientism of the unitary structure of bio-psychosocial medicine (paradigm A).

  The project then is to provide a framework within which that pluralism can flourish, without on the one hand reverting to the anarchy of the market-place, in which health is for sale and anything goes,[17] or on the other hand falling back on the distorting single vision of a revised unitary system.
- Humoral systems give expression to and *balance the relationship between individuals and generalisation, and cause and meaning*. When considered together with pluralism, this determines that evaluation and revision are built into practice in a flexible way. One of the claims of biomedical science is that it provides a rationale for dealing with the difficulties inherent in such an approach, especially the dubious tactics of 'empirics' and 'quacks' who flourished in the eighteenth century. The charge against 'empirics' was that they made extravagant and unfounded claims for their medical nostrums, and in the absence of agreed standards this allowed 'quacks' to sell untested medical wares to a gullible public and so make exorbitant profits.

One aspect of biomedicine was that it dealt with these issues by enforcing a dualistic approach which, by focusing on generalisation at the expense of individuals and cause at the expense of meaning, introduced problems of its own (*see* Introduction). Even when these are set aside and biomedicine is considered on its own terms, it is debatable how far it has escaped the accusations levelled at 'empirics' and 'quacks'. The lack of scientific evidence for many of the most widely used biomedical treatments, and the huge profits made by drug companies, much of which is dependent on gullible patients and professionals and given licence by free markets, suggests that less has changed than we like to think.

Spurious medical claims which open the way for financial exploitation are likely to feature in any medical system. To be credible, any system must be judged on how well it performs in designing and implementing methods for dealing with such abuses. There is often a tendency to think that biomedical science has a monopoly on methods of systematic evaluation, and that the lack of anything comparable is alternative medicine's Achilles heel. But this is not so; for example, homeopathy showed an early concern with substantiating its therapeutic claims through the idea of 'provings', and such precedents provide valuable insights into the way in which humoralism has the potential for the development of evaluation. Contrary to biomedicine's Messianic claims, the guiding principle must be that no one method is perfect and that a variety of tailored approaches will be required to reflect the plural nature of any new system.

Conclusion

Humoralism has had a greater global impact on medicine and healthcare than the comparable set of ideas which underlies biomedicine. However, it is commonly thought that it is outmoded, having been exposed in the last two centuries as pseudo-scientific and so misguided or fake. Over the same period developments in biomedicine, and more recently 'scientific' biopsychosocial medicine (paradigm A), have, it is claimed, led to their dominance in Western societies and are gradually spreading to the rest of the world because of their self-evident superiority. This view, which is grounded in scientific rationalism, then dictates that alternative medicine will always remain either marginal or at best complementary to 'scientific' medicine.

The analysis presented here of the relationship between biomedical, humoral and alternative systems of medicine reveals an entirely different story, which is well summed up by Nutton:

> The downfall of humoralism has been a long time coming and, given the resurgence of interest in holistic medicine, humoral medicine without the humours, it may be postponed for some time yet. The flexibility of humoralism ... may in the end enable it to adapt successfully to the discoveries of modern medicine.[18]

The reference to holistic medicine here applies to both the counter-culture associated with alternative medicine and a holistic approach to 'non-scientific' biopsychosocial medicine (described as paradigm B in Chapter 11) which does not tie it to positivist science. So in this narrative, far from humoral medicine being replaced by biomedicine, or 'scientific' biopsychosocial medicine (paradigm A), it is humoralism which has provided the enduring framework, and so the true orthodoxy, in the long run. Alternative medicine has then been the main bearer of this legacy of orthodoxy, with biomedicine and 'scientific' biopsychosocial medicine more appropriately described as alternatives, despite their recent dominance and power.

The fatal weakness of the currently accepted biomedical orthodoxy is the denial of medical pluralism, which is shored up by a lopsided dualism. This has led to an overemphasis on Asclepian as opposed to Hygeian aspects of medicine, and crucially has driven a wedge between these two aspects as a way of legitimising and enforcing the ideology of scientific rationalism. Humoralism, on the other hand, encompasses both aspects within a more loosely plural system, and although its recent expression from within alternative medicine has emphasised the Hygeian pole, this has mainly been because it has developed in reaction to the opposite biomedical emphasis on Asclepius. Consequently, once the dominance of the current medical orthodoxy is exposed, what is now alternative medicine will no longer be alternative or complementary, but open to be considered as part of the mainstream. The nature of the science and technology of the current medical orthodoxy will thus be changed, and this will give a new status and prominence to the technical achievements and possibilities of present-day alternative medicine. All technical achievements, from whatever source they derive, will be put on a new footing, with a new and common mode of assessment and evaluation.

To return to my original question concerning how medicine is likely to develop during the present century, the argument I have put forward is that the biomedical orthodoxy of the past 150 years cannot survive, even in a modified form. It is not, though, that biomedicine or 'scientific' biopsychosocial medicine will be replaced by another comparable unitary system, but that it will be transformed within a more comprehensive and plural framework which has its roots in humoralism, and so be capable of reassessing and absorbing lessons from both biomedicine and alternative medicine. This will then constitute a new medical cosmology, which is the subject of the final chapter.

References

1   Nutton V (1993) Humoralism. In: WF Bynum and R Porter (eds) *Companion Encyclopedia of the History of Medicine*, vol. 1, p. 281. Routledge, London and New York.

2   Dubos R (1960) *Mirage of Health*, p. 109. George Allen and Unwin Ltd, London.

3   Foucault M (1973) *The Birth of the Clinic*. Tavistock, London. (First published in French, 1963.)

4   Jewson ND (1976) The disappearance of the sick man from medical cosmology, 1770–1870. *Sociology*. **10**: 225–44.

5   Neve M (1995) Conclusion. In: LI Conrad, M Neve, V Nutton *et al.* (eds) *The Western Medical Tradition, 800 BC to AD 1800*, p. 480. Cambridge University Press, Cambridge.

6   Rosser Matthews J (1995) *Quantification and the Quest for Certainty*, p. 22. Princeton University Press, Princeton, NJ.

7   Saks M (2003) *Orthodox and Alternative Medicine*, p. 65. Continuum, London and New York.

8   Ibid., p. 112.

9   Ibid., p. 150.

10   Ibid., pp. 110–11.

11   Sullivan MD (1993) Placebo controls and epistemic control in orthodox medicine. *Journal of Medicine and Philosophy*. **18**: 213–31.

12   Wulff H (1987) Alternative medicine. In: *Rational Klinik* (3rd edition). Munksgaard, Copenhagen.

CHAPTER 11

Reflections on a new medical cosmology

Abstract

Since the nineteenth century, the theory and practice of mainstream Western medicine have been grounded in the biomedical model. In the later years of the twentieth century, however, it has faced a range of serious problems which, when viewed collectively, remain unresolved despite a variety of responses. The question we now face is whether these problems can be dealt with by modifying and extending the principles underlying the biomedical model, or whether a more radical solution is required. Recent critiques of Western medicine have focused mainly on the biopsychosocial model in relation to the former approach, but it will be contended that this cannot deal adequately with the challenges that medicine currently faces because although it addresses both the scientific and humanistic aspects of medicine, it fails to harmonise them. I shall therefore argue for the necessity of a more radical approach, and suggest that what is required to accomplish this is the development of a new medical cosmology, rooted in an older and more global framework. Such a fundamental change would inevitably involve a long-term process which it is not yet possible to fully comprehend, let alone specify, in detail. Some of the necessary features of such a new medical cosmology can, however, already be distinguished and the outline of these is described.

Introduction

My aim in this chapter is to provide an overview of a range of responses that have been generated by the challenges facing Western medicine, and to reflect on their ability to deal with those challenges and hence their implications for the future of medicine and healthcare.

The central question I wish to consider is well expressed by Lamm:

> Do we need a whole new paradigm to reorganise medicine around, or do we perfect the existing paradigm? Are we headed toward a utopia or a brave new world? ... Whatever side the reader comes down on, the debate is of immense importance. Does the world have to start to recognise limits, or will science and technology continue to save us? Forty years ago this year, CP Snow raised the issue of 'two cultures' and

the gap of 'mutual incomprehension' between the two. The health-care debate is a subset of two new cultures which tug at our minds and hearts; do we ultimately have to bow to limits or can science and technology remove all barriers? Do we continue to dominate nature or learn to live within her limits? Are we in the end children of nature or nature's conqueror?[1] (p. 81)

The two opposing cultures referred to here are usually characterised in terms of arts and sciences, but a more accurate description would be of imagination and scientific rationalism, which makes it clear that imagination can be involved with sciences as well as arts.

I will begin by asserting that in the end we are necessarily nature's children, and we need first of all to recognise this. I will then go on to suggest that the word paradigm is too restricted a term and that cosmology is more appropriate, and I will argue that we need a new medical cosmology rather than a modified one. Finally, I will outline some features of such a new medical cosmology, whilst recognising that it is not possible at present to specify the details of how it might be operationalised in practice.

What is a new medical cosmology?

The word cosmos comes from the Greek (*kozmos*) and refers to an ordered world or universe, covering everything that there is. It has, however, come to have two somewhat different meanings. The first, and earlier, conception refers mainly to religious and cultural matters, whilst the second focuses on scientific ones to the exclusion of the wider context. The claim has then been made that it is only the history of religions which continues to interpret cosmology in the older sense and to incorporate the idea of science within religion and culture:

> The history of religions is the only discipline seeking to relate two branches of learning that have been kept apart for a considerable time; that is, the humanities (including history) and the natural sciences.[2]

I want, though, to suggest that if we are to fully comprehend the nature of medicine, it is vital that we also embrace this original conception. This is because in attempting to formulate a new medical cosmology, it is essential to go beyond scientific matters. Indeed, it is the endeavour of the past four centuries to restrict the understanding of medicine mainly to science and technology and to separate them from the arts, which I see as being at the root of Western medicine's current problems. Having said that, I can also discern counter-currents which have never wholly abandoned, for instance, the older conception of the nature of medical cosmology, as illustrated by this passage from Jewson:

> Medical cosmologies are basically metaphysical attempts to circum-scribe and define systematically the essential nature of the universe of medical discourse as a whole. They are conceptual structures which constitute the frame of reference within which all questions are posed and all answers are offered.[3] (p. 225)

Nevertheless, the use of the expression medical cosmology is rare, in contrast with the more common use of medical paradigm (as, for example, in the opening quote from Lamm above). It was Thomas Kuhn who popularised the word paradigm, which he explicitly limited to scientific ideas,[4] so there would seem to be a close parallel between his use of paradigm and the scientifically related definition of cosmology. The expression medical paradigm may then have gained general currency rather than medical cosmology, precisely because the orthodox view of medicine has been principally defined in relation to science and medical cosmology continues to retain the original wider associations. If this is right, medical paradigm has become accepted as an alternative which is preferred to medical cosmology, interpreted solely in terms of science, and the contrast I want to make is then between an all-encompassing concept 'medical cosmology', and a scientific concept 'medical paradigm'. It is the former which is the focus of this chapter.

Three important distinctions will now be suggested in comparing these notions of cosmology and paradigm.

1 As already indicated, cosmology will be taken to include moral and cultural as well as scientific and technical matters (or, in shorthand, arts as well as sciences).
2 Cosmology will be used to refer to both theory and practice, whereas paradigm is principally used in relation to theory.
3 Kuhn described the historical replacement of one dominant paradigm by another in terms of 'paradigm shifts' which usually take place relatively rapidly (often in a period of a few years), whereas dominant cosmologies change much more slowly over decades or centuries. Thus Callahan has suggested that there have been two main eras of Western medicine since ancient times which can be associated with different medical cosmologies.[5] These are humoral medicine, dominant from 200CE (Galen's time) until 1600CE, and biomedicine, dominant from 1800CE to the present, with some two centuries of transition from 1600–1800CE.

The next question to be considered is whether the biomedical era is encountering insuperable problems. In the following section I will suggest that it is, and that these can only be adequately dealt with by fundamental changes which will inevitably lead to the emergence of a new medical cosmology.

Why do we need a new medical cosmology?

Since the 1960s there have been a variety of challenges to the established position of biomedicine which became accepted in the nineteenth century. The following are some of the most significant of these, which in many cases overlap:

• disquiet about the focus on disease as an ontological concept, rather than on health, illness and sickness
• the failure of biomedicine to adequately address non-communicable disease, when compared with communicable disease, the latter being the main source from which biomedicine was originally derived
• questioning of the priority given to acute rather than chronic or disabling conditions

- challenges to the understanding of the proper boundaries of medicine and medical care, most notably in relation to mental illness, which were first raised by the anti-psychiatry movement but are equally of relevance to physical illness
- insensitivity to the patient's rather than the professional perspective, with consequent loss of attention to personal meaning
- the failure of biomedicine to adequately acknowledge and incorporate political, social and cultural dimensions
- the inability of biomedical science and technology to encompass and comprehend suffering and healing
- the ever-increasing expenditure on medical care, coupled with rising levels of dissatisfaction with services (a phenomenon which has been termed 'doing better and feeling worse').

Taken collectively these issues pose formidable problems for biomedicine which, despite a range of responses, have not been resolved.

How should we respond?

I want to propose that there are four main types of response to the challenges to biomedicine set out above, and that some elements of each of them can be found in the current development of health policy.

They are, first, a stricter adherence to the *biomedical paradigm*, and in particular to two inter-related features of its traditional conception: (i) a separation of facts from values and the priority of facts over values, and (ii) adherence to the biological as the proper realm of medicine, and the exclusion of social and, in its most extreme form, psychological elements. This is essentially an attempt to deny the force of many of the challenges by reasserting the original theoretical characteristics of biomedicine. Conditions such as chronic fatigue syndrome which have until very recently been labelled as 'psychosomatic' would be regarded as suspect from this perspective, and Thomas Szasz takes this further in describing all mental conditions as not properly the realm of medicine. Hence his famous portrayal of mental illness as a myth.[6]

Second is what I shall call *biopsychosocial paradigm A*, which is a modification of biomedicine's paradigm, and aims to retain its scientific assumptions whilst enlarging its scope to include psychological and social elements. The key problem with this approach is that it reduces qualitative accounts to quantitative data, and in doing so converts insights into meaning into causal description. There is then a loss of understanding of the patient's illness, and as a corollary a flawed account of disease. This is a serious problem with the recent attempts by economists to provide a universal account of all health states solely in quantifiable terms, for example quality-adjusted life years (QALYs).[7]

Third is what I shall call *biopsychosocial paradigm B*, which is a modification of biomedicine's paradigm through a humanistic addition. This gives recognition to the difficulties and distortions involved in framing qualitative issues, whether psychological or social, in quantitative terms, and so provides a separation between those appropriately considered quantitative on the one hand and qualitative on the other. This then allows for the personal and the social in medicine, which give it meaning, and provides legitimacy for them to be given prominence. It also leaves unquestioned, however, the conception of the scientific component of medicine. Hence this paradigm provides for what Evans and I have termed the 'additive' approach to medical humanities, in which there remains a division and so a potential dysjunction between the scientific and humanistic aspects.[8]

There are three variants of this paradigm. The first sees the division as applying in the same way to all medical conditions, so that every condition has a biological and psychosocial component. The second categorises conditions as either biological or psychosocial, usually equated with acute and chronic diseases, respectively. The third envisages a gradient between conditions which are the most biological and those which are most psychosocial, with a whole spectrum of conditions between these two poles.

Finally, the idea of a *new medical cosmology* aims to deal with the issues raised above in relation to the biopsychosocial paradigm, by setting them in a wider context. Engel was the first person to clearly distinguish the biopsychosocial model and to argue that it represents a radical change and a superior approach in comparison with the established biomedical model.[9] Whilst acknowledging its importance in giving formal recognition to psychological and social processes in medicine, it is much less radical than Engel suggested, providing an extension of the biomedical model rather than a true alternative to it. Thus it fits best with biopsychosocial paradigm A above.

There are a number of reasons for this, of which the following are of particular relevance in considering what would be required in establishing a real alternative in the shape of a new medical cosmology.

- Engel was clear that the biopsychosocial model should continue to rely on the same scientific principles as previously, so that the scientific presuppositions of the biomedical model remain secure. In biopsychosocial paradigm A, the psychosocial dimension of disease is then dealt with in a similar way to that of the biological dimension. Hence the potential challenges that the behavioural sciences pose to biomedical orthodoxy become neutralised by a process of incorporation.[10] In biopsychosocial paradigm B, the psychosocial dimension is added to the biological dimension, so that the presuppositions of the latter remain intact.
- Although the scope of medical knowledge is extended within the biopsychosocial model, its scientific foundation continues to have an absolute status, as with the biomedical model. The structure of medical knowledge is not then altered by the competing ideas introduced, most notably by social constructionism. As Morris observes, the notion of illness as created by a convergence between biology and culture, in which there is a reconfiguration of medical knowledge, is not what is being proposed.[11] He suggests that what is required to introduce this perspective is a biocultural model rather than a biopsychosocial one. As I have indicated in Chapter 2, this implies that medical knowledge cannot be separated into 'scientific' and 'social' components but unites them through its human aspect.[12]
- The biopsychosocial model can potentially be further extended to include the arts as well as psychosocial dimensions, but only in a manner similar to that previously described; that is, either by incorporating them within scientific principles (model A) or by keeping them within a separate realm and so maintaining a division between arts and sciences (model B). The latter is the

most common way in which the medical humanities are interpreted, and, as I have already mentioned, Evans and I have criticised this 'additive' approach for perpetuating this separation.[8] The alternative approach we have called 'integrated' because it aims to overcome this, and in doing so is closer to Morris's biocultural conception than a biopsychosocial one.

- In the biopsychosocial model, the continuing reliance on scientific principles determines that the medical profession will remain as the final arbiter of what is to count as medical disease and disorder, and so determine what is considered to be the proper boundaries of medicine and healthcare. The differing perspectives of patients and society in general will then continue to be excluded.

For all these reasons the biopsychosocial model falls short of providing the basis for a new medical cosmology, and so is inadequate in providing a foundation for dealing with the problems of Western medicine which have been outlined. Only a more radical vision which addresses the issues dealt with in terms of a new medical cosmology will be capable of doing this. Although it is not yet possible to see in detail what this might look like, some elements of what it must necessarily contain are already discernible.

Some elements of a new medical cosmology

The central issue which both the biopsychosocial model and the 'additive' conception of medical humanities have failed to address is the separation of medicine's technical and non-technical aspects. This has implications for all aspects of medicine, and is particularly important in determining the structure of medical knowledge, the conception of the patient, and the organisation of practice and services. In each case the underlying problem relates to fragmentation and compartmentalisation. Thus, however comprehensive the conception of medical knowledge, the individual elements which contribute to it are not altogether commensurable and remain detachable from one another. The person who is the patient then also tends to be viewed in a fragmented way, either as a highly complex series of technical components or with an additional but entirely separate human component. Following this pattern, the organisation of practice and services is also greatly specialised and differentiated. This produces inherent difficulties in assimilating them to a common purpose and so they resurface continually, however much attention is paid to overcoming them. Inevitably this has serious detrimental consequences for the management of patients.

As all these issues are inter-related, if any new approach is to be successful it must be capable of dealing with them in the round. Hence the need for a comprehensive conception uniting theory and practice, and so for the use of a global term such as cosmology, rather than paradigm, which is used more restrictively. Several features of a new medical cosmology that follow from this are highlighted here.

Goals and values

Western medicine and healthcare have been driven by the Enlightenment project, which entails a constant drive towards the perfection of medicine. It derives from the notion that human reason can describe nature so that man has the ability to control it, in the case of medicine by understanding and correcting the structure and function of the body. The goal is then one of constant improvement along a well-understood theoretical route, the direction of which is taken for granted as self-evident. McKenny describes this process as follows:

> In the case of biomedicine, efforts to spell out the utopia modern medicine will usher in are no longer needed; it is enough simply to keep pushing the frontiers of life extension, genetic control, forestalling of ageing, and so forth. Modern technology, including biomedicine, moves toward no ideal to be realised, but simply keeps moving forward.[13]

So although practical difficulties may abound, they are seen as challenges to be overcome, rather than raising conceptual questions about the whole enterprise.

Yet it is becoming increasingly clear that such a process is both theoretically unsound and unsustainable in practice.[14] Man is himself part of nature, and so must learn how best to accommodate to it. This understanding, which underpinned humoral medicine and from which some systems of alternative medicine continue to derive inspiration, contains a different set of values from Western medicine. So if they are to be recaptured there will need to be fundamental changes. Above all, this will lead to an attitude of seeking balance and sustainability rather than never-ending improvement, and this will necessitate a concomitant redefinition of medicine and its boundaries (as described in the next section) as well as what is meant by medical progress. Callahan describes what is at issue here as follows:

> The unlimited, expansionary progress sought by modern medicine – progress with no articulated or envisioned end and no well-reasoned priorities – is not a viable route to continued beneficial progress, nor does it supply an adequate basis for a future sustainable medicine. The idea of progress itself must now be redefined.[15]

Progress only had meaning within the context of particular goals and values, and in showing that this can be contested, Callahan is reminding us of this. So what constitutes the 'best' medical system and 'best' medical care cannot be taken for granted, and at the present juncture requires a fundamental re-examination.

Some of the issues that this will raise concern the present priority given to acute as opposed to chronic conditions, and technical intervention as opposed to personal and social care; also how far to extend methods of medical surveillance, as well as the technical prolongation of life. A further important issue of more general concern is how to deal with inequalities in health. In all these contexts it is important to stress that what is at stake is not the revision of present policies aimed at curbing what is presently seen as progress and best medical care, but redefining these concepts so as to aspire to a different set of goals.

Definitions and boundaries of medicine and healthcare

Western medicine embodies the idea that it has an absolute and unitary status, so that the boundaries of medicine and healthcare are fixed. The concept of disease is then privileged when compared with health, illness and sickness as a means of providing this status. By focusing on health and describing it as a mirage, Dubos was one of the first authors to challenge this conception:

> The kind of health that men desire most is not necessarily a state in which they experience physical vigor and a sense of well-being, not even one giving them a long life. It is, instead, the condition best suited to reach goals that each individual formulates for himself ... the satisfaction which men crave most, and the sufferings which sear their lives most deeply, have determinants which do not all reside in the flesh or in the reasonable faculties and are not completely accounted for by scientific laws.[16]

From this perspective, medicine and healthcare cannot have fixed or determinate boundaries, but are constantly being renegotiated, and because they are derived from goals and values concerning our lives as a whole, there must be an inter-penetration between medicine and other areas of life. This should not lead to the conclusion that any resolution of these issues is as acceptable as any other, but rather that the task of redefining medicine is inevitably unending, and one in which although progress is possible, it is not towards an exact or predetermined end.

The reconfiguration of medical knowledge

If medicine is no longer conceived as having a determinate boundary, then the form of medical knowledge must also be reconceptualised, not simply as one set of knowledge being replaced by another, but as a reconfiguration of medical knowledge. The following are some inter-related aspects of this new understanding.

- Medical knowledge contains an inescapable element of indeterminacy and uncertainty, or a mysterious quality.[17]
- Medical knowledge is in part constructed through a joint project involving patients, professionals and society, and so involves a multiplicity of gazes, rather than any one privileged gaze.
- Medical knowledge is a meld of the technical or objective, and the humanistic or subjective, united by its human dimension.
- Technical knowledge is traditionally understood as being concerned with causes and as being generalisable, and in contrast humanistic knowledge with personal and social meanings. There is now increasing recognition that this dualistic inter-pretation of universal and existential knowledge is problematic in medicine,[18] so that all medical knowledge is concerned with judgements about the appropriate form and degree of transferability, according to the particular context. Medical research methods will then need to be revised to reflect this.

Healing and the healer

All major systems of medicine, both historical and contemporary, contain as a central feature the notion of healing, and a respected role for particular people who are designated as healers. Healing has its origin in religious ideas and concerns the restoration of wholeness in an all-encompassing sense, so transcending the technical/humanistic division which is characteristic of Western medicine. Despite this division, even in Western medicine the tradition of the healer has not yet been lost, although it is under threat. Healers, whether shamans, humoral physicians or contemporary Western practitioners, rely on the indivisibility of their technical and charismatic power, the technical aspect of their work only having meaning in relation to the personal and social aspects and vice versa. Thus healing has a spiritual and mysterious quality which transcends scientific rationalism, and in our society is most obviously embodied in general practice in the figure of the old-style family doctor.[19]

Whilst healing is often considered to be less important in hospital medicine, especially in relation to acute conditions, this needs to be challenged, as Lown has argued in relation to the work of hospital physicians.[20] The problem in giving due recognition to the role of healing in hospitals arises because the values and practices associated with scientific rationalism have mainly been developed within laboratory and hospital medicine, and these tend to undermine the very notion of healing in the sense in which it is characterised here. To compound this, the same underlying principles are being extended to the management of medical care, and even general practice is increasingly under pressure to conform.[21] This is because the Western system of medicine as a whole continues to be framed in relation to the knowledge and practice derived principally from the methodology and techniques of laboratory- and hospital-based research, and also is becoming ever more highly managed by external authorities. Hence it is important that the role of healing and the healer be rehabilitated in a revised form as central to any new system of medicine and healthcare, and be seen as integral to all parts of it.

Medical education

Downie has argued for the teaching of humanities as part of medical educa-tion because 'the doctor needs to be able to make considered judgments, and a developed sense of judgment has a humanistic element as a component means'.[22] If both the arts and sciences in medicine are to be reconceptualised as proposed here, however, it is the non-rational as well as the rational aspects of both of them which will need to be jointly captured. The development of imagination and critical reflection should then permeate the whole curriculum, and will require an interdisciplinary perspective, involving all aspects of theoretical and practical learning. The acquisition of factual knowledge and technical skills will not then be downgraded, but rather be placed within a different and wider context. The objective will be to provide a very general framework for lifelong learning, which will incorporate but also go beyond a set of specific competencies. The General Medical Council's current recommendations for medical education,[23] although in line with these proposals, do not go as far as this.

Collective responsibility

The medical paternalism associated with the biomedical model, which was clearly articulated in Parsons' account of the sick role,[24] viewed medical responsibility as resting almost entirely with the doctor, the patient's responsibility being limited to following doctors' orders. The increasing dissatisfaction in recent years with such medical paternalism, famously expressed by Illich in *Limits to Medicine*,[25] has led to a general upsurge in interest in patient autonomy. One effect has been a partial redrawing of the boundaries of professional and patient responsibility. This change in the moral and social norms of medical practice has mainly been seen as one of patients wresting unwarranted power from doctors, and so of a straight transfer of certain elements of responsibility from doctors to patients. Certain aspects of this situation have, however, largely gone unquestioned. First, it has been assumed that the core of medical knowledge is technical and so remains the province of doctors and is their sole responsibility. Hence reapportioning responsibility concerns only the humanistic aspects of medicine, including when and how to apply technical knowledge, and is regarded as a competitive process. The technical/humanistic division in medicine is therefore left intact, and there is no sense of a new collective approach to the restructuring of medicine as a whole that would follow from the understanding of medical knowledge described above. Any new system must then encompass a different approach to responsibility which takes account of these issues.

Conclusion

For some 40 years, the traditional system of Western medicine and the biomedical model on which it is based have come under increasing challenge. During this time there has been much debate about the need for a new medical paradigm, and the biopsychosocial model has captured most attention as a possible successor to the biomedical model. Although it has been interpreted in different ways, the biopsychosocial model is in essence a revised and extended version of the biomedical model, so that many of the assumptions of the original model remain intact. My central claim is that any such modification of the orthodox biomedical paradigm is inadequate to the problems which now face Western medicine. What is needed is a more thoroughgoing re-examination to replace the theoretical and practical structure of biomedicine with a new medical cosmology. Unlike a paradigm shift, the emergence of a new medical cosmology involves a slow and long-term process of change, and it is not yet possible to comprehend in any detail what the outcome of this might be. Some of the necessary features of any new medical cosmology are already discernible, however, and have been described in outline.

References

1 Lamm R (1999) Is life without disease a false hope? *Medical Humanities Review*. **13**: 80–2.
2 Eliade M (ed.) (1987) *The Encyclopaedia of Religion*, vol, 4, p. 100. MacMillan, New York.
3 Jewson ND (1976) The disappearance of the sick man from medical cosmology, 1770–1870. *Sociology*. **10**: 225–44.
4 Kuhn TS (1962) *The Structure of Scientific Revolutions*. University of Chicago Press, Chicago, IL.
5 Callahan D (1998) *False Hopes*, pp. 27–8. Simon & Schuster, New York.

6   Szasz TS (1960) The myth of mental illness. *American Psychologist*. **15**: 113–18.

7   Williams A (1983) The economic role of 'health indicators'. In: G Teeling-Smith (ed.) *Measuring the Social Benefits of Medicine*, pp. 63–7. Office of Health Economics, London.

8   Evans M and Greaves D (1999) Exploring the medical humanities. *British Medical Journal*. **319**: 1216.

9   Engel GL (1977) The need for a new medical model: a challenge to biomedicine. *Science*. **196**: 129–36.

10   Armstrong D (1987) Theoretical tensions in biopsychosocial medicine. *Social Science and Medicine*. **25**: 1213–18.

11   Morris DB (1998) *Illness and Culture in the Postmodern Age*. University of California Press, Berkeley, CA.

12   Greaves D (1998) What are heart attacks? Rethinking some aspects of medical knowledge. *Medicine, Health Care and Philosophy*. **1**: 133–41.

13   McKenny GP (1997) *To Relieve the Human Condition*, p. 49. State University of New York Press, New York.

14   Midgley M (2001) *Science and Poetry*, pp. 160–2. Routledge, London.

15   Callahan D, op. cit., p. 80.

16   Dubos R (1987) *Mirage of Health*, pp. 278–9. Rutgers University Press, New Brunswick, NJ. (First published in 1959.)

17   Greaves D (1996) *Mystery in Western Medicine*. Avebury, Aldershot.

18   Evans M (2001) The 'medical body' as philosophy's arena. *Theoretical Medicine*. **22**: 17–32.

19   Greaves D (1999) The enduring appeal of the Victorian family doctor. *Medical Humanities Review*. **13**: 44–56.

20   Lown B (1996) *The Lost Art of Healing*. Ballantyne Books, New York.

21   Willis J (2001) *Friends in Low Places*. Radcliffe Medical Press, Oxford.

22   Downie R (2001) Medical humanities; means, ends and evaluation. In: M Evans and IG Finlay (eds) *Medical Humanities*, p. 216. BMJ Books, London.

23   General Medical Council (1993) *Tomorrow's Doctors*. GMC, London.

24   Parsons T (1951) *The Social System*. Free Press, Glencoe, IL.

25   Illich I (1976) *Limits to Medicine*. Marion Boyars, London.

Index